A Dissenting Voice

Books by Denis Smith

Bleeding Hearts . . . Bleeding Country: Canada and the Quebec Crisis (1971)

Gentle Patriot: A Political Biography of Walter Gordon (1973)

Diplomacy of Fear: Canada and the Cold War, 1941–1948 (1988)

Rogue Tory: The Life and Legend of John G. Diefenbaker (1995)

The Prisoners of Cabrera: Napoleon's Forgotten Soldiers 1809–1814 (2001)

Ignatieff's World: A Liberal Leader for the 21st Century? (2006)

Ignatieff's World Updated: Iggy Goes to Ottawa (2009)

General Miranda's Wars: Turmoil and Revolt in Spanish America, 1750–1816 (2013)

A Dissenting Voice

Essays, Addresses, Reviews, Polemics, Diversions: 1959-2015

Denis Smith

Rock's Mills Press
Oakville, Ontario
2017

Published by
ROCK'S MILLS PRESS
www.rocksmillspress.com

Library and Archives Cataloguing in Publication (CIP) data is available from the publisher. Contact us at customer.service@rocksmillspress.com.

Contents

An Introductory Note

Sixty years is a long time in politics, but a short time in history. This collection of scholarly articles and papers, reviews, polemical journalism, and satire spans the period from 1959 until 2015, from the height of the Cold War to its ending, from the "American Century" to the age of American interventionism, from "Dief the Chief" to Stephen Harper's *Party of One*. The themes extend from Canadian party politics to our parliamentary institutions, political biography, Canadian-American relations, NATO, the wars of the Middle East, and back again to the recent decay of Canada's democratic fabric. My subjects were sometimes as accidental as the daily headlines. I have tried to maintain a delicate balance between fair observation and passionate commitment, in the belief that these two aims need not be contradictory. Whether I have achieved it, you may be the judge.

I / Essays and Addresses

Prairie Revolt, Federalism and the Party System
(1959)

I lived for the first eighteen years of my life in Edmonton, Alberta, and from the age of three I lived under the strange provincial government of William Aberhart's Social Credit party. In the Alberta schools of the 1940s we were taught no regional or national history, and at university the gap remained. My local political knowledge was sparse and anecdotal: but I knew that the Canadian prairies had been a source of political revolt since the 1920s. When I began postgraduate studies, I chose to educate myself with a study of the peculiarities of western politics, and soon afterwards found myself teaching Canadian government. In 1963 Hugh Thorburn of Queen's University noted that "no book currently in print" dealt with Canadian political parties. He gathered a collection of essays to fill the void, including this piece based on my graduate thesis.

The leaders of the three western movements of political protest, the Progressives, the C.C.F., and Social Credit, insisted in their national campaigns from 1921 to 1958 that their purpose was not to complicate the Canadian party system by creating permanent minor groups, but to simplify it by forcing a realignment of political loyalty throughout the country. The professed national aim of each party was to create a national two-party system divided on lines of principle, through which the reforms desired by each group might be adopted. The three parties of prairie origin argued either that the Liberal and Conservative parties were alike, offering the voter no choice, or that one of the two older parties was not fulfilling its proper function. Frequently they argued both.

The hope of political realignment first expressed on the prairies by the grain growers' organizations and John W. Dafoe after 1917 is echoed today by the leaders of the New Democratic Party, whose object is to create "a broadly based people's political movement, which embraces the C.C.F., the labour movement, farm organizations, professional people and other liberally-minded persons interested in basic social reform and reconstruction through our parliamentary system of government."[1] The political history of the prairies since 1917 cannot encourage those who still seek such a change. In forty years the three parties originating in the prairies have all failed to bring about a political transformation at Ottawa, and each has eventually been rejected by its own prairie followers in federal general elections. The recurrent wish in western Canada for a new national party may be partly discounted as the rationalization of ambitious politicians; but its persistence cannot be so easily explained. Pursuit of the aim reflects, in one sense, a failure to see the reality of the Canadian political system, and in another, a grasp of the necessities of political action in a parliamentary system of responsible government.

The model which prairie political reformers hoped to reproduce was their simplified image of the British party system. Liberal Unionists and Progressives after 1917 desired new Liberal and Conservative parties on the late nineteenth-century British pattern; the C.C.F. after 1935 hoped for a division of loyalties on Conservative-Labour lines; Social Credit after 1953 pictured itself as the conservative opponent of an increasingly socialist Liberal party. None of the advocates of realignment saw clearly in their enthusiasm; their half-conscious equation of Canadian politics with an ill-formed image of British politics ignored the organization and attitudes of Canadian political parties.

The federal composition of the Liberal and Conservative parties, and of the new prairie parties after 1920, was a clear sign to prairie reformers of the nature of Canadian parties. Neither of the old parties was a monolithic whole. Within the national parties, the prairie units of both Liberals and Conservatives were relatively progressive, especially in the inter-war years. In their empirical way, prairie Liberals and Conservatives have often been more enterprising in proposing reform that would benefit the rural prairie economy than have been the Progressives in Manitoba or the U.F.A. and Social Credit in Alberta. The basic measures of crop insurance and credit reform desired by prairie farmers were adopted by Liberal governments in all three provinces before 1921. To make their appeal in the West, Liberals and Conservatives have frequently played down their relationship with their more conservative eastern branches. Even in the apparently homogeneous political region within the prairies, separate provincial traditions, tactical needs, and provincial jealousies have made co-operation between the three prairie units of the old parties difficult.

[1] Resolution of the Canadian Labour Congress, 1958 convention, quoted in Stanley Knowles, *The New Party* (Toronto: McClelland & Stewart Ltd., 1961), p. 127.

In the Progressive party, the C.C.F., and Social Credit, for similar reasons, provincial autonomy from the beginning vitiated attempts to unify policy and organization. The single-minded provincialism of Henry Wise Wood in Alberta prevented the establishment of a national Progressive organization; the U.F.A.'s parochialism was an equal hindrance to the C.C.F. in its early years; the Social Credit party escaped serious inter-provincial conflict before 1962 only because it was an insignificant force in federal politics outside Alberta. In spite of the common economic interest of the three grain-growing provinces, the provinces have three distinct political systems to which any party must adapt. The new parties have never had to face the more serious problem, constantly confronting the two old parties, of adjusting themselves within national parties having influential blocs of supporters and members of Parliament in the Maritimes, Quebec, and Ontario. The national unity of the Social Credit party was severely challenged for the first time in 1962 by the federal success of M. Caouette and his followers in Quebec.

Prairie reformers were too inclined to impose a European pattern when they claimed that nothing distinguishes the national Liberal and Conservative parties. The familiar distinction between Right and Left does not apply in Canada. Like the Republican and Democratic parties, Canadian parties are, first, alternate groups of officeholders. They are distinguished not by precise differences of policy when in office, but by continuing and deep differences of sentiment and approach which reflect the special ambivalence of Canada's history and position in the world. A new national party, to be successful, must either capture old citadels of sentiment from the existing parties or lay claim to new sentiments and attitudes that, unrecognized by the old parties, reflect new challenges faced by the country. The failure of the new prairie parties resulted from the country's failure to see any but the traditional problems and to consider any but the traditional responses.

The Conservative party represents and contains the latent anti-Americanism which has been the precondition of the country's existence since 1867. Without always exposing this feeling in its crudity, the party has come to power in 1911, 1930, and 1957 on surges of anti-American emotion and when in office has been prepared to contemplate legislative restrictions on American economic and cultural influence in Canada, if such restrictions promise political advantage. When the anti-American devil slumbers in Canadian breasts, the Conservative party loses some of its sense of purpose. The national Liberal party, in contrast, has represented the opposite desire of Canadians: to conciliate the United States, to avoid antagonizing the giant, to enter into a North American partnership.

The Conservative party's weakness in western Canada during the period from 1917 to 1958 can be partly explained by this difference of sentiment. The prairie provinces contained a large proportion of former American citizens; the closest neighbours of isolated westerners were not central Canadians but fellow farmers in Montana, North Dakota, and Minnesota; the ideas of American farm radicals were congenial on the Canadian prairies; the most obvious market for prairie wheat and source of cheap commodities was the United States. Anti-Americanism was irrelevant to prairie needs; prairie interests and associations called instead for anti-eastern feeling. In 1930, when the country was caught by the anti-American mood, Alberta and Saskatchewan were the provinces least affected.[2] The relative absence of this sentiment in the West before 1957 gave an advantage to the Liberal party, or to any other party which did not share the Conservative tradition.

The other side of this coin is the difference in emphasis given to the British relation; and again the Conservatives were at a disadvantage on the prairies in this period because the Anglophilia of Arthur Meighen, R.B. Bennett, and George Drew met indifference or positive distaste from the large numbers of Americans and continental Europeans on the prairies, and from all whose concern in the inter-war years was, with John W. Dafoe, to make Canada independent of Great Britain. It was only when the issue had long been settled that a faintly pro-British reaction to the Liberal party's reiteration of its prejudice set in on the prairies and elsewhere, to the benefit of the Conservative party in 1957 and 1958.

In domestic policy, too, the differences between the parties have been native ones. In this century, the Liberal party has been the public guardian or, more accurately, the propagandist of racial unity between French and English, while the Conservative party has repeatedly antagonized or ignored French Canada. These contrary tendencies had their effect on the prairies, particularly in the defeat of the provincial Liberal government of Saskatchewan by the Conservatives in 1929. The national Liberal party, by the inclination of its leaders and the necessity of accommodating its Quebec followers, has been pragmatic in its encouragement of national development and backward in social policy. The Conservative party has the bolder radical legislative tradition (although it is piecemeal), typified by Macdonald's assistance to the C.P.R., Borden's nationalization of the C.N.R. and civil service reforms, Bennett's abortive social legislation, and Diefenbaker's welfare legislation, assistance to farmers, and commitment to northern development. In the inter-war era of retrenchment, Mackenzie King's quietism was more in tune with the western Canadian spirit than with a policy of national expansion and legislative activity. The reforming surge of 1917 had died on the prairies by 1921, and the

[2] The Conservative party received 34 percent of the popular vote in Alberta, 38 percent in Saskatchewan, 46 percent in Manitoba and 49 percent in the whole country.

provincial governments, too, of whatever political flavour, were unimaginative and cautious for a decade afterwards.

Conservative devotion to the British connection has included a notably stronger reverence for British parliamentary institutions than that of the Liberal party. The Conservative party is quicker to detect and deplore departures from traditional parliamentary practice (or to show guilt for them, if the party itself is responsible) than the Liberal party; the Liberal party is more inclined to accept American partisan practices, especially in its relationship with the senior civil service. (There are exceptions. Some prominent Liberals since 1921 have been parliamentary traditionalists, but they have not been influential in the party's leadership. The Conservative party and the C.C.F. have had many more articulate defenders of the parliamentary system.) The Liberal party, by intent and long habit in office, has established with the federal civil service ties of sentiment which the Conservative party cannot match when it is in office.

All these differences are in feeling, experience, and approach rather than in clear-cut policy. The western advocates of the new parties after 1917, looking for more logical and cerebral distinctions between the old parties, did not see that the existing national parties already had a prescriptive hold on the deepest sentiments dividing the Canadian electorate.

The Progressives left the Liberal party because they saw that it was a loose federation of provincial groups, dominated by members from the populous, industrial provinces. The party's belief in a low tariff seemed nothing but an empty gesture to the West; in the party caucus the western members could rarely gain acceptance for their views. T.A. Crerar of Manitoba drew the same lesson from his experience in the Unionist cabinet from 1917 to 1919.[3] The sentiment for a low tariff seemed after the First World War to be the only dominant political feeling that had not been appropriated by either of the old parties. Yet it soon turned out to be old hat; the West was not seriously interested in major tariff reform after 1925. The Progressives had no other permanent objective of national policy.

One element in the Progressive revolt was, of course, the belief that the expanding West lacked the power to which it was entitled in the Liberal caucus. Equity required that each region should have power in the party commensurate with its economic and social position in the country. No politician would deny this right, and Mackenzie King, whose political life was typified by his efforts to balance delicately the power and interests of all parts of

[3] See *A.B. Hudson Papers*, No. 55, T.A. Crerar to A.B. Hudson (March 12, 1919); *Dafoe Papers*, John W. Dafoe to Sir Clifford Sifton (July 21, 1919); *Borden Papers*, O.C. Series, File 571, T.A. Crerar to R.L. Borden (June 4, 1919).

the country and to remain in power by doing so, would scarcely ignore it. The Progressives could expect that, gradually, the old parties would out of prudence and a sense of justice, grant the West a balanced place in party councils. King did this in the Liberal party by increasing prairie representation in the House of Commons in 1924 and offering cabinet posts to influential westerners like Crerar, C.A. Dunning, A.B. Hudson, J.S. Woodsworth and J.G. Gardiner. The display of western power within the Liberal caucus, and outside it, made it expedient for King to make concessions of policy to the prairies: the restored Crow's Nest Pass Agreement, the 1924 budget, the Hudson Bay Railway, the Old Age Pension Act of 1926, the budget of 1930, and the social welfare measures and financial agreements of 1940 and afterwards. The prairie political revolt, by achieving such concessions of position and policy at Ottawa, may be considered successful. But it was not, and could not be successful in its wider purpose of transforming the Canadian party system. The concessions did not mean that the Liberal party had been captured by western Liberals: they were the limited rewards of compromise.

Because they failed to accept the inevitable heterogeneity of national political parties or to recognize the differences between the two old parties, the prophets of a reformed party system on the prairie set out to achieve the impossible. But if Canadian parties are loose federations like American parties, why did not the West find satisfaction through them, as American regional protest groups usually do? In Canada, western politicians realized that the parliamentary system imposes on regional groups restraints which cannot be overcome within the major parties. In the congressional system, regional interest groups have better opportunities for enforcing their wills in primaries, and in Congress by log-rolling that avoids party lines, by filibustering, or by seeking a presidential veto. If they do not always succeed, American regional groups can at least talk freely within the existing party framework. But the need for party discipline in a parliamentary system limits regional interests to only two opportunities to put their cases: in the privacy of the cabinet and the party caucus. Prairie members of the old parties found it impossible to persuade their supporters that they were acting in their interest, when the dominant eastern sections of the parties were able to force their policies through in private.[4]

[4] Regional tension within the parties seems also to have contributed to the erosion in Canada of the parliamentary practice of collective cabinet responsibility. It appears that one of the responses of the Liberal and Conservative parties to the centrifugal forces of Canadian regionalism has been tacitly to abandon strict cabinet unanimity in public statements of policy. See, for example, the conflicting statements on the South Saskatchewan dam made by Hon. James G. Gardiner, the Minister of Agriculture, and Rt. Hon. Louis St. Laurent, the Prime Minister, as reported in the Toronto *Globe and Mail*, June 4, 1954, July 18, 1956, May 8, 1957, and commented upon by Arthur Blakely in the *Montreal Gazette*, February 14, 1957.

Prairie political rebels made further use of the available instruments of power in a federal system by capturing the provincial governments in the prairies. The parliamentary system forced western politicians out of the old parties; the federal constitution gave the new parties footholds of prestige and patronage in the provinces and made possible their survival, in a lingering half-life, even though the federal parliamentary groups of Progressives, C.C.F., and Social Credit were virtually impotent. The achievement of power in provincial elections was easier for the new parties than gaining power at Ottawa, because they could tum the profound prairie sentiments of insecurity, xenophobia, pioneering righteousness, and resentment of exploitation against the Liberals and Conservatives, who appeared with some justification to be the local agents of a colonial power—eastern Canada. Once the Progressives, the U.F.A., the Social Credit, and the C.C.F. had come to power in the West, they sought to retain power for the same reasons any party does: habit, the enjoyment of power, the rewards of patronage, belief in their mission, the defence of their self-respect.

For ten years after 1917, the *Manitoba Free Press* advocated a complete separation between the federal and provincial units of all political parties.[5] It did so partly because it considered the problems facing a provincial legislature to be closer to those of a municipal council than of a sovereign parliament; partly because it assumed that the federal system, by its nature, involved continuous conflict over national policy between the provinces and the federal government; and partly because it wished the West to take the lead in creating a new two-party system at Ottawa by forming the core of a new national Liberal party. After ten years of testing, the Free Press abandoned its theory in the face of intransigent fact. The germ of truth in this prescription for separating the federal and provincial party systems was that by the very existence of two levels of government, two separate systems of policy-making and competition for power were created. There was illogic and injustice in a party system which made a provincial branch of a party suffer for the unpopularity of its federal associate, or vice versa.

But to expect that politicians would make two insulated realms was as unrealistic as to expect a simplified national two-party system. National party leaders will encourage the growth of provincial party units, as Mackenzie King and James Gardiner did, to make shows of strength and to provide organizations that they can use in federal elections. Men who enter provincial politics early in their careers will be drawn to Ottawa and the greater opportunities for

[5] See, *inter alia*, *Manitoba Free Press* (April 7, 1922) editorial, 11; (April 27, 1922), 13; (April 28, 1922), editorial, 15; (June 2, 1921), editorial, 13; (June 22, 1927), editorial, 15; (July 8, 1922), editorial, 11; *Dafoe Papers*, John W. Dafoe to Sir Clifford Sifton (July 7, 1922).

responsibility and renown that it offers; they will find it useful, while in provincial politics, to conciliate the national party leaders who may later help them. Even a Progressive like John Bracken, who claimed in the 1920s to keep Manitoba politics free of federal complications, accepted national Liberal help after 1928 and at last agreed to take the leadership of a national party.[6] A provincial party leader will deny his federal loyalties when the federal party is unpopular and parade them when it is popular. The relationship is one of prudence, resting on a basis of common sentiment, and not of principle. The first objective of a party is to seek or maintain power, and Canadian parties will pursue this objective by denying their associations if this seems desirable. The temptation to do so would have been the same for the new parties if they too, had become major parties.

There is slight evidence that a provincial government controlled by a separate provincial party can gain more concessions from Ottawa, as the *Manitoba Free Press* implied by arguing for two levels of party system. The prairie provinces took nine years after 1921 to obtain the natural resources that the federal government had retained, although during this time two of the governments were opposed to the federal Liberal administration. The decision to transfer control of resources came when the Dominion's immigration and settlement programme had been completed and control was no longer necessary for its purposes, not when opposition parties came to power in the prairies.[7] Prime Minister King decided to build the Hudson Bay Railway in order to bring Premier C.A. Dunning of Saskatchewan (a Liberal) into his cabinet and to gain the Saskatchewan Liberal Party's aid in the federal campaign of 1925, not to appease an unrelated provincial government.[8] Prime Minister Bennett gave financial assistance to prairie governments during the depression irrespective

[6] The federal power to make judicial and other patronage appointments has been one effective means by which the party in power at Ottawa has sustained weak provincial branches in the prairies, and incidentally made it difficult for the new parties to attract lawyers. Politicians who are lawyers, and who have hopes of being appointed to the bench, will be reluctant to lose the chance by breaking with the two major federal parties. Four prairie Liberal leaders received appointments to the bench from 1920 to 1930: J.R. Boyle (1924) and C.R. Mitchell (1926) of Alberta, W. M. Martin (1922) of Saskatchewan, and H.A. Robson (1929) of Manitoba. A. B. Hudson, the Manitoba Liberal who turned Progressive with John W. Dafoe and T.A. Crerar after 1919, was soon enticed back into the Liberal party by Mackenzie King, and was eventually appointed (1936) to the Supreme Court of Canada. Premier T.C. Norris of Manitoba (1915–1922), who flirted with the provincial farmers' party from 1920 to 1922, but never clearly repudiated his federal Liberal associations, was rewarded in 1928 by appointment to the Federal Board of Railway Commissioners. There is a certain predisposition to expect such appointments in the old parties.

[7] V.C. Fowke, *Canadian Agricultural Policy* (Toronto: University of Toronto Press, 1947), pp. 240, 270.

[8] See *A.B. Hudson Papers*, Memorandum (1925), No. 71; *Dafoe Papers*, John W. Dafoe to Sir Clifford Sifton (November 20, 1925); *Canadian Annual Review* (1925–1926), pp. 30, 31; *Manitoba Free Press* (October 10, 1925), 1.

of party, and Prime Minister King, despite his "five-cent" speech of 1930, did so after he returned to power in 1935. In all these cases, the federal attitude to the provinces depended upon dictates of equity, national interest, and national party advantage, not upon the complexions of the provincial regimes.

Prairie politics since 1917 shows that Frank H. Underhill's hypothesis that the real centres of political opposition in Canada are in the provincial governments requires more careful definition.[9] He sees "a peculiar and uniquely Canadian phenomenon" developing: a party system in which a powerful majority party at Ottawa, faced by a divided and ineffective opposition, is meeting its real opposition in the governments of the provinces. The theory was stimulated by knowledge of the long period of Liberal dominance at Ottawa before June 1957, and of the existence then of a growing number of provincial governments under the control of other parties.[10] It is defended by reference to voting statistics, showing that at times a significant proportion of the electorate votes for one party in provincial elections and for another party in federal elections. The implication of this cross-voting apparently is that the public acts more or less consciously to create a balance between the party in power at Ottawa and opposition governments in the provinces.

Local politicians at times do find it convenient to criticize federal policy. But this is not to say that the real opposition comes from the provinces. Provincial governments are not designed to oppose the party in power at Ottawa, for they are usually preoccupied with duties of a different nature than those performed by the federal government. If Professor Underhill's theory is interpreted to mean that opposition parties use provincial stepping stones to achieve national power, it also requires qualification. Provincial elections in 1921, 1929, 1934, and 1935 did reveal prairie dissatisfaction with the incumbent governments at Ottawa and added to the tides that later brought their defeat. An opposition party may gain by provincial election victories if the timing of elections permits. But provincial victories are not prerequisites of national victory, as the Conservative party showed in the West in 1957 and 1958. Voters sometimes support one party in provincial elections and another in federal elections, but this may be as much the result of a desire to cast a vote for a candidate with a chance of election as of a desire to oppose the federal government in local elections. In the voters' minds, at least, if not in the politicians', the fields of federal and provincial politics are frequently unrelated.

[9] See his *Canadian Political Parties* (Ottawa: The Canadian Historical Association, Historical Booklets No. 8, 1957), p. 19.

[10] Before the federal election of June 1957, seven of the ten provinces were governed by the Conservative, Social Credit, C.C.F. or Union Nationale parties; three provinces of small population, Manitoba, Prince Edward Island, and Newfoundland, were Liberal.

Professor Underhill's theory reduces to the simple fact that the attitudes of provincial governments and the results of provincial elections are two signs, among others, of the public mood in a federal system.

A theory of the prairie party system of greater ideological complexity has been proposed by C.B. Macpherson in his *Democracy in Alberta*.[11] From a position of economic determinism, he concludes that there has emerged in Alberta, and the other two prairie provinces, and "less definitely but perceptibly, in Canada as a whole,"[12] a new kind of party system that is neither plebiscitary democracy, nor the familiar two-party system of democratic theory, nor a one-party system. He calls it a "quasi–party system." He notices that in 1921 and 1935 radical parties came to power in Alberta virtually unopposed, and opposition to them in the legislatures remained weak. He notices, too, that both the U.F.A. and Social Credit gave up their radicalism under the pressures of office. He is not satisfied that this retreat into conservatism can be explained by Michels' theory of the need to create a bureaucracy to carry out reforms, and by the desire of the leaders to increase their power. He believes that "they were . . . compelled to take a relatively conservative position when they saw where they really stood in relation to the established economy. . . . It was not that the exigencies of government, as such, caused the leaders on attaining office to become orthodox both in their economic policies and in their practice of democracy. Rather, the exigencies of governing a society of independent producers, in revolt against outside domination but not against property, brought out the conservatism inherent in *petit-bourgeois* agrarian radicalism."[13]

He explains the long dominance in Alberta of a single party, faced by a weak legislative opposition, as essentially the result of the homogeneous *petit-bourgeois* illusions held by Alberta farmers, who believe themselves to have more independence than they actually have, and who have revolted in politics in an effort to realize the independence they crave. The farmers and their political representatives fluctuate between radical discontent with the external forces that control their economic security, and conservatism when they find that they cannot fundamentally alter their insecurity without destroying the economic system. They give their support, in outbursts of dissatisfaction, to one dominant party that talks of reform but is really conservative.

Macpherson introduces the phrase "quasi-party system" because he believes that the political system of Alberta is peculiar and permanent. It is not

[11] C.B. Macpherson, *Democracy in Alberta* (Toronto: University of Toronto Press, 1953), pp. 3–27, 215–250.
[12] *Ibid.*, p. 215.
[13] *Ibid.*, p. 220.

equivalent to the common Anglo-American two- or three-party system, in which the alternating parties act as brokers among sectional and interest groups, hindrances to oligarchy, and moderators of class conflict. He regards a party system primarily as a means of moderating class conflict; but referring to Alberta, he suggests "... the absence of any serious opposition of classes within the province meant that alternate parties were not needed either to express or to moderate a perennial conflict of interests."[14] The Alberta "quasi-party system," in Professor Macpherson's view, maintains democracy and moderates a class conflict that is not an internal one in the province, but one between the province and outside centres of capital. The system either controls class conflict by giving an outlet to the class feeling of the province or conceals the conflict by demagogic appeals for unity in the pursuit of impossible objects.

Macpherson's criteria for recognizing a "quasi-party system" seem to be long tenure of power by one party, a weak opposition, and a tendency of the party in power to become Jacobin, irresponsible to the people and renewing its authority by periodic plebiscites. He considers this to be the only possible system in Alberta, and perhaps in Canada, because, he maintains, the foundations for a two-party system do not exist.

The long dominance of single parties in Alberta, Saskatchewan, and Manitoba has not primarily been the result of the behaviour of a *petit bourgeois* community in revolt against semicolonial domination from the East. Reaction against the East has been a recurrent factor in prairie politics, but not an exclusive one. The charismatic power and political intuition of a few men has been as important, especially in Alberta. Henry Wise Wood, William Aberhart, Ernest Manning, Tommy Douglas, and John Diefenbaker were successful because they possessed unique talents of persuasiveness, timing, and awareness of the western mentality and were also blessed with good fortune; not because the prairies were occupied by independent producers.

Prairie governments have not been consistently opposed to the East and the old parties, as Macpherson implies: the Liberal party which ruled Saskatchewan from 1905 to 1944 (with one interruption) was for most of the time in open, even defiant, union with the federal Liberal party. The Progressive government of Manitoba gradually, though unobtrusively, moved into the federal Liberal camp after 1928, and from 1931 described itself as a Liberal-Progressive coalition.

Opposition in the prairie legislatures has, as Professor Macpherson notes, been weak in numbers and effectiveness. The numerical weakness of opposition groups in the legislatures, however, does not reflect the absence of

[14] *Ibid.*, p. 21.

opposition voters. Popular support for prairie governments has never been unusually high by the standards of other democratic countries. No prairie party has received more than fifty-eight per cent of the popular vote in a provincial election since 1917. In the elections in which single parties swept over four-fifths of the constituencies, they were able to do so because the opposition votes were divided among a large number of candidates and distributed fairly uniformly among the constituencies.[15] Opponents of the dominant prairie parties have frequently been unable to combine in opposition for reasons of federal party interest. (This was especially the case in Alberta from 1937 to 1940 when there was wide dissatisfaction with Premier Aberhart, yet provincial Liberals and Conservatives were pulled apart by the demands of the federal party organizations.)

Insipid legislative opposition has been partly the product of a non-partisan approach to politics on the prairies. But this does not mean that westerners, because they share a common economic position, are incapable of supporting competitive political parties. There are more strictly political reasons for the failure of opposition on the prairies. The nonpartisan movement after 1917 was created by the frontier farmer's distaste for privilege that was much more than a simple economic impulse, by moral reaction against the excesses of the provincial Liberal and Conservative parties, and by a sense of common grievance against the political and economic power of central Canada. The political calm in the provincial legislatures lasted for several years after 1921; but it signified a return to moderation in politics rather than the triumph of a fundamental nonpartisan tradition.

Professor Macpherson's suggestion that the alternate party system never took firm root in western Canada must, in the light of prairie voting statistics, be modified. What have not taken root are the conventions of parliamentary debate and opposition within the provincial legislatures. The centre of the political battle has rarely been in the legislatures. Prairie legislatures had no independent traditions, self-respect, or position in society before universal suffrage, as did the British House of Commons. They have never acquired them; politicians and the public still regard the legislatures as slightly strange, imported contrivances to be treated with awe but ordinarily to be ignored. Political leaders seek sustenance through public acclaim on the hustings, not through legislative debate.[16] Successful politicians on the prairies (being

[15] The leading party won over four-fifths of the seats in Saskatchewan in 1917, 1925, 1934, 1944, and 1952; in Alberta in 1935, 1944, 1948, 1952, and 1959.

[16] The level of legislative debate has been mediocre, and there has been little incentive to raise it. For most of the period, no reports of debates were kept for the information of the public. Saskatchewan, however, has broadcast the first seventy-five minutes of each day's debates since 1946, and transcripts of debates have been available to members since 1947. Manitoba introduced a provincial Hansard for the first time in October 1958. It is significant that in the heat of the 1962

practical men) have developed the talents—and parties, the forms of organization–required for their purposes. Political groups in the legislature have no coherence or permanence but depend for their life on the mood of a public with few inherited loyalties. The achievement of power comes not from the accumulation of cases against the governments in the legislatures (the public is unaware of any continuity that there may be in legislative debate), but more directly from management of the vote by an efficient machine, from long-term public attachment to a leader, or from demagogic appeals that turn sudden changes of public feeling to partisan advantage. Party competition exists, but it is manifested in tidal changes in voting habits rather than in day-to-day debate in the legislatures. A restrained plebiscitary system of democracy exists on the prairies; it does not merit Professor Macpherson's description as a "quasi-party system." The final safeguard of democracy, the opportunity to replace a government by popular vote, is preserved by the fluid party system of western Canada. But the more immediate advantage of a free party system, a conscientious legislative opposition, does not exist. Cabinets tend to justify their acts by appeals to the electorate over the heads of legislators; they are not in the habit of submitting policies to critical scrutiny by the legislative opposition. The public does not demand it, and members do not train themselves for the work. The farmer's conventions in all three provinces before and after the First World War, and the C.C.F. conventions in Saskatchewan after 1944, for a few years substituted their criticism for that of the legislatures. But they had neither the skills nor the machinery of criticism that an alert legislature may develop, and their influence was ephemeral. Tolerance for persistent critical opposition, and the security and institutional aids such opposition requires, are still absent in prairie politics; prairie society is neither self-confident enough nor distant enough from its days of romantic innocence and isolation to recognize their values.

Saskatchewan medical care controversy, there was no discussion of the value of a legislative session until the doctors' strike was in progress. The entire controversy occurred outside the legislature, through press conferences, radio and television statements, and newspaper advertisements. When the legislature did meet in August, it accomplished its work of amendment in a single day with virtually no debate.

The Speakership of the Canadian House of Commons: Some Proposals

(1965)

The raucous parliamentary debate on a natural gas pipeline in 1956 raised questions about the neutrality of the Speaker of the Canadian House of Commons. That troubling experience stimulated popular and academic interest in the role of the Speaker, and in 1965 the House of Commons Special Committee on Procedure and Organization invited me to study the office and make proposals for changes in the rules and customs governing it. A number of these changes (though not all) were subsequently adopted by the House. After the change of government in 2015 and the former Speaker's immediate and startling reversion to a leading critic's role on the opposition front bench, the House may need to re-examine the last section of this paper.

The status and responsibilities of the Speaker of the Canadian House of Commons are governed by the BNA Act, the Senate and House of Commons Act, the House of Commons Act, the Standing Orders of the House of Commons, and the conventions of the constitution relating to the practices of the House of Commons. The significance of the office derives above all from its representative character: the Speaker is the "first commoner," the spokesman and representative of the House of Commons in its relations with other institutions, and the chief servant of the House of Commons in the conduct of its own affairs. The central importance of the office thus rests upon the importance of the House of Commons. Because the House of Commons is the "superior power" in the constitution of the United Kingdom, the Canadian House of Commons is, similarly, the superior power in the Canadian constitution, since the preamble to the BNA Act establishes the convention that Canada shall have a constitution "similar in principle to that of the United Kingdom." The first member of the House of Commons, its presiding officer and representative, should occupy a position of dignity and eminence in keeping with the pre-eminence of the institution itself.[1] Canadian parliamentary

[1] "Excepting only the Sovereign herself, no personage throughout the structure of British parliamentary government occupies a higher pinnacle of prestige than the Speaker of the House of Commons. He embodies in his own person the dignity of the nation's representative assembly. The honour which is accorded his office is such as to sustain the authority of any incumbent, weak and strong alike . . . whoever assumes the Speaker's historic mantle inherits the dignity that goes with it, a dignity that is unfailingly maintained and enhanced at every opportunity." (Philip Laundy, *The Office of Speaker*, p. 7.)

experience, extending from before the Confederation of the provinces, has demonstrated the advantages of a free House or Commons in Canada, and the importance to that free House of Commons of a Speaker who commands universal respect and honour.

In its conduct and supervision of the nation's affairs, the House of Commons is guided by certain long-recognized principles. Among these are the responsibilities

> . . . to protect a minority and restrain the improvidence or tyranny of a majority; to secure the transaction of public business in an orderly manner; to enable every member to express his opinion within limits necessary to preserve decorum and prevent an unnecessary waste of time; to give abundant opportunity for the consideration of every measure, and to prevent any legislative action being taken upon sudden impulse.[2]

These constitutional duties of the House of Commons are distinctly different from the duties of the Cabinet, and even from those of the majority party in the House of Commons; they require a balancing of the rights and interests of majority and minority in order both that the public business may be efficiently transacted, and that the interests of every section of the public may be advocated and protected against the use of arbitrary authority. The rules of procedure established in the Standing Orders reflect the dual responsibility of the House, and the Speaker of the House of Commons, as the House's chief servant, is given the responsibility of applying the rules in this spirit. The Speaker is the servant not of any part of the House, nor of any temporary majority in the House, but of the best interest of the House as this interest has been distilled in the practices of the House over many generations.

Members of the Canadian House of Commons have always recognized that the successful exercise of his duty requires above all that the Speaker shall be impartial and shall be seen to be impartial. "Confidence in the impartiality of the Speaker is an indispensable condition of the working of procedure, and many conventions exist which have as their object not only to ensure the impartiality of the Speaker but also to ensure that his impartiality is generally recognized."[3] From the time of the first election to the Chair of the House in 1867, members of all parties have echoed their belief in the absolute need for an impartial Speaker, and on more than one occasion have reflected wistfully

[2] Sir J.G. Bourinot, quoted in Beauchesne, Arthur, *Rules and Forms of the House of Commons of Canada*, 4th edition, Toronto: Carswell, 1958, citation 4, p. 8.
[3] *Ibid.*, citation 68 (1), pp. 56–57.

that the conventions and rules governing the Canadian Speakership make achievement of the ideal difficult. Canadian observers of the Speakership have almost always been kind in their judgments of those who have occupied the Chair, but have been disappointed by the weakness or absence of practical buttresses which will support and guarantee the good intentions of the incumbents. This paper will examine what institutional weaknesses may make it difficult for Speakers in the Canadian House of Commons to assure their own independence and the appearance of independence; and it will consider whether the Speakership, as presently provided for, possesses the prestige and distinction that the office should reasonably have as the symbol of the House of Commons' authority.

THE ELECTION OF THE SPEAKER

Section 44 of the BNA Act provides that "the House of Commons on its first assembling after a general election shall proceed with all practicable speed to elect one of its members to be Speaker." Section 45 of the Act provides for the election in the same manner of a Speaker during the life of a Parliament in the event of a vacancy occurring in the Chair through resignation, dismissal or death. The ritual of election, the Speaker's claim to the Governor-General for the rights and privileges of the Commons, the Governor-General's grant to the House of its ancient rights and privileges, are familiar and need no special comment.

One aspect of the Speaker's election, however, deserves reconsideration: this is the custom that the nomination to the Chair is proposed by the Prime Minister and seconded by a minister.[4]

It is natural that the Prime Minister, as the leader of the House of Commons, should take the initiative in seeking a candidate for the office of Speaker. But it is less fitting that he should actually propose the nomination to the Chair. This practice is likely to create the impression among members of the House of Commons and the public that the choice of a Speaker is the prerogative of the Prime Minister; and this is especially likely if a change of government has occurred. The selection of a candidate for Speaker by the Prime Minister in this circumstance easily becomes confused with the process of selecting a cabinet. The Prime Minister may be encouraged to think of the Speakership as just one of the offices within his patronage, for distribution

[4] On three occasions, in 1953, 1957, and 1958, the nomination has been seconded by the leader of the Opposition as a mark of the official Opposition's confidence in the candidate. While this practice improves upon the usual one by requiring consultation and by taking part of the responsibility for the nomination out of the hands of the government, it is still not ideal. The nomination remains, in appearance, that of the leaders of the House, rather than of the whole House.

among his colleagues according to the same political calculations that apply to the nomination of ministers; and if the Prime Minister has a higher concept of his duty, the public at least may be confused.

Members of the House of Commons acknowledged long ago that to emphasize the independence of the Chair, it would be desirable to begin by treating the nomination in a conspicuously non-partisan way. The form of nomination should demonstrate, as other conventions do, that "the House chooses and elects its Speaker; he is in no sense the choice of the Government—in no sense the choice of the Prime Minister."[5] The Speaker's position as the independent servant of the entire House could be symbolized by arranging for his formal nomination to be made by two private members, one from the government side and one from the opposition side, after consultation and agreement among all parties on a suitable candidate. While possessing the confidence of the majority party, he would not be its official candidate for this office. The means of nomination would discourage the suspicion that the Speakership is given as a reward for party services.

The adoption of this reform would require only a change in practice on the part of the Prime Minister. He would have to ensure consultation among the parties on the nominee, through the usual channels, and arrange for the candidate's nomination by backbenchers on both sides of the House.

THE SPEAKER'S TERM

Although five Canadian Speakers have been re-elected to the Chair for a second term,[6] and one of these for a third term, the normal Canadian practice has been to elect a new Speaker at the opening of each new Parliament. Occupation of the Chair has never effectively been regarded as a career by members of the House of Commons, but rather as a three, four or five year interlude in a political career. The nomination to the Speakership has been regarded as one of the gifts in the hands of the leader of the majority party, and never has the nomination gone to a member of any other but the party forming the government. In the four cases in which the incumbents were re-elected to the Chair, no change of government had occurred; the former party affiliation of the Speaker thus remained with the government party. . . .

What is the case for continuity in the Chair? It has been made repeatedly in this country and in the United Kingdom, and it is straightforward. Sir Robert Peel expressed it succinctly in proposing the re-election of the Speaker at Westminister in 1841:

[5] Rt. Hon. Arthur Meighen, *Canada, House of Commons Debates*, March 8, 1922, quoted in Beauchesne, *op. cit*., citation 28(1), p. 22.

[6] Cockburn, Rhodes, Lemieux, Michener, and Lamoureux.

> First, I do not think it for the public advantage that the election for the Chair should necessarily be made the object of a party.
> Secondly, I do not think it would be just towards a Speaker who has shown himself well qualified for his office, and has in my opinion acted fairly and impartially, to reject him.
> Thirdly, I think that the late Speaker, if he be re-elected with the general goodwill of the House, will have greater authority and power to preserve order than a Speaker elected after a party contest.[7]

In spite of the virtually unanimous professions of confidence in the particular occupants of the Chair in Canada made by parliamentarians since 1867, there has lingered in Ottawa a feeling that the Speaker's impartiality cannot always be taken for granted. This feeling has been most evident among members of the opposition parties. While no decisive evidence of collusion between the government and the Chair has ever been presented in the House, and while the record of Canadian Speakers as independent men seems, in retrospect, remarkably good, at various times members of the opposition have suspected bias against them in the rulings of the Speaker. The suspicion has been given support by the conventions governing the Speaker's election, and especially by the convention that the Speakership changes hands at the beginning of each Parliament. The nomination, as has been mentioned, frequently becomes confused with the choice of a cabinet. The successful nominee, knowing that he can expect only a short term in the Chair, is discouraged from regarding the election as the beginning of a non-partisan career as Speaker; and members of the Opposition are forever wary that he will make his rulings in the knowledge that his future career depends on the favour of the majority party. There is always likely to be a doubt among the Opposition that the Speaker, whatever his claim to independence, regards his years in the Chair as simply an interruption in a party career: a period of suspended loyalty, but one nevertheless in which party loyalty remains present at some level of his consciousness. The office does not quite inspire the judicial trust that it should, because members know that the Speaker may shortly become a partisan again. It is the uncertain expectation that above all destroys absolute trust. And yet the authority of the Speaker in guiding the House depends essentially upon the absence of suspicion, on "perfect confidence . . . on the part of all the members of the House of Commons."[8]

To have perfect confidence, the House must know that the Speaker "has

[7] Quoted in W.I. Jennings, *Parliament*, Cambridge: The University Press, 1961, p. 66.
[8] J.H. Aitchison, *The Speakership in 1962*, a talk on the CBC National Network, July 19, 1962.

nothing to lose by doing right and nothing to gain by doing wrong."[9] The most certain guarantee of this is to give the Speaker secure tenure in the Chair, and to remove his future entirely from the patronage of any one party in the House. If the Speaker is to possess the confidence that members of the judiciary are normally accorded, he must hold office on judicial terms; he should not have to plan for another career, most possibly political, after a short term in the Chair. He should be encouraged by a guarantee of secure tenure to regard the Speakership as a career which needs to be undertaken for its own sake alone. He should be able to expect ten, fifteen, or twenty years in the office, rather than four or five.[10]

The argument for competence in the Chair reinforces the case for continuity. A Speaker with long experience is not only likely to be above suspicion of partisanship, but also to be a more capable Speaker than a temporary one. Mastery in the Chair is not something that can be acquired without practice. At the least, the present custom involves frequent periods of breaking-in to the Chair during which the Speakers' knowledge of their task and their authority may be shaky.[11]

Continuity in the office is desirable; but it needs to be more carefully defined. Proposals for an extended term do not call for literal permanence in the Chair. The House must remain the master of its own affairs, and the Speaker must remain the servant of the House in the application of the rules adopted by the House. If, in spite of the best will of the House, a Speaker is seriously incompetent, or biased, the House must possess the means of showing its dissatisfaction and replacing him. "Permanency" in the Chair should mean only that the Speaker will be re-elected without opposition by the House at the opening of each new Parliament for as long as he is able and willing to serve and continues to possess the confidence of the House. The elected term would still be for a single Parliament, and an unsatisfactory Speaker could be replaced in the next Parliament. The same convention of confidence in the Speaker would apply as at present: the possibility of a substantive motion of censure would remain, and the support of such a motion by a sub-

[9] J.H. Aitchison, "The Speakership of the Canadian House of Commons," in R.M. Clark (ed.), *Canadian Issues*, Toronto: University of Toronto Press, 1961.

[10] The longest tenures of the Speakership at Westminster have been those of Onslow (1728–1761), Abbott (1802–1817), Manners-Sutton (1817–1835), Shaw-Lefevre (1839–1857), Denison (1857–1872), and Lowther (1905–1921). The average tenure of the five twentieth century Speakers preceding the present one has been eleven years. The former incumbent, Sir Harry Hylton-Foster, was first elected to the Chair in 1959, and was sustained in office after the change of government in October 1964.

[11] "After a Canadian Speaker has spent his first few years in this precarious position he finds that a new election has been held and that he is quietly dropped, just as he is reaching maturity in office." W.F. Dawson, *Procedure in the Canadian House of Commons*, Toronto: University of Toronto Press, 1962, pp. 80–81.

stantial minority would be a sign that the Speaker's position had become untenable.

This reform can be achieved without any change in the Standing Orders. It requires only the agreement of the parties in the House, a public commitment by the party leaders in each Parliament, before dissolution, to support the incumbent Speaker for re-election in the new House *whatever party wins the intervening election*, an electoral agreement in the Speaker's constituency, and the good faith of the parties in carrying out the commitment in the new Parliament. In 1958 and 1962, appeals were made to the party leaders to commit themselves to support the re-election of Mr. Speaker Michener to the Chair in advance of, and whatever the outcome of, the general elections. But the party leaders failed to act. Some firm public commitment seems necessary if the existing practice is to be altered: the mere expression of general interest in reform, without commitment to it, has proven futile. The long-term maintenance of the convention would depend upon the will of the House to do so in subsequent Parliaments; but if one Speaker survived a change of government the custom would have passed its most severe test.

The establishment of continuity in the Chair should make no difference to the practice of alternating between English-speaking and French-speaking incumbents. The existing custom would be maintained as a matter of course; and it should be taken for granted that every Speaker will be fluent in both the languages of Parliament.

THE SPEAKER AT GENERAL ELECTIONS

If the Speaker is to be re-elected to the Chair for more than a single term, the Speaker's role in general elections is inevitably complicated. The chief purposes of continuity are to encourage the fact and the appearance of impartiality, and to ensure competence in the Chair. But in the present situation, however impartial and aloof from party activity the Speaker may be during the life of a Parliament, if he wishes to run for Parliament again, he is forced to fall back into the partisan struggle at each general election, and to risk defeat. He is opposed by partisan candidates, and is faced with an awkward dilemma: he must either discourage his constituency organization from conducting a partisan campaign (in which case he places himself at a disadvantage in comparison with opponents who lack similar restraint), or he must throw himself and his organization fully into the battle at the expense of his reputation for non-partisanship. The immediacy of this dilemma was painfully revealed in the 1962 general election, when Mr. Speaker Michener, whose conduct of the Speakership was universally admired, and who might well have been re-elected to the Chair in the 25th Parliament, was defeated in his constituency.

The reluctance of the parties to protect the Speaker from partisan conflict in his constituency has, understandably, prompted advocates of a continuing Speakership to accuse the parties of hypocrisy. Professor Aitchison remarked in 1962 that "I am angry . . . because those with power to act, though they profess to be committed to the principle of a permanent Speakership, refused to do what was easy and simple to put the principle into effect."[12] Perhaps the lesson of 1958, 1962 and 1963 is less simple. It seems evident that no electoral arrangement between the parties in the Speaker's constituency can be made quickly, after a parliamentary dissolution, since by this time the momentum of party conflict in the constituency, the commitment of volunteers and the organization of the campaign, is too far advanced to be halted. No party is willing to consider such an act of restraint unless it is sure the others will do the same; but the parties have neither the time, nor are they in the mood at this stage, to consider such an agreement. The decentralized nature of party organization in Canada, too, makes it necessary to gain agreement both at the national and the constituency levels; and the diffusion of responsibility relieves any one level of blame for the failure of an all-party arrangement.

In addition, as previously noted, there has never been any formal guarantee that the incumbent Speaker would in fact be re-nominated to the Chair even if he were acclaimed in in his constituency. No Prime Minister has ever publicly committed himself in advance to the re-election of the incumbent to the Speakership in the next House. . . . The public understanding of the Speaker's special position of independence is probably not as general as it is in the United Kingdom, and a party contest in his constituency is taken for granted as the usual practice rather than the exception in Canada. An uncontested election would require explanation and justification, even among those active in party work and presumably relatively familiar with the nature of parliamentary government, and such justification, to be sufficiently convincing, would require time. It would also require authority behind it: the authority of a few concerned citizens has been shown to be insufficient.

The familiar criticisms of uncontested elections in the Speaker's constituency are that they result in the atrophy of party organizations in the constituency, and that they deprive the electors in the constituency of the opportunity to exercise their fundamental right to choose among party candidates at general elections. The further argument is frequently made that after his election to the Chair, the Speaker's constituents are virtually deprived of normal representation in Parliament.

The first complaint is, within limits, justified. The acceptance of the principle of acclamation for the Speaker in his constituency would mean the intentional weakening of party associations in the constituency for the period that

[12] Aitchison, *The Speakership in 1962*.

that member holds the Chair. To be acceptable, such an act of self-denial would have to be undertaken equally by all parties. One of Mr. Coldwell's complaints in 1958 was that as long as the Speaker himself was proposed by a party association as a party candidate, the opposition parties could hardly be expected to treat him as an independent. The Speaker's party organization would be free to exercise its muscles in the campaign, but the opposition organizations would be expected not to do so. When the Speaker finally retired and normal party competition returned to the constituency, the opposition organizations might well be moribund. The fair solution would seem to be for each party association to nominate the Speaker as a non-partisan candidate, and for each association to participate in the campaign for his re-election. While political activity in the constituency would be low, this would at least stimulate some continuity in the associations during the Speaker's term of office; and the party from which the Speaker was originally chosen would not gain any special advantage as 'the Speaker's party.'

The second criticism, that all electors should have the right to choose among party candidates, can only be met with the argument that, while this is a fundamental right in a free parliamentary system, the successful operation of that very system requires that one constituency should temporarily give up this right in order to support an independent Speaker of the House, the protector of the rights of all parties in the House. Two conflicting principles, both of them basic ones in a parliamentary system, must be reconciled, and the parties must weigh the importance of the Speaker's position against the right of voters in his constituency to express partisan choices. It can be argued in support of all-party co-operation in the Speaker's constituency that two-party or all-party co-operation has frequently occurred for other reasons in various constituencies, formally or informally, without any serious objection on principle that the electors are being deprived of a free choice. What is proposed is not, in any case, that all possibility of an alternative choice should be eliminated in the constituency: only that there should be no *official* party opponents. If an independent candidate wished to contest the Speaker's seat, there would of course be no means of preventing his candidacy.

The third complaint about the Speaker's constituency is that, while he is in the Chair, the Speaker ceases to be an effective representative of his constituents' interests. This claim is not justified by experience. The Speaker does give up his public advocacy of these interests from the floor of the House; but he continues to perform many private tasks for his constituents, as any private member does; and he continues to speak informally for his constituents to the various ministries. His position of eminence in the House is probably advantageous for his constituents,

> Because none of us is under any illusion at all that a request to a

> minister from yourself, Mr. Speaker, would probably produce much faster results than would be achieved by any one of the political proletariat here.[13]

The Hon. Marcel Lambert has suggested that this judgment is applicable also to the Speaker of the Canadian House of Commons.[14]

There seems to be no unanswerable objection to the acclamation of the Speaker in his constituency; and it is evident that no determined effort has yet been made by the parties to arrange for his acclamation in any general election in Canada. It would be appropriate, as the most simple step toward the re-election of the Speaker without a party contest, for the parties in the House now to make a real and coordinated effort to arrange for his acclamation at the next general election. A public show of common purpose by all parties in the House, and support for it in the Speaker's constituency by the local party associations, are essential if the precedent is to be established. A commitment to acclaim the Speaker should be declared long enough in advance of the general election to illustrate its sincerity and to permit time for the principle to be publicly defended. And it would have to be accompanied by the commitment recommended earlier, to support the re-nomination of the same person to the Chair in the next House.

AN ALTERNATIVE PROPOSAL FOR THE SPEAKER'S CONSTITUENCY

Acclamation of the Speaker in his constituency would require political agreement. If the parties believe in the importance of an impartial and continuing Speaker, this agreement should be possible to obtain through patient discussion and negotiation officially supported by the party caucuses and organizations. But, as the British experience has shown, such gentlemen's agreements are by their nature temporary and insecure, and must frequently be defended and renewed. . . . The relative autonomy of Canadian constituency associations from their parent bodies would probably make agreements to acclaim the Speaker even more precarious in Canada than in the United Kingdom. If agreement were seriously attempted in Canada and failed, the Speaker would again face political opposition and the possibility of defeat in his constituency; Mr. Speaker Michener's defeat while in the Chair showed that this unfortunate possibility is real.

The expected difficulty of acclaiming the Speaker, along with the 1962 example, has prompted some supporters of a continuing Speakership in Can-

[13] Richard Marsh, MP, speaking in the United Kingdom House of Commons in 1963, *UK Parliamentary Debates (Hansard)*, Session 1962–63, Volume 676, Column 230.
[14] Conversation with Mr. Lambert, February 19, 1965.

ada to propose another arrangement for the Speaker's seat. This involves the creation of a special constituency of Parliament Hill, whose electors would be the members of the House of Commons, and whose member would be the Speaker of the House of Commons. Upon election to the Chair, the Speaker would cease to sit for an ordinary constituency; his former constituency would be opened to a by-election, and the Speaker would no longer face the danger of partisan opposition on the hustings. Aside from the special nature of his constituency, the Speaker's election to the Chair would be governed by the existing practices. An election to the Chair would occur on the first day of meeting of a new Parliament, or immediately upon the resignation or death of an incumbent Speaker. The existing rule governing a substantive motion of censure of the Speaker would stand. But, since the purpose of the proposal is to encourage continuity in the Chair, it could be assumed that the Speaker, once elected as the member for Parliament Hill, would be re-elected without opposition by the House as long as he was a satisfactory Speaker and wished to serve.

The conception of a special constituency for the Speaker of the House of Commons is not new. In 1939, a Select Committee on Parliamentary Elections (Mr. Speaker's Seat) considered and reported upon such a proposal for the Speaker's seat at Westminster. It had been asked to examine

> What steps, if any, should be taken to ensure that, having due regard to the constitutional rights of the electors, the Speaker, during his continuance in office, shall not be required to take part in a contested parliamentary election.[15]

But the Committee recommended no change in the existing arrangements for the Speaker's seat. After considering the suggestion for a special Speaker's constituency, the Committee concluded that

> To alter the status of the Speaker so that he ceased to be returned to the House of Commons by the same electoral methods as other members or as a representative of a Parliamentary constituency would be . . . repugnant to the custom and tradition of the House. . . . The proper aloofness of the Speaker from the political actions of the members would in time deteriorate to the detachment of the official.[16]

A further overriding consideration influencing the Committee was that, since the Speakership at Westminster was already successfully non-partisan

[15] Quoted in *The Times*, April 14, 1939.
[16] *Ibid.*

and continuing, it would be unwise to recommend any departure from tradition which might itself make the Speakership an object of political controversy during discussion of the recommendation. It is impossible to tell from the document which objection to change weighed most heavily with the Committee: the desire to avoid controversy, the generalized complaint that a special seat would be "repugnant to the custom and tradition of the House," or the fear that a specially elected Speaker might grow aloof from the other members of the House. Given the already generally satisfactory conventions surrounding the British Speakership, the Committee's conclusion seems readily justifiable. But it is also apparent that the Committee's conclusion does not necessarily apply to the different circumstances of Canada.

The argument for avoiding controversy, for one thing, carries little weigh here. The Canadian Speakership has unfortunately been a recent object of controversy, is not yet satisfactorily protected from political pressures, and needs public defence. There would be little sense in claiming in Canada that certain reforms should not be considered because they might involve the Chair in political controversy; they need to be considered precisely to remove the Chair from political controversy. The Canadian Speakership has suffered from recurrent suspicions of bias, from a severe motion of censure, and from the electoral defeat of an incumbent Speaker. These are all complaints peculiar to the Canadian situation, and demand the application of special remedies. A special constituency for the Speaker seems at least worth considerate study.

The argument from tradition has strength: it suggests caution in the application of parliamentary reform, to ensure that valuable features of the parliamentary system will not be lost unwittingly in the pursuit of change. But Parliament is not an institution based upon an unchangeable or logical pattern. It is full of incongruities that exist because they work. The test for parliamentary devices should be whether they actually achieve what they are meant to achieve; if they do not, then other devices may legitimately be adopted. It is not "repugnant to the custom and tradition of the House" to have an independent Speaker: members since 1867 have held this to be desirable. If the creation of a special constituency will make this possible, without creating any very obvious difficulties, it should be worth the trial.

The suggestion that a Speaker elected from a special constituency of Parliament Hill would cease to look upon himself as one Commoner among others, and would grow superior, aloof, and bureaucratic in his approach to the Speakership, is difficult to assess because it rests upon conjecture. But it is open to some doubt. For one thing, it is inaccurate to say that the Canadian Speaker in his present situation is a member of the House like any other. He is already an extraordinary MP, not an ordinary one. He has great powers in the conduct of debate not possessed by other members; he is non-partisan; he has a special position in the order of precedence; he has the authority of a long tradition to sustain him; he alone among the members of the House continues to exercise his authority as an officer of the House after a parliamentary dissolution. To create a special constituency for the Speaker would not suddenly and unalterably set him apart from his fellows in the House: it would merely confirm in one more way that he is, and must be, a member apart. The constituency of Parliament Hill would be a "constitutional fiction," but there are already many commonly accepted and convenient constitutional fictions in the Canadian parliamentary system. In many senses, the Speaker already acts, in effect, as "the member for Parliament Hill," since the statutes require him to do so.

On the other hand, a Speaker elected from a special constituency would be influenced in many ways to remain the servant of the House, and sympathetic to it. Above all, his function would be what it is today, and he would carry it out within the House, not apart from it. He would have to be re-elected at the commencement of each Parliament. If he failed to act fairly or competently during the life of a Parliament, he would still be subject to a motion of censure, which it would be in his interest to avoid by acting in the best interest of the Chair. He would invariably be a person with some previous experience in the House, and familiar with it. If it is now possible for a member who is elected Speaker to throw off his former political commitments by an act of will and imagination, it should equally be possible for a Speaker elected from a special Speaker's constituency to continue to regard himself essentially as a member of the House of Commons.

The creation of a constituency of Parliament Hill would permanently solve the problem of partisan competition in the Speaker's constituency. It might be easier to achieve than acclamation for the Speaker in a normal constituency, since it would involve the decision only of members of Parliament; the interests of local party associations and prospective candidates would not be influencing factors. Once established, there would be no need for the renewal of any all-party agreements except the agreement on the initial choice of a candidate by the whole House.

Because the special constituency is an unusual departure from existing practice, it might be held in reserve by the House as a reform to be adopted if the parties fail at the next election to make any progress toward acclamation of the Speaker in his constituency. There might possibly be a commitment by the House, and by the parties in their platforms, to support a Bill to create a special constituency at the beginning of the next Parliament if acclamation fails.

THE SPEAKER'S AUTHORITY

However competent he may be, the Canadian Speaker suffers from one fatal disadvantage. He is simply unable to establish his authority in the House because the Standing Orders provide for appeals against his rulings.[17] The appeals rule is unfortunate from every point of view. The confidence of a Speaker who attempts to apply the rules judiciously and fairly can constantly be undermined by members of the House who are not always careful students of the rules, but who may challenge his rulings on irrelevant grounds. Appeals can be used by members of the opposition as weapons of delay and harassment against the government; in this case, the government majority normally comes to the support of the Speaker and creates the unfortunate impression that the Speaker is an agent of the government in the application of the rules. If, on the other hand, the majority is unhappy enough with a ruling to challenge it, the ruling can be overridden on appeal, whatever its merits, merely on the grounds that it does not serve the interests of the majority. A majority which resorts frequently to such a practice will entirely destroy the authority of the Speaker and the consistency with which the rules are applied. Such a possibility denies the very purpose of the Standing Orders. In both cases, the interpretation of the rules is taken out of the hands of the Speaker, whose object is to be impartial, and thrown into the political battle between parties.... There is no justification for the retention of the appeals rule.

Two simple reforms are possible. (Both are suggested by Professor Dawson in his *Procedure in the Canadian House of Commons.*[18]) Standing Order 12(1) could be amended to remove the opportunity to appeal. If this change in the rules were accompanied by the institution of continuity in the Chair, it would further strengthen the authority of the Speaker and remove one more suggestion of his dependence upon the government. Given a Speaker whose future career is no longer at the mercy of the government, the Opposition should be prepared to signify its full confidence in his independence by giving up its present right to challenge his rulings.

The Speaker, however, may sometimes make mistakes in applying the rules, and occasionally invites appeals on this ground.... The simple abolition of appeals would provide no recourse for the House against patently mistaken rulings, except the extreme recourse of a substantive motion of censure. An intermediate measure of reform might provide that an appeal could only be made by substantive motion accompanied by the citation of authorities and

[17] Standing Order 12(1): "Mr. Speaker shall preserve order and decorum, and shall decide questions of order, subject to an appeal to the House without debate. In explaining a point of order or practice, he shall state the standing order or authority applicable to the case."

[18] W.F. Dawson, *Procedure in the Canadian House of Commons*, Toronto, 1962, p. 84.

precedents in writing, and that such an appeal would be referred automatically by the House either to the Committee on Privileges and Elections or to the Committee on Procedure (if it were to become a Standing Committee). The appropriate Committee would examine the merits of the appeal, and report to the House, which would act upon the recommendation of the Committee to sustain the ruling or allow the appeal. This deliberate and formal procedure would eliminate most nuisance appeals, but would permit legitimate appeals based upon careful study of the rules.

THE DIGNITY OF THE SPEAKER

Two points are involved, one practical and one symbolic. The Speaker must be rewarded sufficiently to balance the tension, the sacrifice of a party career, and the abandonment of a private occupation that commitment to the Chair involves. The rewards of the office must be enough consistently to attract men of talent; and they must be enough to free the Speaker from any financial dependence which might compromise his position as the servant of the whole House. The Speaker's perquisites should, further, illustrate and reinforce his prestige as the leading member of the House of Commons: they must be the sufficient outward and visible signs of his pre-eminence.

The demands upon the Speaker's time and energies are extraordinary. He is tied to Parliament Hill during a session even more securely than is a minister of the Crown; he is responsible for a great volume of official entertainment; his alertness is constantly required while he is actually in the Chair; he has the responsibility for managing frequent delicate negotiations among the parties; and he is the head of a large administrative department. Merely to relieve the Speaker from any unnecessary distractions and to encourage the full concentration of his energies upon his duties requires substantial material rewards.

It would be appropriate, in the light of both of his onerous duties and his symbolic position as representative of the House of Commons, to make the salary of the Speaker at least equivalent to that of a minister. At present, the Speaker's income, including allowances, falls $5,500 short of this.[19] The Speakership should be recognized in the estimates as the equivalent of a Cabinet office.

In addition, the Speaker should be provided at the commencement of his term with a moving allowance which would permit him to bring his family

[19] The Speaker receives $18,000 as an MP ($6,000 tax-free), $9,000 as Speaker, a $3,000 allowance in lieu of residence, and a $1,000 motor car allowance. A minister receives $18,000 as an MP ($6,000 tax-free), $15,000 as a minister, a $2,000 motor car allowance, and a $1,500 allowance in lieu of residence (*Estimates for the Fiscal Year 1964–1965*).

and possessions to Ottawa at parliamentary expense. This allowance should probably be in the range of $1,000 to $1,500. His residential allowance should be somewhat increased—perhaps to $5,000—or renewed provision should be made for a Speaker's residence in the Parliament Buildings. An entertainment allowance should be provided as a specific item in the Speaker's estimates. The Speaker should be assured the permanent use of the country residence at Kingsmere.

Certain other reforms are desirable to enhance the dignity of the office of Speaker. The Canadian Speaker now ranks tenth in the order of precedence, below ambassadors and high commissioners, Cabinet ministers, Lieutenant-Governors, members of the Privy Council, and the Speaker of the Senate. He is given a relatively inconspicuous place in official ceremonies. The elevation of the Speaker to third place in the order of precedence, following the governor-General and the Prime Minister, would emphasize the significance both of the Speakership and of the House it represents. The Speaker's official wardrobe might contain, besides the black gown and the tricorn hat, a more colorful ceremonial robe for use in formal processions and ceremonies outside the House.

The Speaker's integrity as the spokesman for Parliament must be more scrupulously recognized by the ministry and the civil service than has been customary in Canada. The Speaker's jurisdiction over Parliament Hill as a representative of the House should be clearly established. Ceremonies and conferences on the Hill should be the Speaker's responsibility, rather than the responsibility of the ministry, and the Cabinet should not take for granted that whatever arrangements it wishes to make will be satisfactory to the Speaker. The Speaker should have a certain clearly established power to requisition the use of facilities by the House of Commons for its purposes, without having to appeal as a supplicant to the ministry.

The Speaker's ambiguous relationship to the Commissioners of Internal Economy, and through them to the Treasury Board and the Cabinet, should be clarified. Since the Commissioners are given responsibility for the preparation and support of the estimates of the House of Commons, and the House and Speaker are, in theory, independent of the government, the Commissioners too should have a formal independence of the government. At present, the four Commissioners of Internal Economy provided for by the House of Commons Act in addition to the Speaker are all members of the Cabinet. While it is obviously necessary for the Cabinet to be represented on a commission which prepares estimates for the approval of the Treasury Board, it is not necessary that they should dominate it. In view of the Speaker's essential independence, it is transparently undesirable that they should do so. An amendment to the House of Commons Act should provide that two of the Commissioners of

Internal Economy shall be appointed from the opposition benches upon the advice of the opposition parties. A portion of the Speaker's revenues, too, including the salary and allowances of the Speaker and Deputy Speaker, might be made a statutory charge upon the Consolidated Revenue Fund and therefore not subject to annual review by the Commissioners, the Treasury Board, the Cabinet, and Parliament.

THE SPEAKER IN RETIREMENT

If the Speakership is to gain the reputation for absolute aloofness from politics that the office requires, the nature of the Speaker's retirement is also a matter of concern. An ex-Speaker must be as neutral in politics as he was during his tenure of office if he is to avoid casting doubt retrospectively upon his impartiality, or upon the impartiality of his successors. The convention must be established that a retiring Speaker departs altogether from the partisan political scene. This convention, like others involved in the creation of a continuing Speakership, demands a substantial sacrifice from Speakers, and must be offset by compensating privileges, if it is to be acceptable.

The ex-Speaker must be assured of financial security, so that he will not be forced for economic reasons to turn again to a political career. A special pension in addition to his normal parliamentary pension is desirable: perhaps in the range of $10,000 per year; and this pension should be made a statutory charge upon the Consolidated Fund.

Careful consideration must be given to whether a Speaker should be free to accept any kind of public office upon retirement. If such an appointment is made at the discretion of the ministry, the Speaker's future remains subject to partisan considerations. . . .

Public appointments of ex-Speakers must certainly be governed by scrupulous conditions. They must either be automatic, involving no individual discretion by the Prime Minister, or they must be made only after consultation and agreement with the leaders of the opposition parties. The offices themselves must be above political reproach, like the Speakership. An automatic appointment to the Senate is a possibility, providing the ex-Speaker recognizes that his role as a Senator cannot be that of an ordinary partisan. Appointments to major Royal Commissions of investigation are a possibility. Appointments to senior diplomatic positions may similarly be appropriate. The possibility of elevation to the Governor-Generalship is perhaps the most attractive one, since the two positions are alike in their essential natures. It would be wise in Canada to cultivate the special talents needed for such non-political offices of state, and to encourage those citizens of appropriate skill and ambitions to prepare themselves for this kind of service. The changes in the practices surrounding the Speakership recommended in this paper may thus be seen within the larger perspective of the national interest: the cultivation of a habit of service to the nation which transcends the ordinary interests of party. For the political parties themselves to promote the strengthening of such a habit would surely do credit to their own national spirit and generosity.

President and Parliament: The Transformation of Parliamentary Government in Canada

(1969)

As the burdens of government expanded after the Second World War, the Canadian House of Commons was slow to adjust to the new demands it faced. Partly this reluctance to consider reform stemmed from the mythology of parliamentary government inherited from British writers of the mid-nineteenth century. When a determined prime minister set out to revolutionize the House's practices, I saw a parallel and urgent need to jolt MPs and voters out of their misconceptions about how we are actually governed. This paper was delivered to a conference at Niagara Falls on Canadian priorities, promoted by the new leader of the Progressive Conservative party, Robert Stanfield, in October 1969. Its analysis has been widely accepted, but the concentration of power in the prime minister's office has continued to grow.

In the last five years, the Canadian House of Commons has gone through the first thorough and comprehensive reform of its procedures since 1867. The process of reform that was begun in 1964 came to a stormy climax last July with the adoption under closure of the government's proposal for a regular time-limitation (or guillotine) rule. While the government has agreed that there should be a review this autumn of the House's experience under the new rules, and while certain adjustments and refinements are likely, the body of the reformed rules will probably stand for a few sessions at least, while the House learns new habits and absorbs the effects of the changes that have occurred. These changes have been substantial ones, and it will take some time before their full implications become clear. What I would like to do in this paper is to try to make some assessment of the forces that led to the transformation of the House; to consider precisely what kinds of changes have taken place; and to speculate about where these changes may be leading us, whether we want to go that way, and what, if anything, might be done about it. This study will take me some way beyond the contemplation of House of Commons procedure in the narrow sense.

THE BREAKDOWN OF ORDERLY PROCEDURE

Members of the Canadian House of Commons have intermittently criticized aspects of the House's rules and practices since Confederation; and there have been desultory attempts to alter the rules in this century, especially in 1906, 1913, 1927, 1947, and 1955.[1] The rules adopted in 1867, which were taken over by the Legislative Assembly of the Province of Canada, followed the loose British parliamentary tradition of the period, allowing great latitude for free expression in the House, and giving the Government no special advantages.[2]

For nearly forty years the House carried on unchecked. The period up to 1906 was marked by lengthy speeches, obstruction by the opposition, and a total lack of efficiency in the conduct of business by the House.[3]

Government legislative programs were small, much of the business of the House was in the form of private members' bills encouraging national development; there was not much need for a sense of order or urgency in the House. While the British House of Commons abandoned this generous tradition of unrestricted debate under the pressure of Irish obstruction in the 1880s, the Canadian House was faithful to the tradition for decades longer.

The measures of reform adopted from time to time in this century have all tended to restrict unlimited debate in the House, by limiting acceptable motions and debatable motions (1906, 1913); by providing for the possibility of closure (1913); by limiting the length of speeches (1927, 1955, 1960); and by restricting the number of days devoted to major general debates on the Speech from the Throne, the budget, and supply (1955).[4] But the most severe restrictive measure, the closure, has rarely been used, because of its clumsiness and the likelihood of public criticism; and other measures have done little to make the House's operations more orderly or more subject to the efficient leadership of the government. As late as 1966, one observer commented that:

> The trend of these and other formal rules has been decidedly against the Opposition and the private member. But, in fact, these reforms have not materially restricted their right to speak. Nor have these reforms been significantly helpful to the Government's attempts to achieve efficient dispatch of Government business. The whole House is still a scene of protracted discussions on both generalities and details. The committees of the House have seldom been used to good effect. The question period has lengthened, sometimes to over one hour. In the wake of heated political rivalry and expansion of

[1] See W.F. Dawson, *Procedure in the Canadian House of Commons* (Toronto, 1962), chapter 2; Thomas A. Hockin, "Reforming Canada's Parliament: The 1965 Reforms and Beyond," *The University of Toronto Law Journal,* Vol. XVI, No. 2, 1966, pp. 326–345, esp. pp. 329–330; Donald Page, "Streamlining the Procedures of the Canadian House of Commons, 1963-1966," *Canadian Journal of Economics and Political Science,* XXXIII, No. 1, February, 1967, pp. 27–49.

[2] W. F. Dawson, *op. cit.,* p. 21.

[3] *Ibid.,* p. 21.

[4] *Ibid.,* pp. 20–28; Hockin, *op. cit.*, pp. 329–330.

> Government business in the last decade rules not dissimilar from those of 1867 when the budget was $25 million are not equal to the task of the 1960s when the budget approaches $9 billion. Five elections in twelve years have increased the tendency of the opposition to linger in Supply, to prolong other debates and to sharpen and prolong the question period.[5]

Since the mid-1950s, every government has hurled charges of obstruction at the opposition. These charges, when seen through the eyes of governments, both Conservative and Liberal, have frequently seemed to be fair ones. But seen from the other side, the charges were only half fair. For it was the *rules* that created disorder: the opposition only had to use them. Naturally, it could seldom avoid the temptation, because its political instincts teach it to undermine the Government's good reputation in whatever (mostly legitimate) ways it can. By 1960, the rules of the House of Commons, in the hands of a determined opposition, had become the chief source of frustration for governments. Lester Pearson's four horsemen used them against the government of John Diefenbaker, and John Diefenbaker in his turn used them easily against Lester Pearson after 1963.

The House of Commons was slow to appreciate what had happened. Until about 1963, Canadian governments and most Members of Parliament generally tolerated the casualness of the rules. While Governments repeatedly expressed their frustration at the processes of the House, familiar habits were valued, and there was no urgent pressure for reform in the House of Commons. The Clerk of the Privy Council, Gordon Robertson, said in 1967 that "I think the public generally and perhaps we ourselves [in the federal administration] fail to realize fully the extent to which the nature, scope and complication of government have changed in the last few years. . . . Indeed I think it is only in the last ten years that the cumulative effects of the change in the nature of government have been fully felt."[6] He went on to offer evidence that "the sheer mass of legislation for Parliament to deal with, and the mass of material on which the Federal Cabinet must decide, are enormously greater than ever before in our history."

> I found that, in the five year period from 1957–1962, the greatest number of days per Parliamentary session was 174: in the last five years we have had sessions of 248 and 250 days. Between 1957 and 1962 the largest number of bills passed in any session was 64; at the

[5] Hockin, *op. cit.*, p. 331.

[6] R.G. Robertson, "The Canadian Parliament and Cabinet in the Face of Modern Demands," unpublished paper, 1967, pp. 6, 7.

> last session of 1967 the number was 97. Our largest printed volume of statutes in the first five year period had 583 pages of legal text; in 1964–1965, Parliament passed 751 pages of statutes, and in 1966–67, 1,273 pages. By every one of these indices we have an increase from one five year period to the next of something between 40 and 100 percent.[7]

On the side of the Cabinet, Robertson found that from 1957 to 1959, an average of 382 documents per year were placed before Cabinet; from 1964 to 1966, the average had grown to 656, and in 1967 the volume was still mounting.[8] The capacity of the House and the Cabinet to deal in a rational and orderly way with the measures before them was being severely tested by the volume and technical complexity of Government business.

It has been clear in the last ten years that the House of Commons has not been the only bottleneck and source of frustration in the system. While the Commons, up to December 1968, had done relatively little to quicken its pace and give order to its proceedings to match the potential mass of business that faced it each session, there were occasions, nevertheless, when the Cabinet's disorganization meant that for short periods, it had no new business to place before the House. When this could be made evident by the Opposition, it was a source of embarrassment to the Government, because it suggested that the House, by comparison with the Cabinet, was not so badly organized after all.

Big government had overtaken both Cabinet and Parliament. In Canada as elsewhere in the industrialized world over the last half century, the size, responsibilities and opportunities for initiative of the permanent administration have expanded enormously. While departments have multiplied and divided, while independent agencies and crown corporations have been born and grown prematurely into monsters, the instruments of Cabinet and Parliamentary control of the leviathan have remained negligible. By 1964 the orderly system of Cabinet leadership and Parliamentary scrutiny had broken down under the load, and members in all parties had recognized it.

[7] Robertson, *op. cit.*, pp. 7, 8. Donald Page, in his article cited above, used a different set of comparisons in coming to the same conclusion about the overburdened House of Commons. He mentions that before 1963, only six sessions of Parliament produced more than 1,000 questions on the order paper; but the short 1963 session produced a record 1,906 questions, and the 1964–65 session, 3,078. He reports that in the two sessions of 1963 and 1964–65, the average number of appeals against the Speaker's rulings was more than double the number in any previous year. Questions of privilege increased from an average of 32 per session in 1957–60 to 85 in 1963 and 111 in 1964–65. The two sets of statistics perhaps illustrate that the growth in the House's "obstructive" consumption of time on questions, appeals and questions of privilege parallels consistently—and probably reflects—the burdens placed upon the House by the Government.

[8] Robertson, *op. cit.*, pp. 8, 9.

The Pearson government took the initiative in encouraging Parliamentary reform, with the support of the other parties, and five years of innovation began. But before considering the effects of these reforms, I think it is important to put them into a broader perspective.

PARLIAMENTARY GOVERNMENT: MYTH AND REALITY

What may be equally as important as the growing burdens of government is the mythology of parliamentary government. For the mythology has disguised the reality. We are still bemused by the classic models of parliamentary government presented with such grace and clarity by Walter Bagehot and John Stuart Mill to an English audience in the mid-nineteenth century. They were describing, and prescribing for, the British Parliament of that time; but their influence on *our* perception of our institutions has been profound. A century later, the major works on Canadian parliamentary institutions still take for granted as fundamental the framework of the liberal parliamentary constitution which Bagehot and Mill established in describing Westminster.[9] We have, we are told, a system of responsible parliamentary government, in which the public elects individual members to the House of Commons and the House of Commons, in turn, chooses a Government. Thereafter, while the Cabinet governs, the House holds it responsible for all the actions of the administration, and in the event of parliamentary disapproval, can overthrow the ministry, or force it to seek a fresh mandate from the electorate. The Prime Minister is chairman of the Cabinet; the public service is the loyal and anonymous servant of the Cabinet; the Cabinet is the servant of the House of Commons and only indirectly of the electorate. The theory puts the House of Commons close to the centre of the system, where it is meant to act as "the grand inquest of the nation," influencing, supervising and controlling the actions of the executive.

While the Canadian literature of politics points out that parliamentary control may not be quite up to the theory, the theory is maintained as the

[9] See, for instance, J.A. Corry, *Democratic Government and Politics* (2nd ed., rev., Toronto, 1955), chapters VI, VII, XI; R.M. Dawson, *The Government of Canada* (4th ed., rev. by Norman Ward, Toronto, 1963), chapters 9, 18, 19; Alexander Brady, *Democracy in the Dominions* (3rd ed., Toronto, 1960), chapter 4. C.B. Macpherson's *Democracy in Alberta* (Toronto, 1955) takes a more independent position on the Canadian political tradition, arguing that it is plebiscitary rather than parliamentary. M.S. Donnelly's *The Government of Manitoba* (Toronto, 1963) and F.F. Schindeler's *Responsible Government in Ontario* (Toronto, 1969) are also free from the dominating influence of the traditional model. It may be significant that these studies all deal with provincial institutions and politics, where the legislative tradition has been weak, Westminster and the textbooks have been less referred to, and thus the means of escape from the classical model has been easier than it has been in Ottawa.

ideal. As a result, many of the real forces at work in Canadian politics are underrated or ignored. The tendency is, when describing forces and practices which contradict the model, to see them as aberrations pulling the system away from the Victorian ideal, but rarely as primary forces in their own right which may be basically shaping the system.

In describing a political system, one must start from *some* sort of model, and in Canada the starting point has been natural and obvious.[10] But a point may come, in adding up the distortions and aberrations from the norm, when it becomes more comprehensible to abandon the original description and try to put together another one which accommodates the evidence more completely and satisfactorily. I think this point has been reached in understanding how the Canadian system works.

To say this is hardly to say anything revolutionary about parliamentary government. Observers of the British parliamentary system began as long ago as 1902 to take apart the classical model as it applied to Westminster. The work of demolition has increased in volume and intensity since the 1920s, and especially in the last twenty years.[11] As in the Canadian approach to parliamentary reform, so in our *comprehension* of the parliamentary system, Canadians have stuck relatively uncritically for much longer to the classical model than have Britons.[12]

[10] W.F. Dawson, remarking on the absence of major American influences in the form and style of procedure in the Canadian House of Commons, says that "the United States, which contributed much to the federal form of the country, has had only a slight influence [in the House] which may be seen in the provision of desks for members, page boys to run errands, and roll-call votes. These are relatively insignificant borrowings." (W.F. Dawson, *op. cit.,* p. 14.)

[11] See, for example, M. Ostrogorski, *Democracy and the Organization of Political Parties* (London, 1902); L.S. Amery, *Thoughts on the Constitution* (London, 1947); John P. Mackintosh, *The British Cabinet* (London, 1962); Andrew Hill and Anthony Whichelow, *What's Wrong With Parliament?* (London, 1964); R.H.S. Crossman, introduction to Walter Bagehot, *The English Constitution* (London, 1964); Max Nicholson, *The System* (London, 1967); W.J. Stankiewicz, ed., *Crisis in British Government* (London, 1967); Humphry Berkeley, *The Power of the Prime Minister* (London, 1968); Bernard Crick, *The Reform of Parliament* (2nd ed., London, 1968); Lord Fulton, *The Civil Service, Vol. 1, Report of the Committee, 1966–68* (Cmd3638, London, 1968); Robert J. Jackson, *Rebels and Whips* (London, 1968); Hugh Thomas, ed., *Crisis in the Civil Service* (London, 1968); Ian Gilmour, *The Body Politic* (London, 1969). Two more traditionalist responses to the presidentialist literature in the United Kingdom are Ronald Butt, *The Power of Parliament* (London, 1967) and Henry Fairlie, *The Life of Politics* (London, 1968).

[12] Besides the exceptions previously mentioned, another is the Toronto *Star* columnist Anthony Westell, who wrote in the *Star* on June 21, 1969: "To the extent that anyone expects Parliament to make significant changes in government policies and programs, it is a myth. Prime Ministers and Cabinets tend to hold themselves accountable to the country at election time rather than to the opposition in Parliament. They are not much interested, therefore, in hearing the views of the opposition, and most debates in the Commons are conducted in an almost empty chamber. . . . It is the basic structure of the parliamentary system which seems to be at fault. The Prime Minister and the Cabinet are not accountable *to* the legislature, in any meaningful way, and the parlia-

The best short reassessment of the British model—and now a familiar one—is Richard Crossman's introduction to the 1964 edition of Bagehot's *The English Constitution.* Here, Crossman argues that Bagehot's description of the Cabinet in Parliament was falsified soon after publication of *The English Constitution.* The emergence of highly disciplined mass parties took independent power from individual members of Parliament; the immense new administrative bureaucracy took much ordinary decision-making power away from ministers; and an organized secretariat for the Cabinet, and especially for the Prime Minister, gave the Prime Minister the effective powers of a president.[13]

> Even in Bagehot's time it was probably a misnomer to describe the Premier as chairman, and *primus inter pares.* His right to select his own Cabinet and dismiss them at will; his power to decide the Cabinet's agenda and announce the decisions reached without taking a vote; his control . . . over patronage—all this had already before 1867 given him near-Presidential powers. Since then his powers have been steadily increased. . . . [Each Minister] owes his allegiance not to the Cabinet collectively but to the Prime Minister who gave him his job, and who may well have dictated the policy he must adopt. In so far as the ministers feel themselves to be agents of the Premier, the British Cabinet has now come to resemble the American Cabinet.[14]

Crossman sees that the doctrine of collective Cabinet responsibility has been turned inside out.

> In Bagehot's day, collective Cabinet responsibility meant the responsibility of a group of equal colleagues for decisions taken collectively, after full, free and secret discussions in which all could participate. It now means collective obedience by the whole administration, from the Foreign Secretary and the Chancellor downwards to the will of the man at the apex of power.[15]

The constitutional purists, says Crossman, insist that the essential distinction between Presidential and Prime Ministerial government remains: "A President, we are told, cannot be removed before the end of his term of office; a Prime Minister can be."[16] Crossman admits the distinction, but notes

---

mentary process is mostly play-acting—a farce which has become increasingly transparent to the public."

[13] Crossman, *op. cit.,* pp. 50–53.

[14] *Ibid.,* pp. 51, 52.

[15] *Ibid.,* p. 53.

[16] *Ibid.,* p. 54.

that the Prime Minister is so powerful that "he can never be removed in real life by public, constitutional procedure. The method employed must always be that of undercover intrigue and sudden unpredicted *coup d'etat.*"[17] The British system of government is not Cabinet government, nor Parliamentary government, but thinly disguised Presidential government, in which the Prime Minister possesses some powers of discipline and direction unavailable even to an American President.[18]

Does the story sound familiar in Canada? It does. The Canadian Prime Minister, indeed, may be further along the road to being a presidential leader than the British, for distinct Canadian reasons.

For one thing, the Canadian House of Commons has never possessed the reserve of aristocratic prestige which once gave the British House of Commons some leverage alongside or against the Prime Minister. For most of its life the Canadian House has been a popular chamber, based on wide popular suffrage; Canadian Prime Ministers have always made their primary appeal for support not in the House of Commons, but outside, to the electorate. Humphry Berkeley notes the effect of this focus on the electorate after the extension of the franchise in the United Kingdom:

> The new party managers were not slow to realize the value of Macaulay's maxim that, given the need to appeal directly to the electorate, it was easier to project a personality than an idea. And so from the moment the electorate achieved any significant size, one man came in the mind of the nation to represent an entire government and that man had of course to be the Prime Minister.[19]

The House of Commons is diminished in importance, as compared to the British House in the period from 1832 to 1867, because it is the electorate, not the House of Commons, which chooses and deposes Prime Ministers. The essential influence upon government is the sovereign public, not a sovereign

[17] *Ibid.*

[18] Crossman suggests that this secret of the modern constitution has been successfully kept from the public, just as, in Bagehot's time, the secret of Cabinet government was hidden by the camouflage of the monarchy. He illustrates the reality of the Prime Minister's power by noting that the decision to manufacture the British atomic bomb was taken by Prime Minister Attlee without any discussion in Cabinet or Parliament, and that the Anglo-French decision to attack Egypt in 1956 was made by Prime Minister Eden without Cabinet discussion, and in the knowledge of only a few ministers and civil servants. (Crossman, *op. cit.,* pp. 55, 56.) Humphry Berkeley, in his recent book, *The Power of the Prime Minister,* asserts more strongly than Crossman that Parliament has been overridden by a system of presidential rule, and proposes a number of reforms to restore balance to the system.

[19] Berkeley, *op. cit.,* p. 38.

Parliament. Prime Ministers keep their eyes upon the Gallup Polls, and not normally upon readings of the House of Commons' temperature. And the public sees the government as one man's government. This public assumption gives the Prime Minister great power over his colleagues.

The fact is a commonplace in Canadian understanding, and yet it is not satisfactorily integrated into the normal liberal model of the parliamentary constitution. We know that general elections are competitions between party leaders for the Prime Minister's office; we concentrate our attention upon the leaders, and the parties encourage us to do so; once in office, we see that Prime Ministers exercise almost tyrannical power over their ministers and backbenchers; Prime Ministers frequently ignore the House of Commons, or treat it with disdain, unless they perceive that the public is watching (which it only occasionally is); and our Prime Ministers freely admit their own predominance over the House of Commons and the necessity of it. When they fail to exercise the power the system gives them, as Louis St. Laurent failed in the last year of his administration, or Lester Pearson sometimes did in his, the House of Commons falls apart, and we blame the leaders personally. Yet we still cling to the constitutional purist's belief that the governing party in the House of Commons, or the House of Commons as a whole, can routinely control or depose the Prime Minister and replace him with a person more acceptable to it.

Two occasions in the twentieth century are cited to illustrate the ultimate power of the House of Commons over the Prime Minister: the replacement of Mackenzie King as Prime Minister by Arthur Meighen in 1926, and the defeat of the Diefenbaker government in the House in 1963. Each is a bad example, and better illustrates the power of the Prime Minister over the House of Commons than the opposite.

The result of the constitutional confusion of 1926 was to give Mackenzie King an electoral victory with a clear majority, and probably to guarantee that no subsequent Governor-General would refuse to grant the request of a Prime Minister for a dissolution of Parliament. A Prime Minister has two basic sources of authority over his followers and the House, one retrospective and one prospective: the former is the respect, gratitude and control of patronage he gains from bringing a party to power in the previous general election; the latter is the discomfort he can create among MPs by threatening to call the next general election at a time of *his* choosing. The lesson for Opposition leaders of Arthur Meighen's defeat in 1926 is that one should not accept the Prime Ministership when the Prime Minister has asked for and been refused a dissolution: he will convince the public that you acted wrongly, and you will soon be out of office. 1926 reinforced the usefulness of the power of dissolution as a weapon in the hands of the Prime Minister. The constitutional niceties and the quiet life in the House of Commons were not important.

In 1963, John Diefenbaker accepted defeat in the House, dissolved, and lost power as the result of the general election that followed. The superficial lesson seems to be that the House can, in the extreme, overthrow a Prime Minister. The classical theory of the Constitution seems to be sustained. The real lesson is different. The defeat and dissolution appear to have been the result of a miscalculation, based upon the outmoded view that the House could defeat a Prime Minister and replace him with a more acceptable leader without facing the inconvenience of a general election. According to the account of Patrick Nicholson,[20] Robert Thompson and his Social Crediters were only persuaded to vote against Mr. Diefenbaker (they provided the margin of defeat) on the clear understanding that, following the defeat in the House and before Mr. Diefenbaker could request a dissolution, he would be deposed in a Cabinet *coup* and be replaced by the Hon. George Nowlan. Nowlan would ask the House for a vote of confidence, Social Credit would swing back to support the government, and the session would continue. Had it occurred, this chain of events would have sustained the theory of the House of Commons' power to make and unmake governments. But it did not occur, for, as Mr. Diefenbaker has said, the plan failed to take account of one person: the Prime Minister. What happened is familiar to all of you: John Diefenbaker was *not* deposed, he received his dissolution, and most of those innocent Social Crediters lost their seats forever. If they had had a more realistic view of where power in the parliamentary constitution really lies, they would probably have voted to save their seats and keep Mr. Diefenbaker in power.[21]

These events illustrate Richard Crossman's claim that a Prime Minister can no longer be replaced by public and constitutional means if he does not wish to go. They illustrate more than that: given an alert Prime Minister, it is virtually impossible to replace him even by "undercover intrigue and sudden unpredicted *coup d'etat.*" He has too many weapons of influence and patronage in his hands, and his adversaries have too few.[22] He is virtually as immovable as an American President during his term of office.

[20] In his *Vision and Indecision* (Toronto, 1968), pp. 255–256.

[21] The situation was perhaps volatile enough that the government might have been defeated on some other occasion soon after. But the point stands: in that event, too, defeat would have resulted in a dissolution, not in the replacement of the Prime Minister.

[22] Four of the last five British Prime Ministers have faced substantial dissatisfaction within their parties and Cabinets, but no attempts to overthrow them have been successful. Winston Churchill, Anthony Eden and Harold Macmillan retired in ill health, on their own decisions; and Harold Wilson, who is healthy, has not been budged. The illnesses may have been related to the party pressures being experienced by these Prime Ministers; and they may have become more vulnerable during their illnesses, as Henry Fairlie suggests was true of Anthony Eden in 1957 (Fairlie, *op. cit.*, p. 61). But in no case did a *coup* actually occur.

The five years of minority government under Mr. Pearson emphasized the same point. Even without a majority in Parliament, a Canadian Prime Minister is normally secure in office, and scarcely faces the danger of defeat in the House, because one or another of the opposition parties is almost certain to vote with the Government on any division to assure its own survival. The Parliament of 1963–65 could probably have run to a full term of four or five years, as could the Parliament of 1965–68; each one was dissolved on the decision of the Prime Minister when he sensed the possibility of an electoral victory.[23] When the Government was defeated in the House by its own carelessness in February 1968, the Prime Minister simply chose not to treat the defeat as a matter of confidence, whipped in his followers and gained Creditiste support the next week to show that he could still manage the House as he wished (even as a lame duck Prime Minister just about to give up his leadership to a successor). Against the power of the Prime Minister, the House of Commons has little of its own to match.

In both the United Kingdom and Canada, the Prime Minister gains his predominance over his colleagues and the House of Commons by winning general elections and exercising the power of dissolution at his own discretion. But in Canada the Prime Minister possesses still more authority granted him from outside Parliament which brings him closer to the American President. He is chosen by a popular convention. The Canadian conventions have increasingly come to duplicate the effects of the American presidential conventions. Under the open embrace of gavel-to-gavel television, the conventions have become as central a part of national political life as the campaigns, and perhaps more central, because of their concentrated drama and intense TV coverage. In the conventions the political process is almost entirely personalized, issues fade away, and the winner is the only one to walk away alive. (A year and a half after Mr. Trudeau's accession to the Liberal leadership, his two leading rivals have disappeared from politics. In the Conservative party, too, the runner-up was left without a political career.)[24] If anything has accelerated the trend to presidential politics in Canada, it has been the enthusiastic adoption of televised national leadership conventions.

[23] Apparently on the theory that the king can do no wrong, the Hon. Walter Gordon unselfishly sacrificed himself to the conventions of Prime Ministerial power by resigning his portfolio after the dissolution and yet the party had failed to win the majority of seats he predicted.

[24] On the leadership conventions, see D.V. Smiley, "The National Party Leadership Convention in Canada: A Preliminary Analysis," *The Canadian Political Process,* rev. ed., ed. Kruhlak, Schultz, and Pobihushchy (Toronto: Holt, Rinehart and Winston, 1973), pp. 175–200; Joseph Wearing, "A Convention for Professionals: The PCs in Toronto," *Journal of Canadian Studies,* Vol. 2, No. 4, November, 1967, pp. 3–16; and Joseph Wearing, "The Liberal Choice," *Journal of Canadian Studies,* Vol. 3, No. 2, May, 1968, pp. 3–20.

Given the available technical means and the example next door every four years, the practice could scarcely be resisted.

REFORMING THE HOUSE

Set against the overwhelming power and public prestige of the Prime Minister are the traditional duties of the legislature. Even if one admits that the power of overthrowing governments has been surrendered, the House of Commons is supposed to retain the power and responsibility to provide a public forum of discussion on national issues, to scrutinize spending and legislation, and to safeguard the rights and freedoms of citizens by its vigilant criticism. These are worthy goals; but even *they* fade on closer examination. In certain crucial instances, such as the defence production debate of 1955, the pipeline debate of 1956, the nuclear arms debate of 1963, the Rivard revelations of 1964, the flag debate of 1964, and the rules debate of December, 1968, the House does occupy a central place in public consciousness and does serve as a restraining and moderating influence upon the Government. But these occasions are rare ones. In its less spectacular, day-to-day performances, the House of Commons normally, if grudgingly, does the work the Government directs it to do, and does so without making much critical impression on Government measures or on the public. This is so because the Government wishes it to be so, and because, until the December 1968 reforms, the House was the victim of its own diffuse rules, which did not lend themselves to sharp, critical investigation of Government measures.

Students of Parliament have agreed for years that the House's scrutiny of financial measures was inadequate.[25] Members were given little opportunity to influence the form of other legislation, except occasionally, because the Government used its majority to enforce conformity upon its backbenchers. The question period, emergency debates, and the general debates, while sometimes spectacular, brought little information to the public about the government's rationale for policy or about the processes of administration, because the habit and preference in Ottawa is one of strict administrative secrecy.[26] On balance, the House of Commons was not performing even a

[25] See especially Norman Ward, *The Public Purse* (Toronto, 1962).

[26] See Donald C. Rowat, "How Much Administrative Secrecy?" *Canadian Journal of Economics and Political Science,* XXXI, November, 1965, pp. 479-498; *House of Commons Debates,* February 17, 1969, especially pp. 5631–32; *Report of the Royal Commission on Security,* June, 1969, especially pp. 79–81, "Administrative Secrecy." The tendency of the *Report* is illustrated by the following comments it makes on the possibility of general access to government documents: "We are not required to make general recommendations about these problems, but, as far as Canada is concerned, we would view suggestions for increased publicity with some alarm. We think the knowledge that memoranda might be made public would have a seriously inhibiting effect on the transaction of public business. We believe that the process of policy-making implies a need for a wide-ranging

modest job as the watchdog of the public interest, and by 1963, many members knew it. Government backbenchers, especially, frequently expressed their frustration at the apparent fact that they served no purpose in Parliament except to vote blindly for government measures they had had no hand in producing.

The growing frustration of individual members over the inconsequence of their role in the House, and the frustration of the government at the cumbersome and, to it, obstructive procedures of the House, combined at last to produce a widespread interest in the House in parliamentary reform. But this interest in reform had two sources, and two—not always compatible—objectives. The wish of the government was primarily to organize the proceedings of the House in an orderly way—to "programme" the business of the House—so that it could expect as a matter of course to get its large agenda of business through the House with a minimum of delay and confusion each session. Government backbenchers and opposition members admitted the legitimacy of the government's wish, but *their* chief interest was to give *themselves* a more satisfying and informed role in the control and assessment of Government policy. While the Government's major objective was to streamline proceedings to serve the needs of the Prime Minister and his administration, the House's major objective was to give itself more of the powers it was supposed to possess according to the classical model of Parliament.

In the two Pearson Parliaments (of 1963–1965 and 1965–1968) some notable reforms were achieved which served both purposes to a limited degree. Stricter time limitations were imposed on the question period and the discussion of supply; the hours of sitting were extended; dilatory appeals against the speaker's rulings and frivolous questions of privilege were eliminated; Parliamentary committees were modified to reduce their size and to bring their areas of concern roughly parallel to those of the government departments; a weak guillotine procedure was provided for, which soon

---

and tentative consideration of options, many of which would be silly or undesirable to expose to the public gaze. To insist that all such communications must be made public would appear to us likely to impede the discussive (sic) deliberation that is necessary for wise administration. In Canada, the bureaucracy is not vast, and the numbers of serious enquiries quite small. It seems to us that there is no reason why controlled access to specific administrative files or documents cannot be permitted and arranged on an *ad hoc* basis when a genuine requirement can be established" (pp. 80–81). This section, and the *Report* in general, assumes that the Canadian system is a closed, not an open one; it further fails to distinguish between what are the legitimate concerns of state security, and what are, rather, the political concerns of the party in office to protect its own convenience. The *Report* takes for granted that it should be the administration, not the legislature, which determines what documents it would be "silly or undesirable to expose to the public gaze." Opposition members of Parliament might not always share a minister's or a civil servant's judgment in such matters.

proved unusable. The reforms cautiously balanced the interests of the government and Parliament. While they *began* to give the government the order it claimed in the House's business, they also *began* to encourage Members of Parliament to act with greater independence.[27]

But there was no doubt who intended to remain in control. When, in the spring of 1965, the Special Committee on Procedure and Organization grew too radical in its proposals for the cabinet's liking, the Prime Minister conveniently let the committee die at the end of a session, and declined to present to the House some of the committee's more thorough proposals for change.[28] Instead, the Prime Minister introduced the Cabinet's own selection of proposals.

The work of reform was tentative and unfinished. The House recognized this by making the changes in the rules adopted in June 1965, provisional ones, subject to review and confirmation. They were extended into the 27th Parliament, and again into the first session of the 28th Parliament in the fall of 1968. Further committees on procedure continued to work, and in September 1968, the House directed the latest committee to present permanent proposals for reform by December 1968.[29] The committee did so, and following an extended debate in December 1968, all but one of the committee's proposals were accepted unanimously by the House.[30]

The reforms of December 1968, while extending some of the principles first outlined in 1965, were notably more radical. They reorganized and simplified the manner of passing legislation in the House; they diverted detailed debate on all estimates and virtually all legislation from the floor of the House to the specialized committees; they established an annual timetable for the consideration of spending estimates; they created a Special Committee on Statutory Instruments; and they reduced to twenty-eight the number of days in an annual session controlled by the opposition for debate on topics of its choice. Again, the nice balancing of concessions to the House against concessions to the government brought the agreement of all parties to the

[27] See Donald Page, *op. cit.;* Thomas Hockin, *op. cit.;* Pauline Jewett, "The Reform of Parliament," *Journal of Canadian Studies,* Vol. 1, No. 3, November, 1966, pp. 11–16.

[28] All the Committee's *Reports* were unanimous ones, including the support of the Liberal members of the Committee, among whom was the Government Whip, James Walker, MP. The major recommendation of the Committee in the spring of 1965 was that of Stanley Knowles, MP, for regular adjournments of the House to permit parliamentary committees to concentrate on their work, and to allow members regular periodic visits to their constituencies. Both reforms may have been seen by the Government as too likely to enhance the prestige and critical knowledge of individual MPs.

[29] *House of Commons Debates*, September 24, 1968, pp. 394–437.

[30] *House of Commons Debates*, December 10–December 20, 1968.

proposals.[31] (In November 1968, in addition, the Prime Minister had announced that the estimates would contain annual grants to the leaders of the opposition parties to finance research offices.)[32] But on the other side of the balance, the Prime Minister also introduced a rotation system for ministers during the question period, which freed ministers from attendance in the House for two days of each week.[33] Besides limiting the opportunities for members to question ministers, the change had the further (perhaps intended?) effect of concentrating more attention upon the Prime Minister, who continued to attend the question period daily, and who was inclined to substitute his own replies for those of his absent ministers.

The reform measure that was held by the government House leader and by the Prime Minister to be the most important of all, was the only measure unacceptable to the opposition parties (as it had been unacceptable to them in the Committee). This was rule 16A, which provided for the allocation of time in advance for debate on legislation, and in the absence of agreement among the parties, permitted the government to impose its own timetable (or guillotine) on the House by majority vote. The rule was extraordinarily carelessly drawn, and was bound to arouse the suspicion and distaste of the opposition: it allowed the government House leader alone to constitute a quorum of the Proceedings Committee, and it gave him authority to propose timetabling orders which might theoretically cover all the legislation of a session, before its introduction, under a single time allocation motion. During eight days of debate, the government fell back on the old accusation of filibustering against the will of the majority.[34] But in the meantime, with its presidential antennae out to the electorate, the government concluded that the public—including the Liberal public—understood and sympathized with the opposition's case to an unusual extent.[35] Finally, the government withdrew its request for the approval of rule 16A, and the remaining package of reforms was adopted by the House.

But in December, the Prime Minister warned that the guillotine was still dear to him, and would appear again reincarnate at a moment appropriate to

[31] It is useful to note that this careful balancing of interests was accomplished by an all-party committee, not by the government, which merely endorsed the committee's unanimous recommendations. In the heat of debate in July 1969, the Prime Minister claimed that all the concessions to the House's interest were granted by a generous government out of its own good will. He was reminded forcefully by David Lewis, MP, that his memory was inaccurate (*House of Commons Debates*, July 24, 1969, pp. 11571, 11574).

[32] *House of Commons Debates*, November 15, 1968, pp. 2790–2820.

[33] *House of Commons Debates*, September 25, 1968, pp. 446–449.

[34] *House of Commons Debates*, December 10, 1968, p.3787.

[35] The newspapers were almost unanimous in condemning the proposal, and the results of a private telephone poll of Liberal Party supporters confirmed this reaction.

the government.[36] The new Procedure Committee went to work again this year, and the government brought its revised guillotine proposal, Rule 75, to the House in July. The opposition—and the government—had worked conscientiously to make the rule less objectionable to the House than 16A, and it *was* less objectionable. But it still contained too much sting for the combined opposition in section 75C, which gave the government, in the absence of agreement by the other parties, the power to timetable discussion on the stages of individual bills by government resolution, following notice and a short debate.[37] The provision meant that if necessary a determined government could guide a piece of controversial legislation through the House in a minimum of four days of debate over a period of ten sitting days, against the protests of the minority.

The persistence of the Trudeau government in pressing for the guillotine made its impression on the opposition and the press, and during July negotiations went on among the parties to compromise on a measure which would grant the government's wish but extend the minimum period of ten days to something longer. When the opposition seemed hopeful of reaching agreement with the government, the Cabinet suddenly broke off discussion, closure was imposed, and the measure was adopted on division in its original form.[38]

The sudden reversal by the government was curious: it can probably be explained by the Prime Minister's unerring presidential instincts. As in December, the Prime Minister was watching public reaction to the debate more closely than the House's reaction. He apparently found that the public, this time, was not unduly concerned. In mid-July, he commented on the debate that it was a "stupid filibuster," and said that no one outside Parliament cared what was going on in the House.[39] In his speech before the closure, he remarked that "In a democracy the ballot box, not the filibuster, is the ultimate and appropriate technique of assessment."[40] And in the adjournment debate the next day he let fall his testy comments about the inconsequence of parliamentary debate to the public that elects Prime Ministers:

> The opposition seems to think it has nothing else to do but talk. . . . That is all they have to do. They do not have to govern, they have only to talk. The best place in which to talk, if they want a

[36] Toronto *Globe and Mail*, December 24, 1968.
[37] *Votes and Proceedings of the House of Commons of Canada*, July 2, 1969, No. 180, pp. 1, 2.
[38] *House of Commons Debates*, July 22, 1969, pp. 11470–11478; July 23, 1969, p. 11504; July 24, 1969, pp. 11534, 11544–11550.
[39] Toronto *Star*, July 21, 1969.
[40] *House of Commons Debates*, July 24, 1969, p. 11572.

> forum, is, of course parliament. When they get home, when they get out of parliament, when they are 50 yards from Parliament Hill, they are no longer hon. Members—they are just nobodies, Mr. Speaker.[41]

Judging that Members of Parliament are political nobodies, the Prime Minister felt it prudent to ignore the real possibility of agreement within the House on a compromise rule acceptable to the other parliamentary parties, turned his back on the discussions, and imposed his will on the House in a matter of its own procedure. This was as clear an indication as there has ever been that the Canadian Prime Minister is inclined to think of himself as a crypto-president, responsible directly to the people and not to the House of Commons. But Lyndon Johnson would never have spoken this way of Everett Dirksen!

WHERE ARE WE AND WHERE DO WE GO FROM HERE?

We seem to have created in Canada a presidential system without its congressional advantages. Before the accession of Pierre Trudeau, our presidential system, however, was diffuse and ill-organized. But Pierre Trudeau is extraordinarily clear-headed and realistic about the sources of political power in Canada. On the one hand, he has recognized the immense power of initiative and guidance that exists in the federal bureaucracy; and he has seen that this great instrument of power lacked effective centralized political leadership. He has created that coordinated leadership by organizing around him a presidential office, and by bringing order and discipline to the Cabinet's operations. He has made brilliant use of public opportunities of a party leader, in convention, in the general election, and in his continuing encounters outside Parliament. He has recognized that the public responds first to personalities, not to issues, and so he campaigns for the most generalized mandate. And now, finally, he has successfully altered the procedures of the House of Commons so that it may serve the legislative purposes of an efficient presidential administration.

In doing all these things he has taken advantage of trends and opportunities that already existed. All Prime Ministers have been moving—under pressure—in the same direction, but none so determinedly as Prime Minister Trudeau; he has taken the system further, faster, more self-consciously, than it would otherwise have gone. Are we now to be left with this completed edifice of presidential-parliamentary government, in which the House serves the minor purpose of making presidential programs law without much fuss?

[41] *House of Commons Debates*, July 25, 1969, p. 11635.

Probably not, because the system still contains some fundamental inconsistencies. How clearly the Prime Minister and members of Parliament see these inconsistencies, I cannot be sure; but they exist, and they will create difficulties. As we have seen, the changes in the rules and practices of the House have not only served the government's purposes; they have also, in many ways, benefited individual members and the opposition parties.

In the course of achieving rules of procedure much more tractable for the government's purposes, the reforms and the reforming atmosphere have also created a more intractable membership of the House, with new and potentially powerful instruments of leverage against the government in their hands. The opposition parties are better equipped by their research funds and their role in legislative committees to criticize the administration from a basis of knowledge. The restrictions of time allocation in the House give these parties an incentive to organize their attacks with more precision and directness than before. Government backbenchers, long silent and frustrated by party discipline, permitted only to express their opinions freely in secret caucus, have been given the taste of greater freedom in the new committees of the House. (Already the paradox has been recognized by Steve Otto, MP, who has publicly asked his House leader why government backbenchers should not feel free to propose substantive amendments to government legislation in committee.) For the moment, the government may hold the reins tightly, but the pressures in the House are likely to mount.

One result may be that the government will find itself more frequently embarrassed by independent backbenchers. They will probably continue to demand their own research assistance, and increasingly the rights to speak critically and to vote against government measures: first in committee, and then, by extension, in the House. (But always more and more in public, where they can be heard.) The party discipline of the majority will be put under increasing strain, and the opposition will take every chance to encourage the tension. If we have a President, they will be saying, in effect, then why shouldn't we also have an independent Congress?

The government, in response to such pressures, may put on the screws in private, but it will have difficulty withdrawing the public machinery of criticism that it has now acquiesced in. The House will never agree to return to its fumbling and disorganized pattern of pre-1965. With the taste of influence, and facing a more efficient executive, it will be more inclined, not less, to be independent and sometimes intransigent. If we believe, as the parliamentary myth leads us to believe, in the virtues of *public* policy making and strong *public* criticism of government, this will surely be a salutary development. The Prime Minister will be challenged by the kind of countervailing force that he believes in.

The other possible response of governments may be to accept the logic of these parliamentary pressures, and to move more surely to a system of congressional checks and balances. This would involve the granting of independent powers to parliamentary committees to choose their own chairmen, hire their own substantial staffs, pursue their own independent investigations, initiate their own legislative proposals, and freely amend and reject the Government's measures. It would involve the provision of administrative assistance for MPs comparable to that available to Senators and Congressmen, and salaries matching their new responsibilities. It would involve, undoubtedly, the admission of television cameras to committees and to the House floor, to bring the House closer to the public. It would involve, finally, and probably gradually, the abandonment of the convention of confidence, so that governments could expect to stay in office for full terms in spite of regular defeats in the House. Gordon Robertson saw the possibilities with more prescience than most observers in 1967:

> The American system [he said] may be better suited in some respects to these times than the British. It may be that we will have to accept compromises to make the principle of ministerial responsibility flexible enough to work today.[42]

Who is there, I wonder, to play Senator Fulbright to Pierre Trudeau's Lyndon Johnson?

[42] Robertson, *op. cit.*, p. 12.

"The All-time Canadian Political Bestseller"

(1973)

In 1963 I wrote an enthusiastic review of Peter C. Newman's second book, Renegade in Power: The Diefenbaker Years, *in* The Canadian Forum. *When the success of* Renegade *led to its reprinting ten years later, I was invited to write an introduction to the new edition. Before its appearance, I learned from the editor that Peter Newman had been unhappy about some of my reflections in the essay on the art of political journalism and on his depiction of the Old Chief. (I was already thinking about a work of my own on the subject, which emerged more than twenty years later as* Rogue Tory: The Life and Legend of John G. Diefenbaker.*) Newman's book was reprinted again, in 1989, and hailed as "the all-time Canadian political bestseller," with my 1973 introduction replaced with a new introduction by the author. When he published his memoir* Here Be Dragons *in 2004, Newman graciously recorded in a footnote: "I was pleased to see that when the first academic study of the Diefenbaker period was published in 1995 . . . by Denis Smith, who had access to the former prime minister's private papers, none of my major facts or suppositions (including my title) was challenged." Differences settled. This is my 1973 essay.*

By most of the conventional tests, John Diefenbaker's political career was a spectacular failure. The opportunities that opened to him when he became Prime Minister in 1957 seemed to be great ones; he squandered almost every one. After the first promising rush of improving legislation adopted by the minority parliament of 1957–1958, the new Prime Minister could never impose coherence and a sense of direction on his administration and the House of Commons. He dominated his cabinet but did not lead it. From the summer of 1958 on, as complicated problems—chiefly economic and military—thrust themselves upon it, the cabinet moved further and further from resolution and clarity into immobility and obscurantism. Most of the challenges the Diefenbaker government faced were amenable to reason, or to reason and cosmetic political art in combination. But the government was quite quaintly inept, unable in its confusions even to disguise its ineptitudes, as most governments do most of the time. For the Liberal opposition, which expected ten years in the wilderness after 1958, the government's self-inflicted collapse by 1962 was an unanticipated gift. The transparency of the failure meant that the government's record was an unusually easy one for criticism and ridicule; and the purported benefits of a return to Liberal rule were equally easily exaggerated. It may be that in historical perspective the judgment on the Diefenbaker administration will be more generous than the contemporary one; because the government's dramatic but frequently trivial gaffes will recede from view as its substantial acts are examined and understood.

Because the story was an unhappy and constantly surprising one, it was fascinating; and Peter Newman was its chief chronicler. When *Renegade in Power* appeared in the fall of 1963 it became at once, and has remained, a best-seller. The chronicler gained some of the fame of his subject (much to the subject's violent distaste): so that now, perhaps, the two names most immediately associated in the popular mind with the period from 1957 to 1963 are John Diefenbaker . . . and Peter Newman. If John Diefenbaker saw Newman as an antagonist, Newman himself did not. He asserts in the "Author's Note" that "I can only say that my verdicts are the end result of objectively reporting the events as I saw them. . . . I had no fixed political affiliation—though I was buoyed up by the great expectations the Conservative leader had roused in my country. I still have no fixed political affiliation." The text, I think, sustains that claim, although it also reveals some of the historical limitations of political reporting. This new edition of the book offers a useful occasion for some reflections on both the subject and the account Peter Newman gives of it.

Renegade in Power is neither history nor political biography, and the author does not claim it to be. It is not even "contemporary history," a genre of medium perspective lying between the engagement of the moment and the tranquil recollection of history pure. The book is political journalism. Peter Newman does not need to apologize for that, as he tends slightly to do in his new introduction. The genre is a legitimate one, and *Renegade in Power* is vivid political reporting. It was undoubtedly a major stimulus leading other reporters and reporter-participants such as Patrick Nicholson, Peter Dempson, and Thomas Van Dusen to publish their accounts of the Diefenbaker period, and to the correspondents who produced books on the Pearson administration and the changes of party leadership in 1967 and 1968. Peter Newman deserves credit for his pioneering initiative as for his journalistic skill. It is helpful for the public to have this kind of evidence for judgment when the politicians who are its subjects are still on the scene; and it is useful for historians to have this kind of preliminary account from which to begin their more distant assessments.

If we are inclined to judge *Renegade in Power* for what it is not, that is partly the result of a failure which is not Peter Newman's. There has been remarkably little scholarly writing about the Diefenbaker period, in the form of political biography, contemporary history or philosophic analysis, apart from the Lloyd, Preston and Lyon studies in the "Canada in World Affairs" series, some election studies under John Meisel's leadership, and George Grant's *Lament for a Nation*. But as Peter Newman indicates, there is a host of subjects deserving treatment in this period. The evidence needs to be gathered and assessed. If there is a conventional interpretation of what occurred from 1957 to 1963, it is the Newman interpretation, because it has not yet been solidly tested, challenged or built upon from the longer perspective.

For anything approaching a full view of the Diefenbaker administration, detailed studies will be necessary, for example, of NORAD, the Avro Arrow project, the Northern Affairs department, the Coyne affair, regional policy, cabinet and House of Commons operations, Canadian-American relations, financial and economic policy, the Commonwealth conferences, Quebec policy, and the cabinet careers of—among others—Donald Fleming, Alvin Hamilton, Sidney Smith, Davie Fulton, George Hees, Howard Green, and Gordon Churchill. The eventual opening of the Diefenbaker papers will be essential in dealing with all these subjects, but in the meantime much preliminary work can be done in the public records, and through scholarly pursuit of the papers and reminiscences of other participants in public life. Peter Newman offers sufficient evidence for us to know that this was a significant period and that all was not well; it is time we tried to learn more fully just why.

Newman's book recounts vividly the evolving moods of the time and the accumulating outward evidence of disorder in the cabinet; and it provides many intriguing details which help to create the historical picture. Where it is inadequate, I think, is in putting all this information together into a convincing explanation either of the Prime Minister's character or of the reasons for his government's failure. (The two are very intimately related, as Peter Newman recognizes.) That is not a simple task, because John Diefenbaker is a complicated man and the Canadian situation at the end of the 1950s was suddenly full of uncertainty. In "the turmoil of the moment" not many observers can demonstrate great unifying understanding of events. The work of historical understanding is a collective work of many minds, and the initial contributions, by the very fact of their pioneering nature, are bound to be incomplete in their assessments. Peter Newman began the examination of the Diefenbaker period, and gives us a starting-point for analysis and reassessment which is invaluable.

While he offers a great deal of evidence of the complexity of politics under John Diefenbaker, Peter Newman sometimes creates an impression in *Renegade in Power* that there is only one relatively direct and "true" version of events. He seems to imply that there is not any intrinsic ambiguity in history, that there are not even differing vantage points which reveal various sides to events. This is perhaps the inevitable effect of the journalistic medium, with its need to make immediate sense of the confusing rush of events. The objective in such political reporting is to locate the chief sources of information and to recount their stories of what happened straightforwardly. The virtues of this approach—when it is at its best—are that it calls for great diligence and shrewd discrimination among sources. These were rare qualities in Canadian journalism and Peter Newman has set a conscientious example for his successors. The weaknesses of the approach—which are only likely to become clear in the longer historical perspective—are that it may result in an apparently seamless and unambiguous account of history, and that it tends to rely too uncritically on some sources rather than others. Seen with hindsight, *Renegade in Power* perhaps underemphasizes the notions that a person or group can be moved to act out of multiple motives, not all of them consistent with one another; and that events can have multiple meanings.

These difficulties of interpretation can be illustrated by three examples from the book. First, there is Newman's short account of John Diefenbaker's youth and early career in Saskatchewan, leading finally to his entry into the House of Commons in 1940. It is a familiar and entrancing bit of mythology, the features of which have by now been repeated many times. While Newman reports that he spoke to, among others, John Diefenbaker's barber, the main source for it all is certainly John Diefenbaker himself. Even some of the other sources, I believe, often give accounts which derive from John Diefenbaker rather than from their own unalloyed memories. From the distance of thirty or forty years, the account of John Diefenbaker's youth was moulded to enhance his attractiveness as a candidate for Prime Minister: it was the classical log cabin to President story of North American righteousness rewarded. (And now the family homestead is preserved as a relic in Regina.) This is not to say the account is false; only that the actual history is likely to be more complicated and less easy to characterize. The full truth will have shadings and ironies that the myth lacks. Its recovery will require a certain scepticism of the simple story which is absent in Peter Newman's book, and it will require the most thorough search for alternative sources of evidence—which the journalist could not have been expected to undertake at length.

Newman's chapter on "The Fiscal Sins of a Prairie Prime Minister" shows a similar dependence on a limited source. This time, I think the evidence points to his reliance on the Liberal party, and particularly on the views of Walter L. Gordon, then the financial critic of the party and the architect of its economic attack on the Diefenbaker administration. Newman's outline of the government's economic failures sticks very close to the critical account developed in Gordon's speeches and writings during 1960, 1961 and 1962. He gives no indication in this chapter that there might have been any other framework of economic criticism of the Diefenbaker government. Surely there was, at least potentially, a socialist one too; and perhaps there were explanations for some of the government's policies which may have gone further in plausibility than it was in the interest of the official opposition to concede. But it would be unfair to make too much of this point. Walter Gordon's attack on the government's economic policies was the most coherent and influential one in the period, and there was not much other criticism that was markedly different.

Finally, Newman's account of the defence and nuclear weapons controversy appears too simple and too intolerant of the Prime Minister's case, too passively tolerant of the criticisms made by Douglas Harkness, Lester Pearson, General Lauris Norstad, and the U.S. government. The Prime Minister's awkwardness in handling the situation must, I think, be carefully separated from the substance of the issues at stake. On the matters of substance, while his policies were confused, inconsistent and inadequately explained, I suspect that Canadian history will judge John Diefenbaker much less harshly than did his opponents at the time. Again, Newman's tendency was to rely on the sources he chose, namely the Prime Minister's challengers. The historians will have to review the evidence of all parties with a more acute scepticism than Peter Newman was able to apply to the situation in the immediate aftermath of the crisis. History should add more threads to the fabric.

In his introduction Newman fairly contends that it is up to the historians, and not to him, to acknowledge sources. But it will be peculiarly important—because of his method, and to the extent that later accounts begin from Peter Newman—for historians to discover precisely who his sources were. Newman's own notes and diaries should thus prove to be valuable historical materials themselves.

Newman's thesis about John Diefenbaker is, briefly, that "the right instincts" were in him, but that "he only rarely had the courage to follow his privately held convictions"; that he was a disappointing "renegade in power—a renegade both to his own cause and to the greater aspirations of the nation he was meant to be governing"; that he might have succeeded if he had taken the advice of the civil service instead of the "political hacks who sought his favours"; that he had "not the least inkling of what he wanted to do when he achieved that high office, and was rendered impotent by the magnitude of the claims it places upon its incumbent"; that he cultivated his mystery and isolation and was "preoccupied with . . . personal stature"; that he always distrusted the establishment, and never tried to understand the aspirations of French Canada; that he upset "the ordinary Canadian Tory, who believed that his party stood for individual responsibility, the British connection, and free enterprise"; that he had the unimaginative mind of a lawyer rather than the supple one of a political leader; that he was administratively inept because he had never "administered anything more complicated than a walk-up law office"; that he could not accept responsibility himself, and constantly found it necessary to shift blame and humiliate his colleagues.

Most of these judgments can be sustained by the evidence; some cannot be.

That he distrusted the central Canadian establishment, that he misunderstood French Canada, that he was unusually vain and concerned with self-justification, that he was overbearing, that he was administratively inept; these claims, I think, can be easily supported. But I find Peter Newman not entirely convincing in his assertions that John Diefenbaker had "the right instincts" but failed out of lack of courage; or that he reneged on his cause, or that he had no objectives beyond personal acclaim. A sentence in the first paragraph of chapter one may be a more accurate reflection of Newman's view than all the assertions he makes about John Diefenbaker: that "the central mystery of this period in Canadian history remains." John Diefenbaker, I think, remains a mystery for all of us.

Our task of understanding him is complicated by the existence of a carefully cultivated stage character. Much of the time, John Diefenbaker was a dramatic performer of great skill, practised over fifty years in the courtroom, on the hustings, and in the House of Commons, taking—and giving—great pleasure in the performance. The actor's talent for playing a role involved the submergence of private character into the obscure background. It is very difficult to discover what, in John Diefenbaker, were the assumed qualities of the stage character and what were the more fundamental qualities of the man. Perhaps we can only know the performer. One of the persistent tasks of the historians and biographers will be to try to trace the mysterious interminglings and transpositions of the two from his prairie youth onwards. The dramatic success may be the real triumph of John Diefenbaker's career: that he endlessly perfected this magnificent and stentorian public figure, riveted our attention on it, and concealed whatever lay behind.

Diefenbaker the public figure, like De Gaulle (who referred to himself in the third person), was not genuine, but a work of art. For such a character the maintenance of the illusion has a high priority, sometimes greater than the commitment to smaller truths. It was understandable that simpler men, as Newman reports, would not trust him, or would regard him as "an insincere show-off." His dramatic sense may help to explain what, in some of the crises of the regime, his opponents saw as deviousness or dishonesty. In Diefenbaker's eyes, perhaps, it was not that the monetary crisis of 1962 threatened Canada's economic stability so much as that it threatened the integrity of the performance—and therefore a certain stage deception in the days before the election was called for. Perhaps further, the actor believed in the performance as a kind of magic (the way central bankers do), which if carried off could actually transform reality. But it was puzzling for his opponents and the audience, after the election, to hear him deny the deception. Was that the performer or the man himself speaking in his desperation?

There are glimpses of the private man, and they are significant though never unambiguous. By the time he took the party leadership, he was a confirmed outsider, sensitive and lonely in his isolation from the Canadian establishment, but also conscious that he might use his outsider's status for political advantage in the right circumstances. The personal sense of disadvantage could be parlayed into a political asset. (Would he really have preferred the name of Campbell-Bannerman, if that had opened doors as he said it would?) His outsider's status was a dangerous asset, however, because the cultivated resentment, the jealousy, the distrust that it required could easily overreach themselves. When he felt triumph within his grasp in 1958, he seized the occasion to press home the victory relentlessly against Lester Pearson: and afterwards, when his possession of office called for magnanimity, he could not manage it. Whether this was dramatic excess or something more personal is hard to judge, but it is one thing that increasingly soured the performance. There was no restraint in it. If John Diefenbaker had had more control of the character he created, he might have been a better Prime Minister. But then, of course, be might never have come to power at all. That was a triumph which probably required the concentration of ambition, the narrowness of interest, the self-centredness that Peter Newman reports.

It is insufficiently precise to say that John Diefenbaker had "the right instincts" but lacked courage: the right instincts for what? Presumably Newman means that Diefenbaker was a humanitarian with a strong sense of fellow-feeling for the deprived and dispossessed. Yes; though other instincts put him into uncomfortable situations from which he could not extricate himself. That he lacked courage is, I think, indefensible without great qualification. Does Newman mean he lacked self-assurance? He has always possessed a defiant spirit which rises against insults and direct challenges and which was often the source of courageous political acts—like those in defence of his party leadership from 1963 to the last stand in 1967.

Newman's thesis that Diefenbaker somehow deserted his party and his cause is particularly misplaced. He did upset "the ordinary Canadian Tory" of central Canada, but not by apostasy. The Conservative party in the twentieth century has not, to say the least, possessed an entirely coherent ideology against which one might judge his loyalty to it; but Diefenbaker was true in faith to the Macdonaldian myth of national development, to the liberal mystique of small business enterprise, and to the symbols of the British connection. If he was eclectic, so are most Canadian politicians, and there is no natural law that requires them to be doctrinaire. Dief had the strand of prairie radicalism in him which disconcerted the less adaptable old Tories, and his name and manner offended the narrowest of them. But his accomplishment for the party was, for a decade at least, to make it accessible to Canadians of every class, region and origin in a way that it had not been since John A. Macdonald. That was no act of desertion.

It is unjust, I think, for Newman to claim that Diefenbaker had "not the least inkling of what he wanted to do" when he became Prime Minister. Newman himself offers much of the evidence for what Diefenbaker did intend. He wanted to clean out the stable; he wanted to balance the interests and power of the outlying regions against those of central Canada; he wanted to dignify the dispossessed; he wanted to give Canadians a sense of unifying mission, the form of which had been engraved in him by his prairie youth. Where he did fail—chiefly in economic affairs, defence and the American relationship—his confusions were not the result of having no objectives, but of having no capacity to analyse and work through complicated technical problems in their complexity. This was a failure of intellectual means, traceable perhaps to his education, his legal experience, his political preoccupations, and his inability to seek independent advice.

It is surprising that, for such a completely political animal, John Diefenbaker turned out in many ways to be an inept politician. His sense of timing and occasion in election campaigns was brilliant; but in the Coyne affair, the reaction to Britain's application to the Common Market, the nuclear weapons controversy, and the relationship with President Kennedy, he disastrously misjudged the limits of public and political tolerance. He was insufficiently tough with some of his less competent cabinet colleagues, and he was unable to establish a fruitful relationship of complete trust with most of them. He lacked the prudential sense of Mackenzie King or Harold Macmillan.

In retrospect, Peter Newman's failure to emphasize the nationalist theme during the Diefenbaker years is revealing. Newman himself was not yet a nationalist; and more important, John Diefenbaker too may not have been the nationalist that George Grant made him out to be. Here *Renegade in Power* offers material for balance. Diefenbaker's economic liberalism, his anti-communism, and his deep faith in American leadership of the "free world" always undercut his nationalism and reduced it to rhetoric and pose. His inability to think beyond this postwar liberalism as the Canadian situation degenerated from semi-independence to satellite status led him into the terrible confusions and frustrations of the nuclear arms crisis. He seemed always to be oblivious of the ironies of the situation. By his lack of emphasis on Canadian nationalism, Newman reminds us of how tenuous and incoherent that cause was in the Diefenbaker years. John Diefenbaker was a representative man in his inability to appreciate the implications of his beliefs. Canada was a long way along the path of effective absorption into the empire; the Diefenbaker government assisted that evolution; it was largely unaware of what was happening; and to the extent that it was aware, its strongest inclination was to consider the process a generally benevolent one. Newman's reporting from the scene helps us to recall those circumstances accurately.

Rereading Newman long after the events he recounts, one is probably more aware than in 1963 of the prose style. That it can sometimes be heavy, is an infection perhaps picked up from concentrated exposure to John Diefenbaker's "rococo style of oratory." Newman is not always sure of himself in the use of abstraction and metaphor. But when he is engaged in concrete and unembellished description, on the other hand, he tells the story with splendid pace and touch. For that, *Renegade in Power* should be read for a long time.

Choosing Our Distance

(1977)

In 1976, as editor of The Canadian Forum *magazine, I took part in a border conference at Niagara-on-the-Lake on Canadian cultural nationalism and Canadian-American relations, and afterwards commented on the context and nature of the discussions. The essay appeared as a chapter in the book* Canadian Cultural Nationalism, *published by New York University Press.*

The Niagara conference on Canadian cultural nationalism and Canadian-American relations came at a time of pause when reflection was possible and appropriate. By September 1976 the activity of the federal government in developing a cultural policy seemed to have concluded; and the 1976 Quebec election, with all its cultural implications, was still two months away.

On the eve of the conference the Canadian government brought into force Bill C-58 concerning tax exemptions for advertising expenditures, which meant that, while the American delegates retained a lively curiosity about the intent of the legislation and the degree of support for it, the prolonged affair had finally passed into history and was no longer regarded as a subject of current grievance. It was, however, in the air throughout the discussions as the most immediate instance of Canadian-American disagreement and a possible harbinger of disputes to come.

For about six months before the conference—or since the beginning of 1976—a notable change in the cultural climate of English-speaking Canada had been evident. The period of intense and often strident pressure from a nationalist minority for tangible measures of cultural support from the federal government, maintained in a popular atmosphere of indifference or contempt for such measures, had given way to a more relaxed period of fresh consensus in which the nationalist case seemed to have gained fairly general public acceptance. That gradual change of atmosphere was exemplified by the federal government's decision, announced in January 1975, to tackle the anomaly of the special tax privileges granted to advertisers in the Canadian editions of *Time* and *Reader's Digest* and on border American television stations whose signals are available in Canadian metropolitan centres. (The Liberal cabinet of Pierre Elliott Trudeau, although it contained several moderately nationalist English-speaking members, had always been predominantly anti-nationalist. In this stance it reflected the powerful conviction of the Prime Minister. The decision to proceed with such nationalist legislation, of substantial commercial import, could only mean that the cabinet majority had conceded reluctantly to its perception of a significant change in public sentiment.)

A second sign of the changing orthodoxy was the Canadian Broadcasting Corporation's production, in the spring of 1976, of a major six-hour series on *The Great Canadian Culture Hunt*, which was as much advocacy as it was reporting. It gained large prime-time audiences and favorable reviews. By May 1976 when Susan Crean published her account of the English-speaking Canadian cultural quest, *Who's Afraid of Canadian Culture?*, one of the recurrent themes in the (mostly anti-nationalist) reviews was, ironically, that her story of cultural deprivation and exclusion from the domestic market was already passé. The judgment was wrong but its existence was symptomatic: Critics of nationalist measures in support of the arts could no longer simply reject the nationalist case and expect a sympathetic response from their audiences. They had to concede much of the case and seek to undermine it with more subtlety.

Finally there was the publication in the late spring of 1976 of the first two volumes of the Symons report on Canadian Studies, which catalogued the extent of recent scholarly neglect of Canada. The report was greeted with almost universal support in newspaper features and editorials.

So, by the time of the conference, if the circumstances of Canadian cultural institutions were still frequently precarious, there seemed to be wide public understanding of their plight and recognition that many of their difficulties stem from Canada's openness to American cultural influences. This did not mean that there were obvious and widely accepted policies to meet those difficulties (that is a matter of leadership still to come); it did mean that the institutions and their spokesmen no longer felt isolated from and antagonistic to common sentiment, as they usually had in the late 1960s and early 1970s.

The change of cultural atmosphere in English-speaking Canada was signified most vividly at the conference by two examples which would, I think, have been inconceivable five years ago. One was the fact that Ramsay Cook's account of Canadian cultural nationalism was stated moderately and positively in terms that were acceptable to the Canadian nationalists present. For Mr. Cook, the Liberal anti-nationalist historian, Canadian cultural nationalism had passed out of the realm of tendentious sectarianism into that of indisputable and perhaps inevitable historical fact. Things must have come a long way for that.

The second striking example was the forceful and unapologetic nationalism of two Canadian civil servants, members of the conference, one from the Secretary of State's Department and one from the Department of External Affairs. Their confident assertion of what they saw as the Canadian interest in cultural affairs, and their willingness to contemplate actions which were bound to ruffle American feathers, were revelations, I think, to most of the delegates.

Something approaching a revolution in consciousness must certainly have occurred in Ottawa to produce bureaucrats so much at odds with the postwar orthodoxies and so free to express their thoughts in public. One of them, the Under Secretary of State, André Fortier, more recently repeated some of his remarks publicly in Washington at the Symposium on 20th Century Canadian Culture. "The main effect of all this government intervention," he said, speaking of the recent record of cultural support from Ottawa, "has been to assure a place on the shelf for Canadian cultural products."

> At its heart, are the notions of choice and access, the opportunity for Canadian artists to live, work and attain a modicum of critical and financial success in Canada, and the opportunity for Canadians to experience their work. All of these measures have been good; indeed necessary to survival. I think they are inadequate for growth and self-fulfillment....
>
> The fact remains that our national self-awareness is still threatened; our cultural delivery systems, if I may be permitted so prosaic a phrase, are so full of foreign products that there is scarcely room for the homegrown variety. Our problem is what to do about it....
>
> We know... that whatever mechanisms are employed we will be up against strong economic forces that have traditionally worked to our disadvantage—the ready availability of cheap attractive foreign products and the tremendous expense of producing our own and making them available. Ought the government to intervene more strongly in the production and distribution of Canadian products to ensure that its citizens do indeed have a cultural choice? Or should the government leave this field of activity largely to independent entrepreneurs? Or is there a middle ground where the government would focus on indirect support through legislation and regulation to offset the competitive disadvantage facing Canadians in this area, a disadvantage that is built into the existing market structure?

The "middle ground" previously occupied by the Canadian government in the arts has been the ground of direct subsidy through the Canada Council: a policy which has staved off bankruptcy for many institutions but which has neglected the structure of the cultural market that often prevents those institutions from reaching their primary domestic audience. André Fortier's recognition of a new middle ground of legislative interference in the market is not a statement of government policy, but it confirms the shift in national consensus about the arts in Canada, and probably foreshadows more active government intervention in their support in future. His position confirms the sense expressed by most Canadian participants in the conference that cultural nationalism has now come into the mainstream of political discussion in English-speaking Canada, but has not yet reached its peak. Its evolution was seen as part of the normal growth of national identity. As a number of persons said, there are obvious parallels between the contemporary flowering of the arts and national self-consciousness in English-speaking Canada, the earlier creative blossoming of Quebec in the 1960s, and the development of an indigenous American culture in the nineteenth century as European forms and standards were gradually sloughed off for national ones.

The ways in which Canadians perceive the role of government were much remarked upon. Several Canadians emphasized their view that government must play a central role in the stimulation of both artists and their audiences in Canada. The conviction appeared to be an article of faith arousing little anxiety among Canadians familiar with the formative influences of the National Film Board, the Canadian Broadcasting Corporation (CBC), the National Gallery, the Canada Council, Artbank, and the Canadian Radio-Television and Telecommunications Commission (CRTC). This assumption about government activity may have appeared eccentric to some of the American delegates more accustomed to the dominance of market values in the American cultural industries. (It was at least made clear that when Canadian cultural policies have an adverse effect upon the profits of American companies—as in the case of Canadian regulation of advertising on border television stations—the American reaction is likely to reflect commercial interest rather than cultural sensitivity.)

American participants did note the readiness of the American government to intervene in its own market to protect it by regulation for the support of American entrepreneurs. They could therefore respect, in principle, the right of the Canadian government to do likewise, provided the rules were made clear; but that theoretical respect was unlikely to temper American efforts to defend established American interests in the Canadian market, to emphasize their commercial nature, and to ignore their cultural implications. The Canadians were left with the common-sense view (but one that is relatively novel in a country only slowly discarding its colonial assumptions) that the Canadian interest must be defined and asserted by Canadians.

A distinction was drawn by an American between high culture, which is susceptible to elite management because it is directed only to the elite, and mass culture. He suggested that the extensions of Canadian cultural policy now being considered were efforts to influence mass culture, which is shaped by forces common to all post-industrial societies, and probably beyond the influence of elitist regulation. Aside from noting that this is a real possibility, but asserting that Canadian policy would be aimed at encouraging local control, public choice, and marginal rather than central changes in popular habits, the conference neglected to take up this complicating point in detail. It is one that the CRTC and the CBC struggle with daily in a mood of increasing pessimism; and it is related to the rapid advance of technology which brings us cable and satellite transmission just as we have shakily established the machinery of licensing and control over conventional television broadcasting. It concerns fundamental questions of political versus economic and cultural determinism which were not touched upon explicitly at the conference. The implicit assumption of the Canadian delegates seemed to be that a community's political will (if it chooses to exercise that will) can substantially determine its cultural atmosphere at all levels, to some considerable extent in defiance of strong social and economic forces. The concept of mass society is, further, an American one which fits peculiarly American circumstances; it may be that Canada is not a mass society, except in the features extending into it from American mass society, and therefore susceptible to shrewd national cultural leadership. (It also seems questionable even to claim for American society that mass culture is beyond the influence of leadership or "elitist" manipulation.)

While most of the delegates' attention was devoted to the cultural policies of the Canadian government as they reflect English-speaking pressures and interests, Ottawa's embarrassments over bilingual air traffic control and the signs of growing support for the Parti Québécois inevitably led the meeting to discuss the Quebec independence movement and its consequences for Canadian-American relations. The discussion, which focused on the potential attitude of the United States government to an independent Quebec, was not strictly within the subject of the conference, but the independence movement's potential for disturbing habit and convention was great enough that the matter could not be ignored. The American response was a proper diplomatic one, that the United States government recognizes established governments and does not interfere in domestic politics. There discussion stopped.

One could speculate that the State Department's attitude to the independence movement is in fact more complicated than this, and that many considerations of American national interest enter into the calculation, not all of them constant in all circumstances. The pro forma reassurance about American support for the status quo was not perhaps as reassuring as it appeared to be—since tomorrow's status quo may not be today's.

One point which was stated but not sufficiently emphasized was that cultural nationalists in English-speaking Canada in the 1970s are not antagonists of Quebec nationalism, but generally its supporters. Quebec's awakening has been regarded increasingly in the English-speaking cultural community as an example and inspiration rather than as a threat. What is seen from outside the country as cultural division and disintegration can instead be seen from within as a shared (or at least parallel) search for independence by two colonized communities. It is not quite axiomatic that a victory for the independence movement in Quebec must be a defeat for Canada; it is just conceivable that the two nationalist movements could develop together in a way which would reinforce the confidence and will to survive of both communities.

That is not yet the official view in Ottawa, or the dominant view in the country; but as the need to deal peacefully and realistically with the fact of Quebec nationalism becomes more pressing, the paradox may be recognized in both communities as a creative one. Such recognition might encourage more activist cultural policies in both Ottawa and Quebec City, which would challenge American interests across the whole range of the cultural industries.

According to this analysis, the narrow American interest would thus lie clearly in undermining Quebec nationalism because that action would assist a Canadian federal government, which is anti-nationalist on principle and complacent about the continuing dominance of American cultural and economic influences in Canada. (Perhaps the warm congressional response to Prime Minister Trudeau's promise of continuing Canadian unity revealed Washington's intuition that the American link with Canada inverts the classical maxim, divide and rule.)

For most of the conference, the American participants seemed to be fascinated observers at yet another Canadian session of encounter therapy, genuinely tolerant, and concerned in a good-neighbourly way about the (genially hypochondriac?) patient's well-being. I sensed occasionally that it is difficult for some Americans (as it is for Canadians) to believe that Canada may have interests and a destiny different in important ways from those of the United States. For thirty years Canada has given the United States no reason to think its interests and destiny are separate, so the difficulty is understandable. But the existence of a new Canadian mood was manifest, and I believe that on both sides the meeting reflected a growing willingness to accept the consequences of that change. This does not guarantee easy relations, but it does suggest that both countries may pursue their national interests in ways that will maintain a high level of mutual respect and civility. The forthcoming initiatives in cultural relations, however, are almost certain to come from Ottawa—or Quebec City—rather than Washington.

Political Parties and the Survival of Canada

(1980)

The rumblings of constitutional discontent that began in Quebec with Jean Lesage's quiet revolution of 1960 had, after two decades of intermittent attention and frustration, royal commissions, task forces and federal-provincial conferences, led to impasse by 1980. The provincial victory of the Parti Québécois in 1976, two changes of government in Ottawa in 1979 and 1980, and a looming Quebec referendum on semi-independence brought the country to crisis. This paper was delivered at the University of British Columbia, before the defeat of Quebec's first referendum in 1980 and the subsequent constitutional settlement of 1982 restored a short period of calm to the country's domestic political conflicts. It was published in a collection titled Entering the Eighties: Canada in Crisis.

I should like to take the title of this essay almost literally. If it is true—as I believe it is—that the maintenance of Confederation in something like its present form hangs in the balance in 1980, then what part have our political parties had in bringing us to that precarious stage, and what prospects do they offer for taking us through the present crisis to a state of renewed or fresh constitutional equilibrium?

The crisis is not quite literally a crisis of physical survival. We do not face the imminent possibility that Canada and its citizens will suddenly disappear from the face of the earth—unless there is a nuclear holocaust. (That eventuality lies beyond the influence of Canadian political parties, so that there is not much to be gained from considering their attitudes to it: undoubtedly they're agin it, and that's that.) What we do face is the prospect that the survival of Canada in its present constitutional shape, as a federation of ten provinces whose relationships are formally governed by the terms of the British North America Act, may be at stake. The twenty-four million people who occupy the territory called Canada, or most of them, seem likely to go on living in political association; the question is whether it will be much the same association as at present, or whether it is destined to change substantially in character. The activity of the parties in creating and resolving that crisis of constitutional forms is an urgent matter for consideration.

There are thoughtful Canadians, of course, who deny that we face a constitutional crisis at all. I have talked to several federal politicians in the past two years who have argued that the constitutional alarums and excursions in Canada since 1960 have been nothing more serious than fashionable games; that those who press hardest for constitutional change do not in fact want to achieve it; and that the rest of us need only wait patiently or complacently until the constitutional flurries die away, when we will be able to return to the enjoyment of our blessings under the federal constitution of 1867. I have heard other Canadians argue, slightly differently, that there may indeed be a crisis, in the sense that some provinces or regions strongly challenge the rules and practices of the federal system as it exists; but that the ways of Canadian politics just do not allow for the satisfaction of such basic challenges to the system. This kind of diagnosis usually calls not only for patience or complacency in working out the discontent, but for more active and defiant traits: the courage to hold on firmly, or the will to resist. This attitude is certainly less soft-headed than the first; it may even involve a shrewd assessment of how much change the Canadian political system can normally accommodate in an orderly way; but I suspect that it also underestimates the determination of those who advocate major constitutional change. It therefore stops short of facing the hardest dilemma: if the system can't take much orderly change, and if the advocates of change have the power and the determination to press their claims nonetheless, what kind of political ingenuity will be needed to avert political breakdown? (The answer to that question could be that none is available.)

In contrast to such views, I judge that there is a constitutional crisis in Canada which time alone will not dissipate, which is worsening and approaching its climax, yet which is still open to political resolution. Given the recent historical record, however, the likelihood of a tolerable political settlement must appear slight. Canadian political parties have made a less than satisfactory contribution to that record; but they have also been the victims of circumstances. While they might have done many small things—and thus averted some consequences of the crisis—I am not sure that they could, realistically, have done any big thing sufficient to avert the crisis itself. It is a crisis of world-historical scale, while they have only been weak and mortal institutions.

Here is how the Pepin-Robarts Task Force on Canadian Unity defines the challenge to Canadian political survival:

> While we take the election of the Parti Québécois as our point of departure, we do not regard that event, or any single federal election, or the pending Quebec referendum as defining the sense and substance of the issues the Task Force must tackle. Whether the referendum is "won" or "lost," the underlying problems will remain and will have to be confronted. We believe that such events as these should be taken to symbolize the political crisis Canada is facing, rather than to constitute it. The political crisis which has led to such occurrences displays historical roots which are much deeper and dimensions which are broader than any single event can comprehend, and its rhythms of development are slower and more inexorable than a single election or referendum would suggest. . . .

> Since the early 1960s... considerable efforts at reform have been made in Quebec, in the other provinces, and in Ottawa. Yet more than a decade after the warning of the B & B Commission about a national crisis, the country has moved to an even graver and more critical stage in its history, symbolized by the election of a secessionist government in Quebec.... The crisis which the country faces today is not one of Quebec or of French Canada only: it is a crisis of Confederation itself. In this sense, the challenge to the country differs from that of a decade ago and must be considered in much wider terms. To the fundamental challenge of Canadian duality must now be added the other important challenge of Canadian regionalism....
>
> Canadians now find themselves in a situation quite unlike any they have faced before. While we have had major crises in the past, this one is qualitatively different. The diverse elements ... have converged at one point in time and, partly as a result of this convergence, the rather rough-and-ready consensus which once ensured the reasonably effective governing of the country is at the point of breaking down.[1]

That analysis seems to me to be neither alarmist nor exaggerated, but rather a calm and sober statement of the truth.

It is not too difficult in retrospect to understand why the consensus has broken down. Above all, what gave Canada its confidence and its expansive prospects in the nineteenth century was the existence of the British Empire. The Empire was both a moral and a material force in the world, just reaching its apogee: elevated, in the minds of the smug and adventurous Englishmen and Scotsmen who made and managed it, to the very heights of the earthly paradise. There was nothing better in the world; there had been nothing better in the world. In the Empire the sun never set; material progress never ceased; English liberty and parliamentary institutions were to bring men as close to moral perfection as anyone would care to be. (And the Church of England was there when necessary to tolerate the lapses.) Within this great protective umbrella Canada came to birth in 1867. While Canadian politicians could foresee a gradual and benevolent evolution to autonomy within the Empire, the inspirational strength of the Empire, the certainty about values and institutions, appeared eternal. They remained eternal (with a few twinges of mortality at the time of the South African War) until 1918, and for many Canadians even (though in what was becoming more evidently a period of half-life) until 1945.

I think that the cohesive strength for Canadians of this imperial vision,

[1] Canada, Privy Council Office, *A Future Together: The Task Force on Canadian Unity* (1979), pp. 11–16.

implanted from without, cannot easily be overestimated during the first eighty years of confederation. After 1945 Britain's imperial power and will were gone. As the Empire faded away in the fifties and sixties, and as Britain turned inwards to agonize over her own domestic problems, English Canada lost one—perhaps the most profound—of her spiritual props. Some sense of the confusion and desperation that this loss entailed for British Canadians (a loss that most of the time could find no expression) was displayed in John Diefenbaker's futile objection to Britain's entry into the European Common Market, or in Donald Creighton's fulminations about the road not taken after 1945. Nothing replaced the loss of this source of transcendental assurance: not membership in the pallid Commonwealth; not the Department of External Affairs' earnest participation in United Nations good works; not half-integration into the American economic community; not the weakness and immaturity of domestic Canadian nationalism. And nothing that Canadian political parties could have done would have prevented this loss.

The second source of strength and self-confidence in Victorian and early twentieth-century Canada was the expansionist and centralist ambition of the commercial and political class, the financiers, railroad builders, manufacturers, and politicians of Montreal and southern Ontario who shaped the BNA Act and its continental purposes. These were men of large vision and presumption, spurred by the living example of the British empire and by the competitive challenge of the expanding American nation to the south to create their own continental empire within the broader framework of the British global empire. But their continental empire lacked any spiritual justification of its own: that was provided for it by the British element. The Dominion of Canada, on its own terms, found its nobility in railroads: the conquest and material development of a vast half-continent, the political and financial power at the centre that would accompany so audacious an achievement. Such a vision of development was plausible only in the age of technology; and, like the vision of Rhodes and Milner in southern Africa, it bore its own contradiction at its heart. The new communities of the West that joined or were created by the new federation to achieve its mercantilist purposes were not satisfied in their status of colonial subordination. From early in the twentieth century, the country grew familiar with the insistence of the Western provinces that they should somehow play a full and equal part in the political and economic life of the nation. Concessions were made; but it appeared by the early sixties that the central-Canadian bias of the federation—based as it was on a complex of institutional, geographical, and demographic conditions—could only be altered fundamentally by reforms that central Canada would be unwilling to contemplate and that the West was not yet ready to insist upon. The sense of dissatisfaction remained; and it was clear that, whatever the myth of Canadian unity that was transmitted to the outside world or accepted in Ottawa and Toronto, closer to the ground that unity was extremely fragile. The allegiance of the West was skeptical, and conditional upon the future adjustment of the political balance in its favour. The political parties of western Canada have been leading carriers of that skepticism since 1921.

With the confidence of Empire and the unquestioned predominance of central Canada already gone, two sets of events above all have thrown Canadian stability into doubt since 1960: the awakening of French-speaking Quebec to a confident sense of its national destiny, and the windfall accumulation of resource income in the West (and perhaps soon in Newfoundland too) which has followed from the actions of OPEC since 1973. These events, vigorously promoted and exploited by all the provincial political parties of Quebec (in the first case) and by the governing parties and their administrations in Saskatchewan, Alberta, and British Columbia (in the second case), have finally brought us to the constitutional crisis proclaimed by the Pepin-Robarts Task Force. The crisis involves more than a conflict of centre versus periphery; it involves, as well, the disintegration of the centre itself, resulting from the dramatic appearance in Quebec of a formerly hidden periphery, the Québécois nation. It is not obvious to me what resources of spirit and will, beyond the strength of political inertia and vested interest, the central government can now bring to the maintenance of its authority. Pepin-Robarts concluded that Ottawa's wisest course would be to concede the weakness of its historic position and take the initiative in negotiating a new Confederation settlement that would entrench the enhanced power and authority of Quebec and the Western provinces.

No government, anywhere, abandons power easily or by choice. Ottawa is no exception. In principle, the Trudeau government has insisted since 1968 that it does not have to, and should not do so. But its record in the fruitless rounds of constitutional discussion of the last twelve years hardly sustains its case: that record suggests instead that an unyielding defence of the federal power is untenable. Indeed, the unsatisfactory record of all three federal parties on the constitutional question must be taken, I believe, as strong evidence that the system within which they work has failed.

In the case of the Liberal Party, it is hardly accurate to describe its constitutional position as that of the party, or even of the cabinet. It is the position of Prime Minister Trudeau, his few political intimates, and his constitutional advisers in the bureaucracy. As George Radwanski notes in his recent political biography of the prime minister, the cabinet rarely influenced the government's constitutional stance after 1968;[2] nor did the party in its intermittent

[2] George Radwanski, *Trudeau* (Toronto, 1978), pp. 179–80.

national gatherings. It is surely extraordinary, and the result of something more than Mr. Trudeau's intellectual eminence, that the largest and most significant question before the country in the last decade (as the prime minister insisted during 1979 campaign) has never in that time been the subject of serious debate in the governing party. This is not to say that some Liberals have not sought to bring the question into debate—Gordon Gibson of Vancouver is pre-eminent among them—but where has the effort gotten them? The party, in 1968, effectively delegated responsibility for dealing with the constitutional problem to its leader, and the country endorsed that delegation in the general election that followed. There was a sense, in those heady days, that Mr. Trudeau was going to put Quebec in its place, renew Canadian unity, and satisfy the aspirations of French-speaking Canadians all at once. Beyond belief in those bromides, the party and the country did not probe.

When the Trudeau government's idiosyncratic effort to achieve constitutional reform collapsed in the aftermath of the October Crisis and the Victoria Conference of June 1971, English-speaking Canada and the Liberal Party greeted the failure complacently and for five years shared the government's indifference to the constitutional question.

The election of the Parti Québécois government in November 1976 threw the federal government into panic, and English-speaking Canada into one of its sporadic bouts of confusion and alarm. The country's alarm lasted only a few months; it was soon dissipated by the demonstrated caution and competence of the new Quebec government. But the Trudeau government's panic lasted longer: it was institutionalized in a series of emergency projects ranging from the Canadian Unity Information Office to the Discovery Train to the increasingly elaborate celebration of Canada Day to a fresh round of constitutional conferences. One of the characteristics of the post-November federalist reaction, as in 1968, was that it took the form of a governmental, rather than a party, response. The Liberal Party did not enter into reflective analysis of the country's future. The Liberal government pre-empted the role, at least superficially, by treating the Parti Québécois challenge as a threat to the federal government's propagandist ingenuity rather than a serious challenge to its constitutional authority. The most that Ottawa wanted in the form of public participation in the debate after 1976 seemed to be sentimental declarations of allegiance to national unity. It apparently never occurred to anyone influential in the Liberal Party that it, *as a party*, had any responsibility to reassess the institutions of Canadian federalism.

The prospect of Quebec's independence was, understandably, too sensitive a subject for the Liberal Party to contemplate. Quebec was the basis of the party's hold on federal office, and it believed that hold to be permanent. No one questions the earth beneath one's feet.

Below the superficial efforts of propaganda, the federal government's more substantial response to the Parti Québécois appears, on close examination, to lack the coherence and determination of its previous initiatives in the constitutional wars. The Parti Québécois victory has, I believe, destroyed the confidence of the Trudeau administration in its constitutional mission. It no longer has a clear sense of purpose or a constitutional strategy. The government took four major steps after 1976 to deal with the Quebec challenge:

(i) It renewed its attempts, through the federal-provincial conferences, to reach agreement on a constitutional amending formula and a respectable package of substantive amendments;

(ii) In tandem with that effort it introduced, in June 1978, its own constitutional bill, C-60, and set a three-year timetable for its complete adoption;

(iii) It appointed the Task Force on Canadian Unity to buy time; and

(iv) It introduced a federal referendum bill designed to allow Ottawa to counter a PQ referendum victory with a contradictory result of its own manufacture, either within Quebec or across Canada.

By the spring of 1979 all these initiatives had collapsed. The constitutional reforms that Ottawa discussed with the federal–provincial conferences of October 1978 and February 1979, in spite of their greater flexibility as compared with earlier federal proposals, proved unacceptable to the provinces. Bill C-60, a monument of careless constitutional draftsmanship, was demolished as it deserved to be in parliamentary committee over the summer of 1978 and was never proceeded with; the Pepin-Robarts Task Force, when it reported in January 1979, showed its independence of the prime minister by recommending an approach to constitutional renewal profoundly subversive of Mr. Trudeau's centralism; and the federal referendum bill, which the prime minister insisted had the highest priority, died on the order paper when Parliament was dissolved at last by the prime minister's hand in March 1979. That was not a record to inspire much confidence, and by the time of the first 1979 dissolution more and more Canadians—including Liberals—had judged that the emperor had no clothes. The prime minister's insistence that the constitution was the issue of first importance in the 1979 campaign struck no chords, I think, largely because it was evident that he no longer had a constitutional policy. As I wrote in *The Canadian Forum*, by then he had only a growl.[3]

And where does the Liberal Party stand on the constitution now that it has returned so suddenly to power? Nowhere. The party never passed beyond the preliminaries in reassessing this or any other subject during its short term in opposition. The prime minister, abiding by the advice of his cynical advisers,

[3] "Turning Them Out," *The Canadian Forum*, March 1979.

neglected to mention the subject during the 1980 campaign; he was probably glad of that because he seemed to have nothing to say. The grand constitutional strategist of 1968 is in office once again, but this time without even the shreds of a policy.

There is much less to say about the constitutional positions of the federal Progressive Conservative Party and the NDP. The Conservatives, with a clear run of three years in opposition under a new leader from 1976 to 1979—a period of preparation for power—failed almost totally to consider and develop a general position on constitutional change. The party avoided any coherent response to the program of the Parti Québécois. It offered only a short-term, tactical alternative to the approach of the Trudeau government: opposition to the federal referendum bill on the ground, not that there shouldn't be one, but that it should be more narrowly drawn; a healthy skepticism toward Ottawa's anti-separatist propaganda efforts, based on the plausible view that they were shallow and more likely to promote than to discourage support for the PQ; and a general desire to appease rather than to provoke the provinces, exemplified by the Clark government's abandonment of lotteries, its promise to transfer jurisdiction over offshore resources to Newfoundland, and its politely drawn-out negotiations with Alberta over the price of oil. This approach, like that of the Liberal Party, was the product of the leader's personal instincts rather than of any widespread consideration within the party, either parliamentary or national. Once these points had been made in office, the Clark government gave no further sign of thoughtfulness on the constitution. It reduced the temperature of the debate but seemed to have nothing more positive to contribute. Finally, after the government's defeat in December, Mr. Clark made two death-bed offers. He announced, apparently without reflection or consultation, that Senator Arthur Tremblay would lead a federal task force in preparing the government's constitutional proposals (Senator Tremblay, I believe, never received any formal appointment under the Inquiries Act); and he suggested that a new Rowell-Sirois Commission would be necessary to examine the federal-provincial distribution of financial resources, in order to assure the maintenance of sufficient central power—as though the proposed Tremblay study and the question of federal financial distribution were unrelated! This was a disturbingly amateurish way for the prime minister to treat the country's constitutional future; but he and his party apparently had neither the means nor the desire to offer proposals for public discussion more fully considered than Mr. Clark's electoral expedients.

The federal NDP, one might have thought, was in an ideal position through the 1970s to play an educative role on constitutional reform. From its founding convention it took a generous position on the French language and the position of Quebec in confederation; at the 1971 convention the party took a compromise stance in favour of constitutional change and even a constituent assembly. The NDP had nothing to lose in Quebec, and perhaps much to gain, by opting for a major alteration in the distribution of powers. It would have fulfilled its national vocation as the spur to reform had it insisted upon and developed those early attitudes in confident public debate. Instead it found them embarrassing and buried them. The party seemed unable to stand up against Mr. Trudeau's intimidating scorn of anyone who doubted the righteousness of his federalism, or against the rigid centralism of David Lewis, whether as leader or as ex-leader. The NDP did at least continue to debate the constitutional question at its biennial conventions (on the insistence of a determined and persistent minority), but always came out of those conventions after 1971 with a pale reflection of the Liberal government's policy. And Ed Broadbent's apparent personal indifference to the subject ultimately guaranteed that it would have no place in the party's recent electoral appeals.

We are thus faced, I believe, with two federal opposition parties that have abdicated any serious role in the constitutional debate, and a federal government that is demoralized and intellectually exhausted on the subject. That is not an encouraging prospect, even for those who desire a major transfer of power to the provinces, because it suggests that no one in Ottawa knows how to approach the crisis. The possibilities for panic and imprudent reaction to the pressures of the moment are ominous. There is no indication of any strong commitment in either English-speaking Canada or Quebec to the maintenance of the federal union in its present balance, but rather a striking absence of conviction about the role of the central government. The unusually vacuous nature of the recent federal election campaign, I think, underlines that absence of conviction. On the other hand, what confronts Ottawa's disintegrating defence of the central authority is the powerful mythology of popular sovereignty and nationalism in Quebec, and a new sense of power, enhanced by greed, in Alberta and its neighbouring provinces of the West.

What alone might rally popular support for a renewed assertion of the will and power of the central government (as it has done before) is a widespread perception of national emergency, conceivable in three possible circumstances: an international political crisis threatening world war; an international economic crisis on the scale of the great Depression; or a major crisis of energy supplies. Those circumstances could—and probably would—occur in combination rather than separately; but they are not, I think, events that even the most passionate federalist would wish upon us. Neither are they conditions that Ottawa could easily manufacture in order to justify an assertion of the federal power. Short of this kind of emergency, proclaimed on demonstrable evidence by the federal government and accepted by a strong majority of the population as it probably would be, Ottawa does not appear to possess much psychological leverage in the coming conflict over constitutional power.

Only two political parties, as parties, seem to me to have played a creative role in the evolution of the constitutional debate: the Parti Québécois and the Quebec Liberal Party since the accession of Claude Ryan as its leader. They have both used the party machinery with unusual democratic genius to create and propagate widely their sophisticated programs for constitutional change. The PQ has from the beginning had an instinct about constitutional change in Canada that has proved to be accurate. It takes for granted that Quebec cannot substantially increase its constitutional powers by bargaining from within the established system. This is an instinct about both procedure and substance: that as a province like the others, in federal-provincial conference, Quebec could never gain agreement for its program of constitutional reform; and that even if it could do so in that forum, the alterations gained would not be adequate. In order to reform the system to Quebec's nationalist satisfaction, the Parti Québécois perceives that Quebec must bargain from a position of power outside the normal institutions of federal-provincial diplomacy. The PQ still wishes to bargain, to engage in diplomacy; but it wishes also to reach a satisfactory conclusion to that diplomacy. Twelve years of experience seem to confirm that authoritative decisions cannot be made by the federal-provincial conferences on the constitution; the parties must meet in a new forum, with new leverage. The PQ is well on the way to achieving it.

In Alberta, Saskatchewan, and British Columbia the governments rather than the parties have devoted substantial efforts to the adoption of constitutional programs; and in Ottawa, too, a government, as I have said, once did so after 1968. Elsewhere, including Ontario, I believe that the recent direct contributions of political parties and governments to the debate have been pathetically inadequate. So widespread and profound a failure must point to something more than the political incompetence of all those people and institutions. The forces that make and alter the shapes of nations are, after all, more complex and mysterious than those that make a gasoline tax or a welfare policy, and they are not forces that political parties operating within the rules of the established system can easily perceive or come to terms with. For this reason, that traditional parties elected within an existing constitutional framework cannot in normal times find the focus or the interest to alter that framework, I have sensed for several years that it will require the creation of some extraordinary institutions and procedures to accomplish constitutional reform in Canada: or, alternatively, that change will come about by rupture rather than agreement. One of the problems that will confront Ottawa and the provinces after the Quebec referendum and the next Quebec election—that is, probably within the next year—will be to consider how to arrange the next and most serious round of constitutional negotiations. The conditioned response will be to return to a series of federal-provincial conferences of first ministers: but these have proven frustrating and futile over the past twelve years because the rule of unanimity has prevented eleven heads of government with differing mandates and interests from reaching general agreement. We will be condemned, I suppose, to more of that before agreement will have to be made to transfer the process to another body, more specifically designed for constitution-making.[4]

For the moment, the Canadian federation lies prostrate and disarmed, the purpose and determination of 1867 drained away, the creative political energies resting with a few provinces of the union who are bursting their constitutional bonds (though not with the same ends in mind). The national government and the national parties, I suspect, have already effectively lost both the battle of Quebec and the battle of the West; it remains to be seen whether the necessary readjustments can be achieved in relative order. But the use of political means to achieve accommodation has not yet been abandoned by anyone, and that is a hopeful sign. The outcome, I am inclined to believe, will not necessarily be a bad thing if life can go on in conditions of liberty, democracy, and common decency in the successor state or states of federal Canada. It is now those conditions, rather than the old federal system, that the parties must apply their talents to preserving.

[4] In its claim to negotiate Quebec's status from a position of recognized equality, the Parti Québécois acknowledges the need for a new kind of bargaining process. But aside from suggesting that the other provinces will probably wish to participate with Ottawa on the other side of the bargaining table, and that several negotiating panels might work concurrently, the Quebec White Paper on sovereignty-association leaves the matter vague. The most fully worked-out formula for fresh constitutional discussion appears in the Quebec Liberal Party's document, *A New Canadian Federation*. It proposes the creation of a special constitutional conference, preceded by the adoption of a "solemn preliminary pledge" to write a new constitution by Parliament and a majority of the provincial legislatures. The conference would have "a short deadline" of twelve or eighteen months, during which period it would remain in session. The draft constitution produced by the conference would be submitted for ratification to Parliament and the legislatures, and finally to the public in a referendum. The proposal marks a half-step, and perhaps more, toward the concept of a constitutional convention or constituent assembly, and a departure from the ordinary process of federal-provincial diplomacy. This may be a practical, because unobtrusive, means of making that shift.

Canada: Inside or Outside

(1986)

While serving an administrative term at the University of Western Ontario, I encouraged creation of what was, I believe, the first Centre for American Studies at a Canadian university. The Centre sponsored a lecture series and a conference in 1984–85 on the theme "Canadian perspectives on the United States." I contributed this essay to the resulting publication, reflecting on the curious reluctance of Canadian journalists and academics "to see the United States as a whole and to deal with the central issues of its history and culture."

The theme of this volume, "Canadian Perspectives on the United States," invites us to reflect on the angle from which we perceive the United States and the special contribution which Canadians might make to understanding America. In response to that theme, these remarks are titled "Inside or Outside." This is not meant to be a further contribution to the old debate on political union that was revived recently in *The Economist*'s inane suggestion that Canada should become the fifty-first state.[1] I take for granted that the political separation of the two countries will be maintained and mean instead to reflect on the problem of Canadian perspective. As Canadians, are we inside or outside observers of the United States?

For someone like me, raised in the Canadian prairies in the 1930s and 1940s, the question of what is special about Canadian perspectives on the United States has hung in the air virtually since the moment of my first awareness of public events, because the American presence was so immediate. In those days on the prairies it was as easy, and almost as common, to listen to KSL, Salt Lake City as to CBK, Watrous, Saskatchewan. Even when we listened to our own commercial stations we tuned in for "The Lone Ranger," "The Green Hornet," "Superman," the "Lux Radio Theatre," "Fibber McGee and Molly," Fred Allen, Jack Benny, Edgar Bergen and Charlie McCarthy—and when we managed to miss school, we could add another two hours of soap opera to that list, all of it out of New York City. No one knew whether Wilf Carter was Canadian or American. The wartime voice of Winston Churchill (or his double), the King's Christmas broadcast to the Empire, and the Union Jack reminded us faintly that we were British; and only, it seems, the Happy Gang and Foster Hewitt gave us any indication that we were actually Canadians.

[1] "Namerica, Namerica," *The Economist*, 6 April 1985.

The flow of land settlement had brought tens of thousands of American farmers across the invisible border into Alberta from North Dakota and Montana after 1900, just as in the previous generations, thousands of Canadians, both French- and English-speaking, moved from Quebec and Ontario into New England and the Midwest. Some Edmontonians took escapist weekends in Great Falls, Montana. The forty-ninth parallel hardly existed in our imaginations and after 1941, it seemed to disappear altogether when the B-17s and Tomahawk fighters arrived in Edmonton—and then thousands of U.S. troops for the duration of the war. For a teenager all that seemed entirely natural and unproblematic. Toronto and Ottawa were distant and alien, just as Washington and New York were for our Montana neighbours. That degree of intermixing of the two societies, both of them new and resource-based societies in the West, has had a profound and continuing influence on political and social assumptions in the prairies; and those assumptions, in turn, have complicated the political life of Canada, as it has become more nationally self-conscious and mature in the last three decades.

These personal reflections lead to an initial conclusion about Canadian perspectives on the United States: while the American presence has been near to us all, there are obviously important regional distinctions among our perspectives on the United States, the result of contrasting regional experiences of the American nation. The view from the Maritimes, Quebec, and Ontario is as idiosyncratic as the view from Alberta, and each area can offer its own distinct insights. What that suggests to me is the potential richness of *Canadian* study of the United States, if we encourage it from our various regional points of view. The more common choice of Canadian regional scholars until now has been to examine Canadian subjects with American regional influences in mind, rather than American subjects from a Canadian regional perspective. It may be true that the historical influences have mostly flowed one way with, for example, the arrival of the Loyalists in Upper Canada and the Maritimes, or the spillover of the progressive movement in the west, but the application of our Canadian perspectives to American subjects, where we have had similar experiences of settlement and industrial and resource development, should certainly offer fresh illumination on many subjects of American enquiry. Some possibilities come immediately to mind. Where are the studies by Quebec scholars of the French-speaking minorities of New England, or on a larger scale, of American policies of cultural assimilation in general? Where are the studies by Canadian authors of American regional politics? On the national level, where are the Canadian contributions to American constitutional studies, or foreign policy studies, or to scholarship on American transportation and resource development? There are some striking exceptions to this Canadian scholarly neglect of big American subjects, in the writings of the economists Jacob Viner and John Kenneth Galbraith, for example; or in Ted Chamberlin's book on native policy in the United States and Canada, *The Harrowing of Eden*;[2] or in Thomas Berger's current commission of enquiry into the Alaskan native land settlement.[3] And there are, of course, the three great Canadian originals with their startling insights into imperial America: Harold Innis, Marshall McLuhan, and George Grant (only one of whom has reached the American audience). But those exceptions are certainly unusual.

There is surely something very curious about the fact that this most dynamic society has drawn observers in their hordes from across the globe to dissect it, but has not attracted the same interest from the closest neighbours. Canada has not had an Alexis de Tocqueville, a James Bryce, a Denis Brogan, or a Marcus Cunliffe; an Alistair Cooke, or Alastair Buchan, or Henry Brandon, or Henry Fairlie, or Louis Heren. Scarcely any of our scholars or journalists have attempted to see the United States as a whole and to deal with the central issues of its history and culture. (There was one journalistic exception in Max Freedman, but he wrote for the *Manchester Guardian* rather than for Canadian enlightenment.) We may say simply that we have been too busy in the young life of Canadian scholarship and journalism to turn to many subjects beyond the life of our own national community, but the explanation of our neglect goes deeper than that.

The failure to analyze the United States can he partially explained on the grounds that, until recently, Canada lacked the educational and cultural apparatus to prepare individuals of talent to undertake such enquiries at home, let alone to do so abroad. Our institutions of higher learning and our educated population have just been too sparse to produce such riches. If that is the chief explanation of the failure, we should soon have evidence that it has been overcome, since we now possess the developed apparatus of higher education to produce some Bryces, Brogans, and Brandons (although we still lack the intensive publishing industries, both scholarly and popular, that complement the universities in Britain and Western Europe). Perhaps it is now only a matter of waiting, complacently and confidently, for our inspired studies of the United States to appear.

But this is unlikely. Scholarly interest and fashion do not develop autonomously from the broader movements of popular interest in the community in which the scholarship is produced, and that may be one key to the reluctance of Canadian academics and journalists to plunge seriously into writing about major American subjects. There are at least three distinct aspects to this Canadian reluctance. Two of them arise from a kind of McLuhanite immersion in

[2] Ted Chamberlin, *The Harrowing of Eden* (New York: Seabury Press, 1975).

[3] Thomas R. Berger, *Village Journey: The Report of the Alaska Native Review Commission* (New York: Hill and Wang, 1985).

American society which makes that society largely invisible to us. We are so close to it, we are so fully a part of it, that we cannot see it whole as independent observers. We cannot leave the fishbowl to look in, as Europeans can, from the perspective of a few thousand kilometres.

But Americans somehow manage to gain a critical perspective on themselves, just as we do increasingly on ourselves. So why do Canadians find it so difficult to achieve that perspective in relation to the United States? A further reason for the lapse may be that we have not found it necessary. Americans reflect on their own society as part of an internal debate that leads to action; Europeans have reflected on the United States for generations, because it was a new giant on the horizon that had turned away from the Old World and threatened its power and self-confidence. While, as Canadians, we feel that we are inside the American nation and can hear the national debate going on around us, we know, too, both that our contributions will not make much difference if we do make them, and that Americans can be counted on to make their own pungent and telling comments from all angles on their own national issues. We are so close that we can take a free ride. Other foreign observers, standing at a greater distance or writing for audiences at a greater distance, cannot take for granted that the domestic American conversation will be heard abroad, so they have to reconstruct and analyze it, just for the sake of elementary understanding.

The third reason for our collective reluctance to enter the great debate about American issues is more tentative—though perhaps more crucial. This is the matter of cultural confidence and its relationship to power. The prominent place occupied by British and European commentators in the debate on America derives not simply from the highly developed state of their journalism, scholarship, and publishing, but from the original position of these countries as leading societies in relation to America. They had already established their political and cultural positions in the world when the United States was a mere upstart, and although their empires have faded, their cultural pretensions, their assumed superiority, their established cultural competence, have not. They go on observing and commenting because they have always assumed, in relation to the United States, that they have a right and a responsibility to do so.

We, on the other hand, come from a more modest background. In relation to the United States we are the upstarts. We existed originally on the imperial fringe, not at the centre, and both empires have departed. (Donald Creighton would say that they abandoned us;[4] Hugh MacLennan has told us that we are

[4] See Donald Creighton, *The Passionate Observer: Selected Writings* (Toronto: McClelland & Stewart, 1980).

the descendants of defeated nations and continue to act that way.)[5] We have been left alone to our own devices in the American shadow, without much experience and without much power. While we may privately have comforted ourselves on the superiority of our manners and our ordered constitution (in contrast to the American condition of constant risk and near-anarchy), we have never assumed our role as legitimate commentators on the American scene, as the Europeans did from the beginning.

By an act of will, by belief in our own competence, and by the application of sufficient resources to the cause, we may at last be overcoming this absence of inherited cultural confidence in relation to the United States. That would be an admirable change if we can bring it about. The change will not be entirely a matter of will, and it can only go so far: Canada is not a great power, is unlikely to be one, and its literary and scholarly self-confidence are not going to be buoyed up by the presence in the background of the Royal Navy or the National Aeronautics and Space Administration (although a powerful Arctic icebreaker would help). But we can do enough things well to give us the assurance that others might benefit by our observations. The study of the United States is one of the most fascinating and important subjects, in all its aspects, that academics and journalists must undertake in the modern world. It is high time that Canadians plunged fully into it. As Canadians we are, and will remain, both inside and outside the United States. We have a unique perspective and we should exploit it.

[5] Hugh MacLennan, "Scotland's Fate, Canada's Lesson," *Maclean's*, October 1973, pp. 27–29 and 94–98.

Canada and NATO: Adjusting the Balance

(1988)

The Fourteenth Military History Symposium at the Royal Military College in Kingston in 1988 examined the nature of the Cold War, forty years after its beginning and at a time of improving relations between the West and the Soviet Union. My paper looked at the key role of Canada in the NATO alliance, suggesting that the time had come to reassess this country's strategic interests and to consider a phased withdrawal of Canada's military forces from Europe. (This was not an approach likely to appeal to the Mulroney government.) What I could not anticipate was the imminent and astonishing collapse of the Warsaw Pact and the Soviet Union, followed by the paradoxical expansion of NATO into Central and Eastern Europe that occurred in the following years with Canada's approval.

Forty years ago, on March 11, 1948, Prime Minister Mackenzie King received an urgent message from the British Prime Minister, Clement Attlee, expressing the British government's alarm at the consolidation of Communist power in Czechoslovakia two weeks earlier, and its anxiety over where and when Soviet pressures might next be revealed. Attlee wrote that "events are moving ever quicker than we at first apprehended and there are grave indications from many sources that the next Russian move will be to make demands on Norway. . . . Norwegian Government have consulted United States and ourselves as to the help that we could expect if attacked."[1] While he said that the Norwegians had been advised to resist Soviet demands, Attlee was uncertain whether "encouragement of this kind will alone induce Norwegian Government to hold out." Its defection, however, "would not only involve the collapse of the whole Scandinavia system but would also prejudice our chances of calling a halt to expansion of Soviet influence over Western Europe and would in fact mean the appearance of Russia on the Atlantic." The British concluded from this alarming prospect that "only a bold move can avert the danger and the pace already set by Russia tells us that there is no time to lose." What was necessary was "a regional Atlantic pact of mutual assistance" to be joined by "all the countries threatened by a Russian move on the Atlantic," including the United States, Canada, and Western Europe. Attlee warned that Nazi Germany offered the historic parallel: "Failure to act now may mean a repetition of our experience with Hitler and we should again have to witness the slow

[1] Secretary of State for Commonwealth Relations to High Commissioner for United Kingdom, Ottawa, no. 220, March 10, 1948, DEA files 283(s).

deterioration of our position until we were forced to resort to war in much less favorable circumstances."

The British Prime Minister proposed to King (and simultaneously to President Truman) the immediate convening of secret talks between Britain, the United States, and Canada to explore the creation of an Atlantic security system. Its purpose would be, in Attlee's words, to "inspire necessary confidence to consolidate west against Soviet infiltration and at the same time inspire the Soviet Government with sufficient respect for the west to remove temptation from them and so ensure a long period of peace." The three foreign offices had been preparing the mood for such talks for several months, in an atmosphere of increasing fear over Soviet diplomatic belligerence and heavy-handedness in the occupied countries of Eastern and Central Europe. Mackenzie King had already passed through several interludes of cold panic since 1945 over the prospect of a new world war that would this time be fought, he was certain, on Canadian as well as European soil. The U.S. administration would not itself initiate talks on a peacetime alliance, because it was still shepherding the Marshall Plan through Congress and was worried about an isolationist reaction against further, potentially unlimited, international obligations. What it needed in order to proceed was some kind of unusual justification—preferably a European request based on a fresh and apparently tangible threat to Western security.

Mackenzie King, too, needed unusual justification to commit Canada to any continuing peacetime obligations abroad. Attlee's message to King provided the necessary alarm from the appropriate source, for King deferred more easily to the British than to the Americans on postwar international issues. When Attlee's message arrived, King consulted three persons: Louis St. Laurent (Secretary of State for External Affairs), Brooke Claxton (Minister of Defense), and Mike Pearson (Under-Secretary of State for External Affairs). Pearson drafted a reply which was agreed upon and dispatched that evening. In it King offered Canada's commitment to join in a treaty of mutual assistance under Anglo-American sponsorship.

There followed ten days of hectic Anglo-American-Canadian diplomacy. On March 12 the United States accepted the British suggestion; on March 17 President Truman announced publicly the U.S. commitment to the political integrity of Western Europe; and on March 22, 1948, representatives of the three powers met at the Pentagon to begin planning for a security system. These talks led to broader consultations over the summer and autumn, and eventually, on April 4, 1949, to the signing in Washington of the North Atlantic Treaty.[2]

[2] See Escott Reid, *Time of Fear and Hope* (Toronto, 1977), for a detailed account of the making of the treaty.

In retrospect, there were at least two curiosities about the appeal made by Clement Attlee to Mackenzie King that led to the initial treaty discussions. The first was that the assumption of power by the Communist party in Czechoslovakia occurred in a country already considered by Western diplomats to be within the Soviet sphere of influence, and conceded to be an inevitable target for an exclusive Communist takeover. (But the diplomats had not anticipated the strength of Western emotional identification with Czechoslovakian democracy when the takeover came, a sympathy that contained a strong remnant of guilt for Czechoslovakia's previous abandonment to the Nazis in 1939. Once again, however, the belated diplomatic reaction in the democracies did not benefit the unfortunate Czechoslovaks.) While the coup did not obviously alter the existing balance of power, it created unexpected panic in Western capitals. The second curiosity was the nature (or indeed quite possibly the existence) of Soviet pressure on Norway. Attlee described this variously as demands made along the Nazi model, pressure, aggression, attack, or the potential appearance of Russians on the Atlantic. His account seemed to arise from a British embassy dispatch from Oslo reporting vague rumors that the Soviets had asked for treaty discussions with the Norwegians after the conclusion of their recent negotiations with Finland—something considerably less alarming than Attlee's account of it.[3] According to Escott Reid and Mike Pearson, the Norwegian factor strongly influenced the Canadian government's mood of fear and assisted in the decision to join the talks on a security treaty.[4] But it was never mentioned publicly at the time, subjected to analysis, or apparently referred to again in the urgent consultations that followed.[5] Can we speculate, perhaps, that it was a bit of black propaganda produced conveniently by the Foreign Office to prompt a decision that Britain now urgently desired and knew how to promote? From this distance, given our knowledge of later occasions of deception and disinformation in what were seen to be good causes, the thought might occur to skeptical historians. Or perhaps it was merely the exaggeration of panic. It was curious nonetheless, and, at the least, evidence of blurred perception of a kind that became familiar as the Cold War intensified.

For 40 years thereafter, this initial undertaking of March 11, 1948, had guided, framed, or straightjacketed Canadian strategic policymaking and effec-

[3] Secretary of State for Commonwealth Relations to High Commissioner for United Kingdom, Ottawa, no. 217, March 10, 1948, DEA files 283(s). See also Denis Smith, *Diplomacy of Fear* (Toronto, 1988), pp. 223–224.

[4] See Reid, *Time of Fear and Hope*, pp. 42–43, 49–50, 70; and Lester B. Pearson, *Mike* (Toronto, 1972), vol. 2, p. 39.

[5] Escott Reid says: "The fact that the incident which precipitated the talks on the treaty was a Soviet threat to Norway seems to have been kept secret for ten years or more"; *Time of Fear and Hope*, p. 70.

tively suspended Canadian debate on matters of high foreign policy. What Canada encouraged and agreed to was the declaration of a U.S. military guarantee of the political independence of Western Europe, decked out in the paraphernalia of a mutual security treaty and later, in the 1950s, reinforced by the creation of a collective military command on the ground in Europe. By endorsing the U.S. commitment and entering the alliance, Canada chose loyalty to U.S. strategic policy over any effort to think and act on its own in the realm of East-West relations. (For the Europeans, the choice was more complex and, since the 1960s, more creative.)

Only once in those 40 years, in 1968 and 1969, has a Canadian government been prepared to reopen the question of Canada's fundamental commitment to the North Atlantic Treaty. That reassessment, undertaken at the whim of a new Prime Minister ignorant of foreign policy, was predictably compromised away under the pressure of Canada's allies, the bureaucracy, and Pierre Trudeau's own cabinet.[6] Although the Trudeau government did not treat Canada's NATO role (or its defense policy in general) as a matter of priority during the following 15 years, neither did it attempt again to alter that role in principle. Now the new government of Brian Mulroney has reaffirmed Canada's NATO commitment as the central element of its foreign policy, based on the bedrock of a traditional view of the intentions and capabilities of the Soviet Union.[7]

While the issue of NATO's purpose and strategy has generated a continuous flow of analysis and commentary in the United States and Europe since the 1960s, there is virtually no Canadian equivalent. (There was a burst of discussion in the late 1960s which exhausted itself by the settlement of the Trudeau policy in 1971.) Canada's fitful defense debate has tended to focus on North American defense, North American Air Defense (NORAD), and the Arctic rather than on NATO and European defense; that balance in the domestic debate probably reflects the essentially marginal or subordinate role that Canada chose to take in the alliance from the beginning. That judgment perhaps needs some reflection, because it would certainly be disputed by most Canadian governments since 1949. In their rhetoric, NATO has been the most significant part of the country's foreign policy, a historic departure from its previous peacetime isolationism. It has involved, they would say, a fundamental acceptance of collective security in principle and, since 1950, a major burden of defense spending and military participation as well. And it has been an emphatic expression of Canada's perception of the world conflict. More subtly,

[6] See D.C. Thomson and R.F. Swanson, *Canadian Foreign Policy: Options and Perspectives* (Toronto, 1971), pp. 48–56.
[7] See the 1987 Defense White Paper, *Challenge and Commitment,* passim.

the professional diplomats first hoped, and then asserted, that NATO would give—had given—Canada a privileged place at the table in making Western policy, and a multilateral means of restraining the ambitions and impulses of the Americans. These claims have some weight, but they are devalued by the realities that the rhetoric ignores.

What really distinguishes Canadian membership in NATO is not its historic boldness and novelty but its caution and conventionality. The principle of Mackenzie King's diplomacy before 1948, when he allowed Canada to act in the world at all, was to do so with the approval and protection of the United Kingdom and the United States. The principle of Canada's entry into NATO was identical. NATO provided the traditional umbrella for Canadian diplomacy. An Anglo-American initiative was King's prerequisite for Canadian participation in a security treaty; for Norman Robertson it was "a providential solution for so many of our problems."[8] Put in other words, the creation of NATO meant that Canada could leave the thinking about the big questions to others, as it had always done before, but now with the comfortable illusion of participation in high decisions.

NATO was Canada's new fireproof house. If the existence of strategic weapons and long-range air power made Canada physically less secure from attack than it had been in the 1930s, the country was made more secure in another sense by the resolute guarantee of the United States and the United Kingdom to deter aggression—a guarantee previously missing and whose absence had apparently brought on World War II. The new guarantee was directed against a single great power, which was taken to offer the only serious threat to peace.

Within NATO Canada gained the satisfaction of consultation about the alliance's European strategy, and a measure (more apparent than real) of U.S. military guarantee to Europe. President Truman's declaration of March 17, 1948, did not require a treaty of alliance for its effect, and there were influential voices in the State Department and the Congress (not necessarily isolationist) who argued against the creation of a formal alliance. But the Europeans, with their memories of U.S. isolationism, did not find the President's promise sufficient. The treaty of 1949 was thus an elaborate device of psychological reassurance to the governments of Western Europe, a means of convincing a weak and ravaged continent that America's presence as a counterweight to the Soviet Union was real and long term. Despite the elaboration of its political and military structure in the 1950s, NATO has remained, behind the façade, simply the formal expression of this original

[8] Canadian High Commissioner to Secretary of State for External Affairs, April 2, 1948, DEA files, 264(s), quoted in Escott Reid, *Time of Fear and Hope*, p. 132; J. L. Granatstein, *A Man of Influence* (Ottawa, 1981), p. 236; and Smith, *Diplomacy of Fear*, p. 229.

guarantee—as David Calleo describes it, a U.S. military protectorate.[9] The various efforts throughout the 1950s, 1960s, and 1970s (usually promoted by the relentlessly idealist Canadians) to turn NATO into something broader than a system of U.S. guarantee uniformly failed.

Forty years on, the strategic and political situation of Western Europe has been transformed, but the organization that proved so comforting a device in European recovery has somehow become a sacred and untouchable element in Western mythology. It should not be regarded that way.

In the beginning NATO was the outcome, in part, of misunderstanding. That misunderstanding was entrenched in the Western mind in the late 1940s, lingers on, and is probably the main source of NATO's immunity from change today. The misunderstanding, as I hinted in my remarks on Czechoslovakia and Norway, related to the objectives and immediate intentions of the Soviet Union. It was a product of fear, postwar exhaustion, the misapplication of a historical lesson, and opportunist political calculation.

Europe was physically, economically, and morally devastated by World War II. The influences of Germany, France, and the United Kingdom as great powers were destroyed. There was a vast and premature power vacuum on the continent, and just one continental power that could conceivably fill it in the short run—the Soviet Union. The other remaining great power, the United States, was engaged in rapid demobilization and, for a few years after 1945, was confused and uncertain about whether and how to commit itself firmly to a forward international role. The condition of Europe in 1945 was unstable and, if a new balance of power was to be established that restored the independence of the European countries and avoided Soviet hegemony by default, the United States would have to be a prominent player. (By hegemony I mean dominant influence, not conquest and military occupation.) But utopian U.S. objection to, and failure to understand, the politics of international balance meant that the United States could not be appealed to for support in such old-fashioned diplomatic terms.

In Britain, the United States, and Canada two lessons above all were drawn from the Nazi experience: that aggressive dictatorship should not be appeased and bought off, but rather confronted early with real military force; and that the United States, which might have restrained the dictators if it had not chosen renewed isolation after 1919, should be brought permanently into the system of postwar guarantee. These beliefs, accompanied by a commitment to the international free market and expanding world trade as the other source of

[9] See David Calleo, *Beyond American Hegemony* (New York, 1987), passim; Theodore Draper, *Present History: On Nuclear War, Detente, and Other Controversies* (New York, 1984), pp. 106–194.

peace, freedom, and prosperity, formed the core of the liberal internationalist consensus.

By one of the ironies of history, this accidental pattern of convictions became fixed together in a rigid ideological grid as the dogmatic foundation for the postwar system. The means by which the U.S. Congress and public were persuaded to join the world was to threaten them with Communism, catastrophe, and war if they did not do so. The Marshall Plan was devised in 1947 to promote European economic recovery and thus to avoid another great economic depression; NATO was devised in 1948 to confront the new manifestation of an evil aggressor in the Nazi pattern—the Soviet Union. The real benefits of economic prosperity and a stable balance of power (both of them desirable objects of policy) were transformed, for Americans and Canadians, into cosmic necessities whose alternative was apocalyptic. The product was oversold.

What was going on in the late 1940s in the effort to bring the United States into a permanent activist role in international affairs was well understood by the managers of the process in Congress and the Truman administration.[10] It was understood as well by close diplomatic observers in Washington, by observant members of the press, and by political skeptics. But the success of the campaign of 1947 and 1948 in Washington, and the rigid fixation it created in Western foreign policy for the succeeding 40 years, have tended to disguise from public understanding the degree of self-conscious exaggeration and easy deception that was involved.

The new pattern of domestic explanation for an activist U.S. foreign policy was established before the creation of NATO, in the Truman administration's unexpectedly hasty effort to take over the role of protector for Greece and Turkey when that role was suddenly abandoned by Britain early in 1947. The epoch-making shift in U.S. perception and policy can be precisely dated: it occurred in a meeting on February 27, 1947, of President Truman, Secretary of State Marshall, Assistant Secretary of State Dean Acheson, and Congressional leaders. According to Joseph Jones, Secretary Marshall made a "summary and cryptic" presentation at that meeting of the strategic case for U.S. aid to Greece and Turkey which failed to convince the Congressional delegation. Dean Acheson intervened to speak as the "fervent advocate" of the U.S. mission to defend democracy and liberty throughout the world against Soviet aggression, to which Senator Vandenberg replied gravely that the request to Congress for aid should be accompanied by a presidential message "in which the grim facts of the larger situation should be laid publicly on the line as they

[10] See, for example, the account by Joseph Jones of the genesis of the Truman Doctrine in *The Fifteen Weeks* (New York, 1965).

had been at their meeting there that day." The administration's policy, expressed in the President's speech to Congress of March 12, 1947, and subsequently known as the Truman Doctrine, was thus framed in those terms. Jones wrote: "It was Vandenberg's 'condition' that made it possible, even necessary, to launch the global policy that broke through the remaining barriers of American isolationism."[11] Acheson told the same story at the time to Hume Wrong (the Canadian ambassador), reaffirming his own decisive role in linking U.S. aid to "the openly anti-Communist aspects which were incorporated in the President's speech to Congress."[12]

"The grim facts of the larger situation" which Dean Acheson presented to the Congressional delegation that day did not consist of any secret intelligence about Soviet plans or intentions, but rather Acheson's dramatic early version of the domino theory.[13] Already, and increasingly, the attention to fact in analyzing Soviet policy and the desirable U.S. response were giving way to reactions of instinct and assertions of faith. The fateful discovery of February 27, 1947, was that this was the way to sell U.S. global activism to Congress.[14] By the time of the North Atlantic treaty discussions the predisposition was well established, and NATO was marketed by the same overwrought appeal to prejudice and fear.

I do not suggest that U.S. aid was unnecessary for Europe's economic recovery. It was essential. I do not suggest that a U.S. guarantee to Western Europe was superfluous. There was a vacuum of power. Soviet intentions were unclear, its actions in Eastern Europe were brutal, and its rhetoric was menacing. But, regarded closely, its acts beyond the limits of its established sphere of influence were much less threatening to the West than its rhetoric. In order to make and elaborate its military guarantee, the United States and its allies progressively misrepresented the nature of the Soviet challenge. The challenge was diplomatic, in the fullest sense of that word, rather than military.

The evidence is strong that there was no Soviet military threat to Western Europe in the late 1940s and 1950s. The lesson of Soviet deeds was that, except in the areas of wartime occupation by the Red Army, where Soviet dominance was imposed (Finland and eastern Austria were notable exceptions to that note, where the Soviets withdrew and permitted the creation of independent governments), the Soviet Union was a cautious power, probing the limits of its influence as great powers invariably do, but acting with restraint when firmly challenged. Its greatest respect was reserved for U.S. power, or U.S. and British power in combination, when it was applied clearly and with determination—

[11] Jones, *The Fifteen Weeks*.
[12] See Smith, *Diplomacy of Fear*, p. 185.
[13] Ibid., p. 197.
[14] Ibid., pp. 184–189.

as it was in Iran in March 1946 and Berlin in 1948–1949.

And yet the Soviet challenge was explained to the parliaments and publics of the NATO countries as an unprovoked military threat based upon a coherent plan and aimed at world domination. After the outbreak of the Korean War in the summer of 1950, the NATO military structure was erected in Central Europe to resist such anticipated aggression. The vast panoply of U.S. forces and arms in Europe, under the seas, and in the missile silos on the U.S. plains, was created to reassure Americans and Europeans that they were under the protective care of the U.S. deterrent against Soviet military attack. On the other side of the line, the response was the Warsaw Pact, which was popularly taken in the West to confirm the claim of Soviet aggressive intent. On both sides, as the arms proliferated, the forces and weapons themselves (when combined with the fixed ideas that justified them) became the primary source of danger, more real in the 1980s than in the 1940s.

We, the Canadians, with our few dozen F-18s and our 6,000 ground troops in Europe, went to Europe to help encourage the Americans to go, and we remain to help keep the Americans there. Given Canada's other defense undertakings, our European units could not be maintained and supplied during real hostilities; their presence in Europe is symbolic and potentially sacrificial.[15] It always has been. In 1948 it was essential for European morale to ensure the U.S. presence. Now, in 1988, that should no longer be true: Europe is prosperous, and can, if it must, defend its own interests wholly by its own means. But it is also financially and politically comfortable under U.S. protection, and will have to be firmly pushed to allow the Americans to depart. For us in Canada in 1948 there was palpable relief at being able to slip under the British-American security blanket, as there was for the more desperate Europeans. Canada, in contrast, had no record of bold activity in foreign policy, no domestic lobby for it, no expression of an alternative. In foreign policy we were just emerging from the womb. The European nations, old and wounded, were being treated in the emergency ward, but with every intention of re-entering the world of international decision when they could. It seems strange that, 40 years later, we Canadians are still resting snugly in the delivery room while the West Europeans have long ago checked themselves out of hospital and resumed their role in high policymaking.

For them, the debate on NATO doctrine and strategy has been vigorous

[15] The Minister of National Defense was reported in April 1984 to have told the cabinet: "If a major national crisis were to occur, the Canadian Forces could not make a credible contribution to deterrence; and in the event of hostilities, the Canadian Forces would not be sufficiently manned and equipped to carry out the tasks expected of them in support of the Allied effort and consequently would be overly vulnerable to enemy attack"; *Calgary Herald*, April 14, 1984, quoted in R.B. Byers, *Canadian Security and Defence: The Legacy and the Challenges* (*Adelphi Papers* 214, Winter 1986), p. 11.

since the early 1960s, when the United States substituted "flexible response" for "massive retaliation" and began to place tactical nuclear weapons with NATO ground forces in Europe. The Canadian government of John Diefenbaker stumbled into that controversy by arming its European contingents at U.S. persuasion with weapons designed to use nuclear warheads—and then refusing to accept the warheads. But Canadian politicians did not confront the strategic issues with any clarity, and in the end the country sidestepped the debate by replacing Diefenbaker with Pearson, who accepted the nuclear commitment (but with a never-never promise to renegotiate it). Finally, in the late 1970s the Trudeau government quietly ended Canada's tactical nuclear role in Europe, again without contributing anything to the broader discussion of policy. Since then Canada has supported NATO's two-track policy and the various arms reduction negotiations, but without any related effort to think through its role in the alliance. As Rod Byers writes:

> Canada's political leaders have not sufficiently appreciated the need to base . . . policy on national assessments of those strategic issues which directly and indirectly affect Canada's security interests. The inclination has been to rely on European or U.S. assessments and perspectives. The major military-strategic issues of the last 20 years have not been influenced by Canada.[16]

The new international stance of the Soviet Union since 1985, the growing problems of U.S. economic and military overextension, and the undoubted ability of the Europeans now to provide for their own defense together throw the continuing role of NATO into doubt. The clear outlines of an altered and less dangerous balance of power, which responds to such challenges, are emerging. It is not obvious what place Canada would have in that balance, unless we Canadians make it for ourselves. But the existence of a problem seems not to have occurred to the Canadian government, if we can judge from the recent External Affairs Green Paper and Defense White Paper. They stand for all the good things, including arms reduction and the honorable fulfillment of commitments; but their image of NATO and its purposes springs from the exaggerations of the 1940s rather than the 1980s. The Defense White Paper simply asserts as

> a fact, not a matter of interpretation, that the West is faced with an ideological, political and economic adversary whose explicit long-term aim is to mould the world in its own image. That adversary has at its disposal massive military forces and a proven willingness to use force, both at home and abroad, to achieve political objec-

[16] R.B. Byers, *Canadian Security and Defence,* p. 13.

> tives. . . . [U]nless and until there is concrete progress, the West has no choice but to rely for its security on the maintenance of a rough balance of forces, backed up by nuclear deterrence.[17]

The paper follows that statement with proposals for a modest consolidation, and strengthening, of the Canadian military commitment in Europe (not to speak of its substantial recommendations for enhanced naval and air forces on and around Canadian territory, including nuclear submarines, which have received the bulk of public comment).

There is something half-hearted about the White Paper's presentation of the security challenge, as though the authors themselves did not believe it. The call for military balance, and the recognition of the existence of the nuclear deterrent, are unexceptional platitudes. But they get us nowhere in the consideration of policy for Canada—except, fuzzily, to sustain the status quo in NATO. (The whole statement could be turned around to apply, with equally empty effect, to what the Soviet Union perceives when it regards the U.S. alliance—an adversary hoping to mold the world eventually in its image, with a proven willingness to use force for political ends, and giving the Soviet Union no choice but to maintain a stable balance of forces and its own nuclear deterrent.) It masks totally the needs and possibilities faced by both NATO and the Warsaw Pact in the 1980s.

The forces of strategic deterrence are vastly redundant on both sides, and inherently paradoxical: they depend for their effect on the willingness to use them, but both Soviets and Americans admit that they cannot be used. If both sides know that, and yet the peace in Central Europe has nevertheless lasted for four decades, it is probably the result of mutual restraint that has much more complex sources than the existence of the nuclear deterrent—such as a strong disinclination to engage in any kind of war on that battleground, where so much has already been suffered. The present military balance strains both U.S. and Soviet treasuries to an unacceptable extent, from which they seek relief; the balance could be maintained at a dramatically lower level of armament and expense. In Central Europe the concentration of massive forces and weapons on both sides creates unusual danger, inconvenience, and uncertainty. The overwhelming and widely accepted need is to reduce both strategic and tactical nuclear armories and conventional forces in Central Europe in a series of arms control agreements that is now under active negotiation.

There is now, for the first time since 1948, a reasonable possibility that the frozen assumptions of 40 years can at last be thawed by actions that will gradually create a reduced, more plural, more stable, less ideological disposition of forces in Europe and the world. Canada wastes its influence if it avoids

[17] Defence White Paper, *Challenge and Commitment*, p. 5.

participating in the creation of that new balance.

To participate effectively we Canadians will have to think coherently about strategic policy as we have not done since the 1940s; and then we will have to take initiatives. Increasing and concentrating our military contribution to NATO, as the Mulroney government now proposes, does nothing to encourage movement in the right direction. However, a withdrawal from NATO is not the only alternative, and it is perhaps unwise as well. Canada gains from the political connection, and there is no reason why it should not continue to do so. We should emulate the French, who withdrew from the integrated military command in 1966 and threw NATO headquarters out of the country, but remained active as political members of the alliance; or the Spanish, who followed their recent entry into NATO by refusing to renew their bilateral treaty to permit the stationing of U.S. fighter-bombers on Spanish soil; or the Danes and Norwegians, who refuse bases on their territory for their NATO allies. It is quite possible for members of this alliance to judge for themselves the state of East-West relations, the collective needs of the organization, and their own national interests—and to act on them, if necessary against the judgments of other members. Canada must be unique among the members of NATO in believing that membership entails the surrender of independent judgment.

A prudent Canadian reassessment of the strategic situation and its own interests would, I believe, lead Canada to conclude that its military contribution to NATO in Europe no longer serves any understandable purpose. As a fighting force it is negligible; the circumstances in which it might be called upon to fight are now almost inconceivable, and its contribution to something called "the deterrent" is implausible.

Both Europeans and Americans still hesitate to consider large reductions in the U.S. military presence in Europe, and they link the Canadian contingent (despite its tiny scale) to the Americans. Talk of its departure would give the Americans ideas. A Canadian decision to withdraw its forces, announced with sufficient warning of the timetable (perhaps spread over five years) and justified as a contribution to the scaling down of the military balance, could thus be a significant stimulus to creative thought in Washington and the European NATO capitals. If the U.S. tripwire forces were no longer to be present, the American guarantee of 1948 would seem less secure, and that would require the West European nations to provide adequately for their own defense (within whatever limits could be agreed on with the Soviet Union). More than 40 years after the end of World War II that seems a reasonable expectation. For Canada the direct benefit would be to give that country greater flexibility in arranging its defense priorities to meet Canadian needs adequately on and around this continent.

As a complement to such action, Canada should pursue active discussion with the Soviets on measures of arms control and other common purposes in the area of our greatest mutual concern (the Arctic), with Canadian national interests firmly in mind—just as the Americans and the Europeans have pursued their own bilateral arrangements for detente with the Soviets, according to their own calculations of interest, since the early 1970s. We should begin in earnest, too, the complex task of reassessing the whole range of our intricate North American defense arrangements with the United States, with the clear objective of assuming, where technically and economically feasible, a greater measure of autonomy in our policies than we have permitted ourselves since 1945. Canada should begin at home, that is, to weigh and assert its strength in its own national interest, just as other confident and mature nations expect to do. In the present international atmosphere, handled skillfully, that would be a contribution to stability. But Canada's long membership in NATO has given us the debilitating illusion that we need never act in defense of our own perception of our highest interests.

To be practical, this is not an approach that the Mulroney government is now likely to endorse. It has chosen, instead, to discourage change in the alliance, and to do essentially nothing in any field of policy to disturb the evolution of former President Reagan's cloud-cuckoo world. Independent Canadian action in NATO of the kind I suggest would certainly disturb slumbers on the Canadian watch in Washington. (But many in the United States, more discerning about the real world than the present administration, would welcome such Canadian prodding.) At home, an initiative of this kind would not be entirely at odds with the Mulroney government's own rhetoric. There are elements of its northern, defense, and disarmament policies that are more consistent with this approach than with its intellectual sterility on NATO and the Soviet threat. At least it should recognize that a serious debate on foreign policy is desirable as the U.S.-Soviet relationship of 40 years transforms itself. Such a debate, for Canada, must start with the nature of the Soviet challenge and the NATO connection—the very points that mesmerized us and halted our thinking after 1948.

The Gulf Crisis: Chaos or New World Order

(1991)

In March 1991 I was invited to address faculty members in the Department of Medicine at the University of Western Ontario on the recently concluded Gulf War, a now-forgotten episode in which an American-led military alliance ejected Iraq from its occupation of Kuwait. The short war ended with the proclamation of a "New World Order" by the American president, George Bush (that is, George H.W., not George the younger). This war marked the beginning of permanent U.S. military engagement in the Middle East, from which there has been no escape after more than 25 destructive years. In my talk, I chose to challenge the policy adopted by America and its allies (including Canada) and to offer a wishful might-have-been instead. I was greeted with a cascade of criticism from most of the audience. Perhaps my arguments stand the test of time. (The essay in section 3, "Making war the American way," published three months before the Gulf war, is a companion piece to this one.)

In the days preceding the ground war in February, television reporters spoke of the "emotional roller-coaster" provoked by the Soviet Union's diplomatic intervention, whose purpose was to achieve an Iraqi withdrawal from Kuwait before the ground attack. Those were indeed days of confusion, hope and dashed hope; but the moment of war meant, by then, that it would not stop short of an Iraqi rout. Within five days that occurred.

For close observers of the whole affair, the roller-coaster ride began, not in February, but on August 2 when Iraq seized Kuwait. From then until the end of February we experienced seven months of uncertainty and anxiety as we were whip-sawed by the obsessive attentions of the media. The countdown to war between August and January, while mobilization proceeded on both sides, appeared as inexorable as that of August 1914—and most of the talk, a charade.

What I argue is—according to the press and the polls—a minority view on the Gulf War and its aftermath.

I believe that this was an unnecessary and unjustified war whose cost in lives, human suffering, a disrupted political balance, and a devastated environment were immense, almost fully predictable, and avoidable. While the United States and its coalition partners have announced victory and begun their triumphal celebrations, the war is not over. It continues within Iraq, where Kurds and Shiites battle the Republican Guard; where basic supplies of water, electricity, gas, oil, food, and medicine are unavailable for most people; and where communications remain broken. It continues in Kuwait, where the oil fires burn, the skies are dark at midday, the average temperature is ten degrees lower than normal, supplies are scarce, government has no authority, and vigilante groups carry out indiscriminate vengeance against persons suspected of collaborating with the departed Iraqi occupiers.

From this distance, George Bush, John Major, Brian Mulroney and their allies can conveniently say that the war was neatly won in 42 days, because their casualties were few, their troops are coming home, and the devastation left behind is effectively invisible to their voters. But the consequences will plague the Middle East for decades, and in the aftermath we should be asking what brought us to this state of things. What went wrong? Were there alternatives? What are the prospects now?

The provoking event was Iraq's invasion and seizure of Kuwait. That brutally violated the norms of international behaviour, and had to be challenged. For 24 hours it appeared that the world's response might be one of impotent complaint, then tacit acquiescence. The UN Security Council made its formal denunciation and call for withdrawal (as it had in other cases); but the first words of George Bush suggested that no major intervention was being considered. The early hints of stiffening came from Prime Minister Margaret Thatcher, who happened to be in Aspen, Colorado and was due to meet with the president the next day.

Soon it was clear that the U.S. administration too was hardening. Air and naval units in the region were placed on alert or set in motion towards the Gulf; and intelligence reports suggested that Iraq might sweep south to seize the Saudi Arabian oil fields. The president announced that his secretary of defence would visit the Middle East at once, primarily to seek Saudi approval for the deployment of U.S. forces on its soil, as a deterrent. The U.S. had publicly acknowledged the Gulf as an area of strategic defence since the end of the Second World War, and for two decades had sought without success to place forces there. Kuwait seemed to offer the opportunity and the necessity.

By August 5 the war clouds were gathering. Curiously, the thunderheads mounted first in London, not Washington or the Gulf. Margaret Thatcher continued her tough talk from Aspen—no longer alone. *The Observer* and *The Sunday Times* were equally uncompromising and belligerent. It seemed that Saddam Hussein had touched British nerves in some unusual way not seen since the Falklands in 1982 or Suez in 1956. Editorials in the two Sunday papers set out the essential patterns, both of argument and action, that guided events over the next seven months. Here is *The Observer* speaking:

> The simple facts of the case are straightforward and unchanged.... On Thursday morning, without warning and under the flimsiest of excuses, Iraq invaded a friendly neighbouring state and ejected a government recognised by itself, the United Nations and every member of that organisation. Until it withdraws all its forces

> and allows the government of Kuwait to return, there cannot be any negotiation, discussion or even mention of compromise. The full force of economic and military pressure has to be brought to bear and sustained. . . .
>
> Ultimately, this crisis is not just about a threat to world order and oil supplies, but also about the international prestige of America and its ability to protect its allies in a traditional sphere of influence, the Gulf, from a regional dictator who would set himself up as the dominant power. . . .
>
> Comparing people to Hitler can often be counter-productive . . . but in Saddam Hussein the world is facing another Hitler. . . . If the world negotiates a settlement with him this time, he will be back with another venture tomorrow.
>
> Only with Hussein's fall can the world rest any easier. Sanctions, if they are pursued with real determination, might just produce a situation of economic and political chaos in which he is overthrown. . . . Other than that, he will have to be clearly and decisively beaten in the military language he understands. . . . No wonder the U.S. is gathering its task forces and preparing its bombers. It may need them very soon.

The Sunday Times also made the link with the thirties: the invasion of Kuwait was "the equivalent of Adolf Hitler recovering the Saarland and remilitarising the Rhineland." Saddam Hussein would "go on taking what does not belong to him until somebody stops him," and that somebody would have to be "the United States, the reigning global superpower." The paper hoped that the U.S. would act through the United Nations in association with NATO, Japan and the Soviet Union to impose a policy of sanctions and containment. It, too, went further—suggesting that an Iraqi withdrawal from Kuwait would be insufficient. "The thief of Baghdad would remain free to steal again in the night." It was time to remove Hussein from power.

The events that followed are familiar. On August 8 the U.S. announced its rapid commitment of forces to Saudi Arabia, after Secretary Cheney gained King Fahd's agreement. (There is some uncertainty about who took the initiative, but the public evidence suggests that Cheney leaned hard on the king and frightened him into accepting.) George Bush told the nation of his determination to confront and reverse Iraq's aggression, and stated four objectives: "immediate, unconditional and complete withdrawal of all Iraqui forces from Kuwait"; the restoration of Kuwait's legitimate government; the restoration of "security and stability in the Gulf"; and a ritual commitment to protect the lives of American citizens abroad.

Although the president later seemed to have difficulty expressing clearly what his justifications for action were, in that first speech he set them out clearly. They were justifications of principle, of interest, of diplomatic tactics, and of future promise.

In principle, aggression had to be recognised, confronted and rejected. That was the Hitlerian lesson of the thirties. The United States is unusually inclined to seek moral support for its foreign policy, and needs such principles for its own satisfaction more than other, more coolly cynical states.

The justification of interest was that "our country now imports nearly half the oil it consumes, and could face a major threat to its economic independence. Much of the world is even more dependent on imported oil, and is even more vulnerable to Iraqi threats." The U.S. is more hesitant than other states about recognising or expressing such interests (although it does not hesitate, in fact, to pursue them). James Baker went too far for the public taste when he later said that American was in the Gulf for the sake of "jobs, jobs, jobs."

The third justification, of diplomatic tactics, again linked to the lesson of principle from the 1930s: Appeasement of dictators does not work. They cannot be allowed to benefit from their aggressions. Appeasement means the slippery slope, or falling dominoes. This is the most familiar of postwar Western readings of history. It was applied against the Soviet Union after 1945, to justify the Cold War policy of containment. (But in other cases where the calculation of interest pointed to support for dictators, including Iraq before August 2—as in "He may be a son-of-a-bitch but at least he's our son-of-a-bitch"—it seemed conveniently not to apply.)

The fourth justification was more sweeping and open-ended, in the optimistic American tradition, an aspiration for utopian achievement. In this speech, George Bush spoke of "this new era" as something "full of promise, an age of freedom, a time of peace for all peoples." Later he talked of the "new world order" that could result from victory in the Gulf.

We should remember that George Bush insisted on August 8 that the purpose of American deployment in the Gulf was defensive. Here is what he said in conclusion:

> I want to be clear about what we are doing, and why. America does not seek conflict, nor do we seek to chart the destiny of other nations. But American will stand by her friends.
>
> The mission of our troops is wholly defensive. Hopefully, they will not be needed for long. They will not initiate hostilities, but they will defend themselves, the kingdom of Saudi Arabia, and other friends in the Gulf.
>
> We are working around the clock to deter Iraqi aggression and to enforce UN sanctions.

This was the basis on which other members of the coalition, as well, sent their forces into the Gulf. For most of them, it was the only basis on which they could have justified that action to their publics. It was the original ground for United Nations involvement. The forces were sent to enforce the embargo against Iraq, and to assist Saudi Arabia in its self-defence. They were forces of deterrence and containment, "wholly defensive," who "will not initiate hostilities."

Between the lines, there was more ambiguity from the outset about what was going on in the Gulf. The American commitment was not to a small trip-wire force along the Saudi-Kuwaiti border: it was to a huge naval task force, large offensive air forces, and more than 200,000 ground troops in the desert. British words and military commitments were equally ominous. This was more than a sanctions and containment force; it was a vast offensive force in the course of buildup.

One response to this fact was that it was simply part of the peaceful means of persuasion, a demonstration to Saddam Hussein of the seriousness of the alliance and thus good reason for him to concede and withdraw from Kuwait. Put another way, it was an application in the Gulf of the West's Cold War policy of deterrence (minus the nuclear element). On that reasoning, a potential aggressor will be dissuaded from aggression by a show of determination to resist with overwhelming offensive force. The superficial lesson of the Cold War seemed to be that deterrence had worked against the Soviet Union; so why not against Saddam Hussein too?

Two points are significant in the theory:First, deterrence must be convincing. The expansionist power must be sure that its opponents are actually willing to use their power. They cannot be bluffing. Second, in the case of the USSR, deterrence was intended to hold the expansion of its empire—never, except in the faltering and disastrous case of North Korea in 1950, a policy of rolling back to previous lines. In the Cold War it was a means of maintaining the status quo.

As deterrence in that sense, the Gulf buildup was unnecessarily large. It always seemed intended for other purposes, which could only gradually be revealed to the democratic publics of the coalition who are properly reluctant about going to war. That basic deceit—perhaps self-deceit too, since the leaders seemed often to be themselves uncertain as the buildup continued—was one of the things that took us into the war without adequate understanding of the consequences. The coalition kept pretending it wasn't happening.

Now that the war is over, we are at the stage when the meaning of the "new world order" should become clear. What is it? Does it mean anything? Is it anything to be desired? What could it be, at best? Or is it no more than a careless propaganda phrase tossed out in the countdown to war, to be discarded in the dustbins now that apparent victory has been achieved? These are deceptively simple questions lost in depths of obscurity.

For me, the phrase is unfortunate and paradoxical. By some curious twist of George Bush's memory, in comparing Saddam Hussein to Adolf Hitler and thus calling for his downfall, the president pulled another phrase out of the thirties. But it is Hitler's phrase. The Third Reich was to introduce its own New World Order, under Nazi domination, a system of oppressive racist and mercantilist dictatorship, to serve German national interests. (The phrase may have resonance now only for those of a departing generation like mine—but I still find it unfortunate. It suggests that President Bush lacks a certain sensitivity to history.)

But second, of course, the phrase is intended to suggest a generous American vision of leadership and international opportunity. For two generations the world, as seen and largely formed by Americans, has been frozen in the paralysis of the Cold War. After 1985, and especially since the autumn of 1989, the Cold War has utterly and astonishingly evaporated. Eastern Europe has shaken off Soviet domination, the Soviet Union has ceased to pose any military or ideological threat, the Warsaw Pact has formally dissolved, Germany has been reunited, the Soviets and the Americans have cooperated to give some of the original meaning to the United Nations as a political institution.

That was already beginning to happen in the UN before the Gulf crisis, after President Gorbachev's bold speech to the General Assembly in the fall of 1988, or earlier in the UN's mediation to end the Iran-Iraq war. But the real test came with the invasion of Kuwait. The result in the Security Council was remarkable and salutary—at least for three months. Beginning from a joint American-Soviet commitment to cooperate in confronting Iraqi aggression through the Security Council, the Council adopted a series of eleven mandatory resolutions requiring Iraqi withdrawal, imposing comprehensive sanctions, establishing a land, sea and air blockade of enforcement, creating reporting procedures, and so on. This was an historic achievement, a genuine return to the use of the Council as a collective security agency under great power leadership as conceived by the founders at San Francisco, but never achieved during forty years of Cold War.

In most respects that part of the "new world order" deserves support and encouragement. It involves a commitment of the great powers to oppose the use of force in international affairs, and to use the UN to promote civilized political standards, the recognition of national sovereignty and the rule of law. It suggests that powers should not act unilaterally to oppose injustice, but rather jointly, through the formal channels of the UN. When Joe Clark talks about the great gains in cooperation which the Gulf crisis has brought, he is talking about the new world order in this sense.

But there are other, more troubling senses of the phrase. For one thing it is vague and ill-defined. If it remains simply Pablum, that might not matter much—except that the palpable failure of George Bush's promise of order might induce exaggerated disappointment, especially in the United States where this kind of rhetoric gets taken seriously. American disappointment, we know, can sometimes have unpleasant results.

Two senses of the phrase are genuinely worrying. One is the sense it acquired as the coalition, with the Security Council's authority, shifted from a defensive stance of containing Iraqi expansion to an offensive stance. On November 29, as the result of three weeks of intense American diplomacy, the Security Council delivered an ultimatum to Iraq to abandon Kuwait in six weeks or face war. This would not be war under the UN flag, however, but war authorized by the UN and conducted by a private coalition on its own terms. Collective containment and embargo would become collective war, initiated by the coalition—or to be more realistic, by the United States in consultation with a few allies. (Most members of the coalition, including Canada, were in no position to block action. Once in the Gulf they were forced to go along. In a sense they had been duped—or, more likely, had duped themselves and their publics.)

In adopting Resolution 678, the Security Council departed from the provisions of the Charter's chapter on enforcement. That chapter foresaw the possibility of military action only after other means had been exhausted, and then under supervision of the UN Military Staff Committee. The Military Staff Committee had never been used as it was intended to be, and as a result had no rules or customs of operation, and no machinery; but in any case the United States had no intention of acting through it under a unified UN command. As the president and secretary of state made clear in the early autumn, they were prepared to eject Iraq from Kuwait by force without any UN authority to do so. They were finally persuaded to seek broad UN sanction for the use of force as a prudent political device, both domestic and international, rather than out of any commitment of principle to the Charter of the United Nations.

At home, there was strong congressional doubt about war in the Gulf, an emerging constitutional conflict over the war-making power, and the likelihood that the president would lose an early vote in Congress if he sought its authority for war. The administration chose what it saw as the easier path: It would first gain authority from the Security Council and then confront Congress with that fait accompli.

Internationally, there were strong reasons for the U.S. to seek UN authority for war. The Soviet Union was reluctant to see the U.S. act outside the UN, after so much had been achieved within. No doubt Mikhail Gorbachev and Edward Shevardnadze saw the UN, as Canada did too, as a means of reining in

American unilateralism. Joe Clark insists that Canada lobbied diligently to bring the U.S. to the Security Council in November. Other members of the coalition, as well, were reluctant to go to war without the cover of some kind of UN umbrella.

Together these factors persuaded James Baker. To gain the kind of overwhelming Security Council support he needed, the secretary of state set out in November on a diplomatic journey of wheedling, threatening and buying votes from members of the Security Council. In the end he gained twelve, plus a Chinese abstention. (The abstention, which avoided a veto, was sufficient to give the Chinese foreign minister access to the Oval Office the next day. Since Tiananmen Square he had been frozen out. Others received warnings, gifts or promises whose full nature we will not know for years.)

The resolution of November 29, which George Bush, Brian Mulroney and others described as a "pause for peace," was more generally seen in realistic terms as a blunt ultimatum. It sanctioned and promised war unless Saddam Hussein withdrew his forces from Kuwait. But its interpretation was left entirely to the U.S. coalition, and George Bush insisted throughout that "peace" meant what he said it meant. There could be no negotiation, and the only face-to-face diplomacy occurred just six days before the deadline with no opportunity on either side for give-and-take. The six week interval was designed to coincide with completion of the American buildup for war, as dictated by the U.S. high command.

On the one hand Resolution 678 transformed a peaceful UN economic embargo against an aggressor into authorized counter-aggression. On the other hand, it marked premature abandonment of sanctions and military enforcement of the embargo. Sanctions were obviously given insufficient time to bite. We will never know whether, or when, they might have been sufficient to force Iraq's withdrawal from Kuwait. During November a parade of senior ex-members of the U.S. chiefs of staff committee, the National Security Council and the state department testified before congressional committees that sanctions would need, and should be given, from nine to eighteen months before having their effect upon the Iraqi military machine. This early abandonment of the path of sanctions was a significant defeat for the UN's peaceful efforts to enforce collective security, and a tragic triumph for violence. When the UN resorted to force, collective security had failed, not succeeded. It failed through the explicit choice of the Council. It might have succeeded if sanctions had been sustained.

Thus I have a distinctly ambivalent attitude towards Canada's efforts to encourage passage of Resolution 678. By bringing the U.S. back to the UN to seek authority for war, we also transformed the nature of the UN's efforts and discarded a sanctions policy that was unprecedented.

War authorized by the UN but outside its control is still brutal war. If the UN is to engage in war, it must surely, for the sake of its dedication to peace and the rule of law, be certain that it is a just war (in the traditional theological definition): that is, war of last resort, proportionate to the wrong that it aims to right, by means proportionate to the end. This was not a war of last resort, nor did it seem proportionate to the situation. Both the means and the consequences (known in advance or foreseeable) were vastly disproportionate. George Bush called this a just war in a speech to a religious writers' association in January, but he did so in what seemed a lame attempt to retrieve the lost moral ground. The Catholic bishops and the American Council of Churches did not agree with him, and it appeared that the philosophical complexity of the concept was unknown to him.

This sense of the new world order—an order inappropriately given the sanction of the UN but violently enforced by individual nations—is not to be devoutly desired. It suggests rather chilling possibilities of other sessions of the Security Council, on other occasions, managed and manipulated into support for the vigilante acts of great powers against small. But only when those great powers think that their own interests are being served.

Finally there is a still cruder sense of the new world order. Perhaps that is the one that has most popular meaning in America in these weeks after victory, when a certain triumphalism is in the air. That is the new order of *Pax Americana*, in which Uncle Sam plays the role, more or less unhindered, of the world's policeman, ignoring the UN and the wishes of other nations when it chooses. Irving Kristol described this role (approvingly) a few years ago as "global unilateralism." Americans may be tempted to it, after sloughing off so suddenly the guilt and sense of inferiority of the defeat in Vietnam. American leaders may be tempted to it, if they think there is great domestic political gain in the risks. George Bush has rolled the dice this time and won. Where might they be rolled again?

Still, I don't think there is great danger in that—not on the scale of the Gulf War. The United States cannot afford it, and it is difficult to conceive of comparable situations offering the same occasions for American glory. The American public will be reluctant to send off half-a-million troops to the far side of the world again. As much as he may gain politically from the public's perception that this was an American war fought for American interests on American terms, George Bush has never claimed that his new world order is unilateralist. He has insisted on the cooperative role of the Soviet Union, on the existence of a coalition whose leaders he consulted intensively, and on the rebirth of the United Nations in the crisis. If he continues to talk of the new world order, he will have to talk of it in those universal terms. That should influence and temper his actions.

Besides—and perhaps above all—this was a victory in only the narrowest of military terms. This was victory declared before the calamity could become clear. In the Middle East there is spreading chaos. There are few signs of hope in the short term. The physical destruction of Iraq and Kuwait is catastrophic. The U.S. military now suggest that the bombardment cost the lives of 100,000 Iraqi soldiers. New weapons of mass destruction (like fuel-air bombs, as horrifying as nuclear weapons) were used on the battlefield. The environment is devastated. Iraq is torn apart and bleeding in civil strife. One month after the end of the war Saddam Hussein remains in power, more or less, in Baghdad. The temptations facing Iran and Syria to fish in Iraq's troubled waters are great and probably increasing. The Palestinian issue remains unsettled: James Baker could report no progress from his postwar visit to the region. Despite George Bush's promises to bring all the troops home quickly, coalition forces still occupy a large part of Iraqi territory. They are likely to be caught there in the disorder, with an obscure mission, as long as anarchy continues in Iraq. The United States seems to have little idea of what to do next. (And we, like other minor allies, have scuttled for home.) There are already signs of a new binge of arms sales in the region, prompted by many of the powers that have just finished destroying the weapons they sold to Iraq over the last ten years.

Almost all these results were foreseeable. Some of them were shouted from the rooftops by American critics. But the administration, for what were above all American reasons, dictated the international response to the invasion of Kuwait, carried its allies in its policy of war, and ignored most of the probable consequences. For this, they (and we) will bear a heavy responsibility before history. Better that George Bush and Saddam Hussein had not shot it out at high noon in the desert.

After what is now often called the First Gulf War, a weakened Saddam Hussein remained in power. With U.S. leadership, the UN applied a harsh sanctions regime against Iraq while the U.S. and Britain imposed a 'no-fly zone' in northern Iraq to protect the regional Kurdish population. After 9/11, a UN weapons inspection regime was imposed on Iraq. It was pre-empted in September 2003, when the U.S.-led "coalition of the willing" attacked, occupied the country, and managed the adoption of a new constitution. In 2016 the wars continue.

Beyond the Golden Age: Diefenbaker's Diplomacy . . . and Ours

(2005)

In 2005, to mark publication of the twenty-fifth volume of its monumental series of Documents on Canadian Foreign Policy, *the Department of Foreign Affairs and International Trade (now Global Affairs Canada) asked me to speak at the Diefenbaker Centre in Saskatoon. This paper on Canada's relations with the United States at the height of the Cold War in 1957–1958 was the result.*

Like the previous volumes in this valuable series, this is a thick book, with more than one thousand pages: and that is just the half of it. Volume 25 covers the first eighteen months of the Diefenbaker government, from July 1957 to December 1958—a period also covered by the previous Volume 24, published in 2003. The editorial process for the volumes involved a relatively arbitrary division of subjects between the two books: Volume 24 was devoted to the UN, NATO, the Commonwealth, atomic energy, and Western Europe, while Volume 25 is devoted to Canada's relations with the United States, the Middle East, the Far East, Eastern Europe, the Soviet Union, and Latin America. Those divisions—obviously—do not reflect the jumbled flow of day-to-day events, during which politicians and senior members of the Department had to cope with all these subjects (and more) at the same time. But it is an orderly way of sorting the record into accessible form, with only one physical disadvantage: someone studying the first eighteen months of foreign policy during the Diefenbaker period must try to juggle two hefty volumes weighing three or four pounds each while frequently moving back and forth between them. By weight alone, I can't recommend them for bedtime reading. For their content, we owe congratulations to the work of Michael Stevenson and his assistants in the Historical Section of the Department of Foreign Affairs. Professor Stevenson and his associates have edited the volumes with great thoroughness and care, and maintain the excellent historical record already established for the series. These two new collections became indispensable sources for historians of the period from the very instant of publication—and no doubt also for working members of the Department as well.

What can usefully be said about a dense thousand pages of documents dealing with five major areas of policy and perhaps a hundred subjects? I could try to titillate you by going back to my taped interviews with John Diefenbaker recorded in the late 1960s, but I can assure you—despite Dief's unending political battles, his sharp tongue and his talent with words—that they contain far fewer scatological outbursts than Peter Newman managed to draw out of another Conservative Prime Minister twenty years later. My Diefenbaker tapes contain the occasional reference to "that gol-darn son-of-a-buffalo" and similar mild expletives, lots of harrumphs and "well, I never"s, frequent dashes of malicious humour and innuendo—but curses and four letter words are as infrequent in those recordings as they probably would have been in taped interviews with Robert Stanfield. Although no one thought so at the time, John Diefenbaker's term in office came in what was still an age of relative political decorum, when irony, sarcasm, and cutting putdowns—not vulgarity—were the favorite weapons of combat. And Dief's best performances, after all, were in the House of Commons, not on the recording couch. So there is nothing much from those tapes to shock you with today.

What I will try to do, instead, is to set the scene for this volume—in the country, in the Department of External Affairs (as it was then known), and in the world—and then to focus on a few of what seem to me to be some highlights of the collection.

John Diefenbaker became prime minister of Canada on June 21, 1957 with a minority of seats in the House of Commons after a stunning electoral upset of Louis St. Laurent's Liberal party, which had ruled the country continuously since 1935. The victory was very much a personal triumph for the new Progressive Conservative leader. Diefenbaker was chosen leader of the party at a convention just seven months earlier; and despite the fact that he had won the leadership easily on the first ballot, there remained widespread doubts in the party about his policies and his independent personality. He caused particular antagonism at the convention—and provoked a walkout of delegates—by failing to name a French-speaking seconder for his nomination. But in the House of Commons, and increasingly in the country, he made formidable assaults on the complacent Liberal government, which went into the 1957 election campaign without a program beyond the promise to continue Liberal good times forever. During the campaign—through shrewd management and the new leader's own evangelistic fervor—the Conservative party was transformed into the Diefenbaker party. John Diefenbaker stirred the Canadian spirit as it had not been stirred for decades, and was rewarded with power. Ottawa had not expected it; *Maclean's* magazine had not predicted it; and the Department of External Affairs had not anticipated it.

During the new session of parliament that autumn, the Diefenbaker government produced a quick program of reforming legislation and reinforced its popularity. (The atmosphere of soaring enthusiasm for the government during that short minority parliament was nothing like the mood in the present [2005] minority parliament.) When the Liberal party chose Lester Pearson as its new leader early in 1958, John Diefenbaker took advantage of Pearson's initial fumbling in the House of Commons to dissolve parliament and call a winter election. It was no contest: Diefenbaker swept the country with his "Vision of the North," and returned to parliament with 208 seats (including 50 of Quebec's 75 seats), reducing the Liberals to 48 seats and the CCF to 8. John Diefenbaker was now confident and triumphant, and the Conservative party seemed poised to govern the country for twenty years.

This was the domestic political background to the work of the Department of External Affairs in 1957 and 1958. The government had changed. For the first three months of the new regime, the prime minister himself acted as secretary of state for external affairs, until he plucked Sidney Smith from the presidency of the University of Toronto in September 1957 to take the job. But even then, Diefenbaker retained a dominating influence in the conduct of Canadian foreign policy. Smith, the political novice, took many months before he grew comfortable in his new political role—and then, in March 1959, after only eighteen months in office, he died suddenly of a heart attack. He was succeeded by Howard Green, a loyal Diefenbaker lieutenant who, nevertheless, had strong ideas of his own on foreign policy. But that rocky part of the story, as the Diefenbaker government tumbled over long passages of white water, awaits the appearance of further volumes in the *Documents* series. 1957–1958 was just the beginning of the Diefenbaker era in Canadian foreign policy, when the waters were still placid.

In his recent book *While Canada Slept: How We Lost Our Place in the World*, Andrew Cohen describes the period from 1945 to 1957 (the years preceding the arrival of the Conservatives in power) as Canada's Golden Age of diplomacy. He speaks of the foreign service officers of that period as renaissance men: among them Hume Wrong, Norman Robertson, Mike Pearson, Jules Léger, Georges Vanier, Escott Reid, Herbert Norman, Charles Ritchie, and John Holmes. Cohen quotes *The Economist* magazine of 1953 praising the department in these words: "If it is permissible to generalize about the diplomatic service of any country, it is probably true to say that the representatives of Canada exercise an influence and enjoy a prestige out of all reasonable proportion to the size of their country or the power they wield." *The Economist* explained their influence and prestige, above all, by "the personal quality of the men themselves."[1] Cohen was not the first person to see the department of external affairs of the early 1950s in this way: the golden image, indeed, owes something of its endurance to successful promotion of its reputation by the department itself. It saw itself then, and for years afterwards, as the premier department of government, trailed at some distance only by the department of

[1] Andrew Cohen, *While Canada Slept: How We Lost Our Place in the World* (McClelland & Stewart, 2003), p. 130.

finance. And the nostalgic glow remains: if you go to the current web page of the department of foreign affairs and international trade and search for the department's account of its own history, you will find a chapter titled "The Golden Age—1945–1957." The last date—1957—is apparently when it all ended.

The next chapter on the department's web history bears the ominous title "Dealing with Diefenbaker—1957–1963," and the first few paragraphs reflect the unease felt in the DEA following the change of administration in 1957. "For the first time since 1930," the account reads, "the department had to deal with an unsympathetic prime minister. Diefenbaker was deeply suspicious of External Affairs and its senior officers, whom he derided as 'Pearsonalities.' Although Diefenbaker had some experience of foreign affairs during his long parliamentary career, he did not have Pearson's depth of knowledge, and other members of his government had little or no knowledge at all." That's an emphatic judgment: but it is a faithful reflection of the mood in the department as the new government took office. There was doubt and anxiety on both sides.

But Canada possessed a disciplined and professional foreign service, and much as it may have been unsettled by the accession of a prairie populist, it was committed to loyal service of whatever government held power. The department took a few deep breaths and carried on. At the beginning there was no purge of senior officials. Jules Léger, the under-secretary or deputy minister, remained until he was posted overseas in October 1958; and he was then replaced as under-secretary by Norman Robertson, the very model for John Diefenbaker's description of the "Pearsonalities" that he suspected roamed the halls of the East Block. In the prime minister's office, Robert Bryce remained as clerk of the privy council and secretary of cabinet, and Basil Robinson was seconded from external affairs to act as liaison between the prime minister and the department. From 1957 to 1963 the prime minister had few direct encounters with Norman Robertson, and the interchanges between government and department were less easygoing than they had been for two decades under the Liberals; but in external affairs Diefenbaker found a department that he could depend upon—even if he never fully trusted it. At the level of the career diplomats, there was in fact no sudden end in June 1957 to the department's "Golden Age." That came later.

In policy, too, beyond an initial and ineffectual effort to shift trade away from an overwhelming dependence on the United States, and a greater emphasis on the Commonwealth connection, the new government sought to maintain continuity with the previous Liberal administration. The image of Canada's diplomatic "Golden Age" reflected the country's enhanced position after the Second World War as a specially influential middle power, catapulted into prominence by its military and industrial strength, by its active pursuit of an enlarged international role after 1945, and by its favoured position beside the United States in North America. When he came to power, John Diefenbaker had no wish to bring that charmed age of Canadian diplomacy to an end: instead he wished to extend it, to bring it to perfection. He wished only (and passionately) to lift himself into the pantheon beside (or above) Mike Pearson. In June 1957 he embarked on that Quixotic journey in foreign policy-making.

In the late 1950s, Canada's role in the world was conditioned by the dominating influence of the Cold War, the political and military standoff between the Soviet Union on one side and the United States and its European allies on the other. In 1945 the United States had emerged from war as the lone superpower, an economic giant in sole possession of the atomic bomb. The U.S. and Britain could see only one challenger on the horizon. The Soviet Union had been devastated by war, but it had become a major military power; it occupied a protective zone in central and eastern Europe where it imposed satellite regimes; it promoted an ideology based on what it claimed to be universal truths of history; and it was seen in the West as aggressive and expansionist. By 1949 it too had developed atomic weapons; and by 1952 both the United States and the Soviet Union possessed hydrogen bombs and were racing to create arsenals of intercontinental missiles to range against each other in mutual deterrence. In the east, the Chinese communists had triumphed in the civil war and created their People's Republic. The U.S. and its allies created the North Atlantic Treaty Organization – first, in 1949, as a pact of mutual guarantee and then, after the summer of 1950, as an active military alliance. The Soviets responded with their own Warsaw Pact. In Korea, there had been three years of destructive war before the conclusion of a shaky truce along the existing North-South frontier in 1953. Mutual suspicion and fear of atomic war gripped both sides in this world-wide conflict.

The Diefenbaker government assumed office under this dark cloud. The Cold War was the overriding preoccupation of all western governments; it was both a source of permanent anxiety and a daily drain on budgets and military resources. Canada was a major participant. From our perspective in 2005 (when the country has difficulty assigning 4,000 soldiers to overseas duty) it is surprising to recall that the Canadian armed forces in 1957 numbered about 120,000; that the RCAF maintained eight fighter squadrons and four air defence squadrons in Europe (totalling 272 aircraft), nine air defence squadrons (of 162 aircraft), and 48 maritime patrol aircraft in Canada; that the army had a brigade group, an armoured regiment, a field regiment and supporting troops in Europe and another division at home; and that the navy had assigned an aircraft carrier and forty-two escort ships to North Atlantic defence in the event of war. In addition, there were Canadian military units serving with the UN in the Middle East, Indo-China, and Kashmir, and an RCAF air transport group based in Naples to supply the United Nations Emergency Force in Egypt. (These figures were presented to the cabinet defence committee by the new defence minister, George Pearkes, in his first review of defence policy in July 1957. He noted that these heavy commitments would be strained by the pressures to re-equip and add new weapons in the coming years.)[2] The new government fully shared the previous government's view of the international obligations Canada had undertaken as a member of NATO and the United Nations, and had no intention of altering Canada's major commitments abroad. The country carried these burdens with a population less than half of what it is today.

Popular memory of John Diefenbaker's six years in office (to the limited extent that it exists at all after forty years) is shadowed by the way in which he lost power in 1963. The issue that brought him down was whether or not to accept nuclear warheads for the Bomarc antiaircraft missiles then being delivered to Canadian bases in Northern Ontario and Quebec. When Diefenbaker repeatedly delayed his decision, the Kennedy administration accused him of lying and reneging on his commitments, Lester Pearson suddenly came around to the American pro-nuclear position, the Conservative cabinet fell apart, and the government was defeated in the House of Commons and at the polls. In the eyes of John Diefenbaker and a substantial part of the public, a Canadian government had been thrown out of power by a conspiracy managed in Washington and executed by the Liberal party. For another slice of the Canadian electorate, the Diefenbaker government had been destroyed by its own diplomatic and political ineptitude. (Many swing voters believed both stories, and refused a majority to either Liberals or Conservatives.) From all points of view, the conflict of 1962–1963 was nasty and messy. John Diefenbaker and John Kennedy went into the history books as venomous enemies.

But when the new government came to power in 1957, as this collection of the *Documents* shows, John Diefenbaker was a friend and admirer of the United States. The possibility of a breakdown in Canadian-American relations was inconceivable to the new prime minister. Diefenbaker was an avid observer of American politics and a collector of lore about Abraham Lincoln; he was an advocate of a bill of rights on the American model; he was an admirer of President Eisenhower; and he shared American concerns about the threat posed to the world by an expansionist Soviet Union. He took for

[2] Minutes of Meeting of Cabinet Defence Committee, September 19, 1957, in *Documents on Canadian External Relations, Volume 25*, No. 18, pp. 41–46; and see also Record of Meeting between Secretary of State of United States and Secretary of State for External Affairs, July 10, 1958, in *DCER, Vol. 25*, No. 7, pp. 20–23.

granted that Canada must be a loyal and active member of the American-led alliance.

There were minor irritants like American dumping of agricultural products in world markets, and American restrictions on the sale of Canadian oil into U.S. markets, which were dealt with politely through diplomatic negotiation. There were Canadian anxieties about the scale of American capital investment and business ownership in Canada. There was the unpleasant memory of American security investigations involving accusations against a Canadian diplomat. But overriding these concerns was the sentiment shared by all parties in Canada that the United States was a benign force in the world, whose leadership was welcomed and encouraged. The Diefenbaker government, like its predecessor, accepted a policy of general harmony with the United States—even if it was more inclined than the Liberal government had been to voice its discontents with America in response to the domestic political mood.

For Prime Minister Diefenbaker in 1957–1958, this sentiment of solidarity was exemplified, above all, in Canada's defence relations with the United States. But his first venture into this realm created minor confusion that caused trouble for him both in the House of Commons and among his senior advisors. The previous Liberal government had seen through to completion the joint Canadian-American construction of three continent-wide radar networks in Canada, intended to give early warning of Soviet bomber attacks on the United States. The next logical step was a unified air defence system that would, in the event of war, allow the destruction of Soviet bombers as far beyond American borders as possible: that is, over Canada. In 1956 the Canadian and American defence chiefs had agreed on such a joint operational command; but the Liberal cabinet, fearing that the subject might cause controversy during the coming election, postponed its approval "until such time as it was not a political issue"—that is, until after its expected re-election in June.[3]

A month after Diefenbaker took power, he and his defence minister, George Pearkes, were presented with the draft agreement by the Canadian chiefs of staff, who argued that the decision had, in effect, been taken by the previous government. Diefenbaker and Pearkes not only conceded to military pressure, but decided that they could make the decision themselves, without reference either to cabinet or parliament. That was the way the creation of NORAD was announced—by simple fiat of the prime minister. The precipitate agreement soon proved to be imprudent—not in substance, but in procedure.

[3] "Aide-Memoire: Integration of Operational Control of Canadian and Continental United States Air Defence Forces in Peacetime," June 12, 1957, quoted in my *Rogue Tory*, p. 264.

The prime minister had neglected even to inform external affairs of the decision (the department learned of it, to its own embarrassment, from the American ambassador), and for a few days there were impatient exchanges between defence and external affairs blaming each other for the confusion. Six months later the prime minister was troubled enough by the mixup and its potential for public criticism that he drafted a memorandum to Sidney Smith insisting that he, Smith and Pearkes should adopt a common position on what had happened and "ensure that our officers . . . do not say or do anything of which the echoes would reach the public."[4] The department of external affairs helped the prime minister to free himself from this scrape by offering good reasons for an *ex-post facto* formal exchange of notes with the United States on the creation of NORAD; and that exchange of notes gave him the opportunity to permit a parliamentary debate on the subject in May, 1958, as demanded by the opposition parties.

The prime minister learned from this episode that continental defence had to be treated with caution. He would not rush into any further agreements with the United States. From this point on, negotiations over a range of defence questions moved slowly, always involving careful analysis of the issues by Canadian senior officials—though John Diefenbaker probably did not yet sense that he had entered a minefield.

The largest section of this volume of the *Documents*, covering more than three hundred pages of text, tells the story of these defence negotiations from July, 1957 until December, 1958. But there are a few surprising gaps. The opening document in the collection is an account of the first meetings between the American secretary of state, John Foster Dulles, and Prime Minister Diefenbaker, in late July, 1957. It is a report by John Holmes, the assistant undersecretary of state, in which he repeats the American ambassador's account of the meetings because, as a footnote indicates, "No official record of Dulles' visit was prepared by Canadian officials."[5] Almost a year later, in July 1958, when President Eisenhower met with the Canadian prime minister in Ottawa, another footnote tells us that "Canadian officials do not seem to have kept detailed or coherent minutes of all meetings related to the visit. . . ."[6] Do these lapses suggest any other failures of coordination between officials and ministers of the new government?

[4] See *DCER, Volume 25*, No. 25, pp. 55–57. The editor of the volume notes laconically that "It is not clear if a final version of this document was sent to Smith."

[5] See *DCER, Volume 25*, No. 1, 1–3.

[6] See ibid, No. 2, fn. 25, 14. The Department's liaison with the prime minister, Basil Robinson, was ill during the Eisenhower visit; but External made no arrangements for a stand-in who might have monitored all the meetings. (See Basil Robinson, *Diefenbaker's World: A Populist in Foreign Affairs* [Toronto: University of Toronto Press, 1989], pp. 50–52.)

Whatever reports of meetings may be missing, the documentary record published here is large and intelligible. The United States set out its proposals to Canada for "Closer Integration of Atomic Capabilities in Defence of North America" in December 1957, and those proposals set most of the agenda for Canadian-American defence relations over the following five years. The framework of joint defence over Canadian territory already existed in the northern radar lines and in NORAD, and what the Americans now proposed amounted to filling out the system in predictable ways. They called for the storage and possible use of atomic weapons in Canada by American and Canadian forces, both air and naval, and the continuing addition of new weapons to the arsenal. Canada added to the negotiating lists the subjects of cost- and production-sharing, and the fate of the Avro Arrow interceptor aircraft then under development. The negotiations involved delicate issues of sovereignty, the future of high technology industry in Canada, the nature of consultation between governments in times of crisis, and control over the storage and use of nuclear weapons. There was no way that the Diefenbaker government could have avoided facing these problems, and there was no easy way of dealing with them.

It was arguable that the Soviet Union did not pose the aggressive challenge that NATO and the American government attributed to it. But for ten years the Soviet Union and the western powers had been locked in mutual antagonism, and together they had created a system of confrontation that was worldwide. Some countries of the developing world could stand aside in non-alignment, seeking favours and advantage from both sides in the conflict. Even Yugoslavia managed to manoeuvre painfully from a position within the Soviet bloc to one of non-alignment. But neither the Canadian public nor its politicians could imagine such daring independence, given our shared experience of the Second World War alongside the United States, and our geography. Robert Thompson said it for us: "The Americans are our best friends, whether we like it or not." (I'm not sure that Thompson's Aphorism still applies in 2005.) What John Diefenbaker (and later, Mike Pearson) had to do in matters of North American defence was to find what was minimally acceptable to the Americans, persuade Canadians that that was reasonable, and do it. There was some bargaining space, but not much.

For the Diefenbaker government, the most urgent defence problem was what to do with the Avro Arrow. The Liberal government had initiated the project, seen its budgets explode, and postponed any decision on its future until after the 1957 election. Over $200 million had already been spent, which would rise to $400 million within a year. No aircraft had yet flown. In October 1957 the minority Diefenbaker cabinet agreed to continue development of twenty-nine pre-production aircraft for another twelve months, rather than risking the loss of thousands of jobs at Malton Airport just before another election. This initial decision was entirely political.

By the time the government achieved its safe majority in the spring of 1958, the Arrow was just one element in the package under discussion with the Americans. If it was abandoned, the cabinet would have to decide what would replace it, who would pay for the replacement, and how it would be armed. What industrial benefits could be prised from the Americans in return for scrapping an advanced, home-grown aircraft?

All these questions faced the cabinet in the summer of 1958, and in a memo to the prime minister at the end of July the cabinet secretary Robert Bryce explained his wordiness by noting that "there is so much detail and so many considerations that there is never finality."[7] Bryce told Diefenbaker that he favoured continuation of the Arrow program, that the plane should be armed with nuclear weapons, and that Canada should accept two bases for Bomarc ground-to-air missiles near Ottawa (these weapons also to be tipped with nuclear warheads). He lamented that "It is worrying to see how far the whole Bomarc complex, on the map, seems designed to defend the U.S. and its bases and not Canada, but it is probably too late to do much about this now, other than to have the two Canadian bases in addition to the 30 or 32 in the U.S."[8]

Within a week, the *Documents* show that the minister of defence and the prime minister had agreed, after Pearkes's consultations in Washington, that the Arrow program should be cancelled, and that nuclear-armed Bomarc missiles should become the central element of Canadian air defence, intended to form part of "a Canada-U.S. plan for a continuous system of missile defence from coast to coast designed for the protection of the principal targets in North America."[9] (Although as Bryce had pointed out to the prime minister, "protecting the principal targets in North America" had nothing to do with protecting Canadian cities.) The decision to scrap the Arrow was made on grounds of excessive cost, Washington's clear lack of support for the project, and dubious arguments about the changing nature of air defence which applied as much to the Bomarc missile as they did to the Avro Arrow. But in

[7] Memorandum from Secretary to Cabinet to Prime Minister, July 31, 1958, *DCER, Volume 25*, No. 69, pp. 142–143.

[8] Ibid. When the American defence secretary Robert McNamara testified to a congressional committee in March 1963 that the Bomarcs were ineffective weapons, except that "they would cause the Soviets to target missiles against them and thereby increase their missile requirements or draw missiles onto these Bomarc targets," Diefenbaker told an election audience gleefully that "The Liberal policy is to make Canada a decoy for intercontinental missiles." He had perhaps forgotten who took the decision to locate the Bomarcs at North Bay and La Macaza. (See *Rogue Tory*, pp. 503–504.)

[9] Memorandum from Minister of National Defence to Cabinet Defence Committee, August 8, 1958, No. 72, *DCER, Volume 25*, pp. 153–162.

1958 the United States preferred the Bomarc.

What followed in Ottawa was a six-week marathon of meetings of the cabinet defence committee and cabinet on these momentous policy and budgetary issues. The anguish and uncertainty displayed in cabinet over these six weeks was probably the first clear signal of the Diefenbaker government's difficulty in reaching decisions on major subjects. But since all this occurred in the privacy of the cabinet room—and well before such debates began leaking to Peter C. Newman—the public learned little about that exhausting summer for the Diefenbaker ministry. Ironically (given that it was the prime minister's indecision over accepting delivery of nuclear warheads for the Bomarc missiles that led to his fall in 1963) there seemed to be no uncertainty about acceptance of the warheads in principle during those long weeks of interminable cabinet meetings. Joining the nuclear club, inviting Soviet targetting of central Canada, raising complex matters of sovereign control over weapons on Canadian soil, did not give ministers pause in 1957—although the documents show that their officials understood the issues and struggled with them. Acceptance of the Bomarc with its warheads was taken for granted, with the understanding that delivery of the weapons would still be years away, probably beyond the next election.

The problems that troubled cabinet were immediate: financial and (above all) political. Scrapping the Arrow would staunch a bleeding military budget; but it would also, potentially, destroy a major aircraft company and throw thousands of skilled employees out of work. The choice was finally made late in September 1958 when Diefenbaker proposed further delay: development of the Arrow would continue for another six months, with a final decision by March, 1959. Meanwhile the Bomarc, with its nuclear warheads, slipped through the Canadian doorway with little public notice. Attention was focussed on the Arrow's stay of execution.

As it related to the Arrow, this was an astute short-term decision. Diefenbaker and Pearkes intended to kill it, but not at the beginning of winter during an economic downturn. The public admired the government's compassion for Avro's employees, while the pundits admired its courage in deciding to cancel the project. The prime minister expected that Avro Aircraft would spend the next six months devising alternative tasks for its factories. Avro's executives, on the contrary, saw the chance to lean hard on a pliable prime minister and pressed on with plans for full production of the interceptor. In this they misjudged John Diefenbaker. In February 1959 he cancelled the project. When he made the announcement in the House of Commons, the prime minister emphasized instead Canada's "need in present circumstances for nuclear weapons of a defensive character," to be placed in the new Bomarcs.[10] At that point he had no sense of the political nightmares this choice would bring him four years later. The Canadian public had not yet awakened fully to the dangers of nuclear war and radioactive fallout, and Howard Green had not yet brought his preoccupation with disarmament to the department of external affairs.

As the Diefenbaker government took its first steps towards accepting nuclear arms, one minister cautioned it that Canada should show some scepticism about the military threat posed by the Soviet Union. Sidney Smith, perhaps taking his cue from senior advisors in the DEA, told cabinet that "the threat does not consist alone of enemy capabilities; enemy intentions are important as well." "Can it not be argued," he wrote in tentative mode, "that the Soviet Union can safely rely on the existing balance of deterrents as sufficient safeguard to her own security" and thus did not plan to initiate war against the United States? In that case, the United States could relax a bit, and pay more attention to economic and political competition with the Soviets. If only. Smith recognized that this was idle fancy.

> Whatever judgment may be made on the nature of the Soviet threat, it is evident that the United States is committed to the erection of defences in North America to meet the most diversified attack of which the Soviet Union is capable.... It can be argued that such an extensive effort is unnecessary and, indeed, too costly even for the economic resources of the United States. Nevertheless, it is clear that it is the determination, at the moment, of the United States Government, influenced, it would seem, by the events of Pearl Harbour in 1941, to work within this concept of defence. It is further a matter of agreed policy between the Canadian and the United States Governments that the air defence of the continent is a single problem and must be met jointly by the two countries.

Canada was locked into American defence policy, he said, "unless the Canadian Government is prepared ... to challenge the basic United States concept"—which it was not.[11] That may be the essential message of Canadian

[10] Quoted in *Rogue Tory*, p. 319.

[11] Memorandum from Secretary of State for External Affairs to Cabinet Defence Committee, "Continental Air Defence—Foreign Policy Implications", Enclosure with Memorandum from Under-Secretary of State for External Affairs to Prime Minister, August 14, 1958, *DCER, Volume 25*, No. 74, pp. 166–173, esp. p. 169. The DEA's point of view was noted at the Cabinet Defence Committee on August 15, 1958: "... there might be more likelihood of a continuation of the cold war and of the outbreak of local incidents along the fringes of the free world than of the launching of a definite attack on North America by the Soviet Union." (Ibid, No. 75, pp. 174–177).

foreign policy from 1945 until 1989.[12]

John Diefenbaker had not come to office to make a revolution in foreign policy. But that memo from Sidney Smith indicated that the department of external affairs was still a place, as it had been in the early years after 1945, where thoughtful discussion about the presuppositions of the Cold War, and the possibilities of an alternative world, could take place. The last section of this volume of the *Documents*, dealing with Eastern Europe and the Soviet Union, contains several notable commentaries on the nature of the Soviet-American balance of power, the Western "obsession" with the Soviet menace, and the risks of an accidental outbreak of nuclear war. The internal debate seems to have begun with an unsolicited paper from the Canadian ambassador in Colombia, Robert Ford, in October 1957, suggesting that the new balance of nuclear terror gave middle powers greater potential freedom of manoeuvre (although he added that, in Canada's case, "our special defence relationship with the United States is bound to limit our freedom of action much more than other countries").[13] The under-secretary, Jules Léger, distributed the paper widely and congratulated Ford for his analysis, which he said "leads to some truly interesting lines of thought."

Robert Ford's paper was followed over the next six months by equally penetrating comments on Soviet intentions from John W. Holmes and J.B.C. Watkins.[14] But the most remarkable piece in the collection, I think, is a twenty page essay by Clifford Webster written in September 1958 and titled "A Gloss on Kennan." Sidney Smith thrust it into the hands of Prime Minister Diefenbaker as he was about to depart on his world tour that autumn with the apology that "I dislike 'shoving' more paper at you but this is good!"[15] Diefenbaker kept the memo—but there is no clear indication whether, or how, it influenced his thoughts about the Cold War and Canada's place in it.

"The basic question," wrote Webster, "is Soviet intentions. The extreme view, which, after four decades, is still by and large the received view, is that

[12] And in that latter year—as the Berlin Wall came down, the Soviet Empire crumbled, and the Cold War alliance became redundant—Canada chose, in the Free Trade Agreement, another way of locking its fortunes to those of the United States.

[13] Memorandum by Ambassador in Colombia, "A Re-Examination of the Balance of Power," *DCER, Volume 25,* October 15, 1957, No. 515, pp. 1026–1032.

[14] Memorandum from Assistant Under-Secretary of State for External Affairs to Under-Secretary of State for External Affairs, March 24, 1958; March 28, 1958; March 31, 1958, *DCER, Volume 25,* Nos. 517, 518, 519, pp. 1033–1042.

[15] Memorandum from Secretary of State for External Affairs to Prime Minister, September 30, 1958, enclosing Memorandum: A Gloss on Kennan, September 30, 1958, *DCER, Volume 25,* No. 520, pp. 1042–1062. Webster was an economic historian with a special interest in Soviet economic history who joined the department from National Defence in 1956. He later served in Djakarta, Moscow, Ottawa, Phnom Penh, and Geneva. He died in 1967 at age 49.

since the U.S.S.R. is fundamentally hostile to the West, it must ultimately intend to destroy, or to conquer, or to convert the West to communism." Yet in the ten years after George Kennan set the pattern for a Western policy of containment of the Soviet Union in 1947, no one had attempted a systematic study of Soviet intentions. The USSR's military capabilities had been assessed, and the Western military response had been based on that judgment of capabilities; but there had been "no effort from observable Soviet policy to divine actual Soviet preferences, concrete Soviet expectations, and so Soviet intentions." When the Soviets proposed a summit meeting and a general settlement of differences (as they had recently done), there had been no attempt to engage in serious analysis of their purposes. Could it be that their intentions were straightforward? The western alliance had shown itself incapable of taking "a reasonable view of Soviet policy, of the Soviet achievement, of the limits of Soviet ambition. To acquire this, we must surely ask the normal questions of the evidence . . . we must focus attention on actual Soviet policy," isolating that policy from the "confusion of fantastic ideology, dishonest propaganda and scurrilous vituperation" in which it was packaged.

Webster offered his careful historical judgment that, since 1917, the utopian Marxism of the Soviet founders had been "reduced from the pursuit of world revolution to the defence of the independence and sovereignty of the members of the Soviet bloc against the predatory U.S." Beyond the extension of a protective zone into central and eastern Europe (which had been achieved in the years immediately after the Second World War), Soviet foreign and defence policy had been cautious and highly conservative, responding defensively in the placement of ground, air and naval forces only to the growth of forces mounted against them. Equally, in its international economic policies and its respect for international law the Soviet Union had sought basic guarantees of national security. "Action which has seemed to the external world to reflect the most aggressive, expansionist, Marxist initiative, has instead been aimed at negative, limited and immediate goals; Moscow has been too desperate, too preoccupied, to translate vague, maximalist thinking into concrete long-term plans. . . . The West has been dealing with an appallingly crude approach to politics, rather than sophisticated malevolence." Webster urged, in conclusion, that Western policy-makers should now approach the Soviet Union as a normal member of the international community, not a mysterious and implacable foe set upon the destruction of the civilized world. The West should seek compromise and disengagement through "patient and piecemeal" approaches that would move beyond military containment.

Such policies of limited disengagement did, in fact, form a part of Western dealings with the Soviet Union in the following thirty years, and were gradually reflected in the various arms limitation treaties of the sixties, seventies and eighties. But they remained only as a minor element in alliance policy, subordinate to maintaining the balance of nuclear terror with all its frightful arsenals of weapons both defensive and offensive. Meanwhile, official Western policies of explanation and justification remained mired in the fantasy-ridden muddle of the anticommunist crusade.

In Canada, this remarkable document must have provided useful hints to the senior officials of the department of external affairs, who were already deeply worried by the deceits and costs and risks of the nuclear arms race. Within a few months, the new under-secretary, Norman Robertson, found himself joined by a new secretary of state, Howard Green, who shared his anxieties. In the next four years, they jointly focused their energies on Canada's efforts to reduce the tensions of the Cold War through negotiations on disarmament. In doing so, they complicated the work of their prime minister, whose political skills were tested beyond his capacity to navigate the shoals as the closest subordinate member of the American alliance.[16]

The succeeding volumes of the *Documents* series should offer more fascinating details of this story. And as we see every day—even though we have passed into an era beyond the Cold War and beyond the department's "Golden Age"—Canada still faces the dilemmas of living within the American embrace. Now our neighbour has adopted a new absolutist vision (with its own exaggerations and confusions and misapplications) to replace its absolutist anti-communism. We can certainly benefit today by fresh and detailed study of how we managed (or mismanaged) the continental relationship in a previous time of troubles. As in 1958, so in 2005: Canada needs to be able to think clearly and to consider alternatives.

[16] For the views of Robertson and Green on nuclear arms, see Basil Robinson, *Diefenbaker's World: A Populist in Foreign Affairs* (Toronto: University of Toronto Press, 1989), pp. 106–117.

II / Reviews

From 1989 to 2007 I was a regular reviewer for the Saturday book section of the Toronto Star *under its book editors Judy Stoffman and Dan Smith, and an occasional reviewer for the* Globe and Mail. *This was a period of admirable Canadian political biographies by John English, Stephen Clarkson and Christina Newman, Lawrence Martin, Geoffrey Stevens, Knowlton Nash, and Richard Gwyn (among others), and provocative political essays by Jack Granatstein and David Frum. The biographers inspired reflection; the provocateurs invited challenge. Ken Dryden, the literate ex-politician, raised discussion about Canada to a philosophic level in a book I reviewed for the* Literary Review of Canada *in 2011. I've always believed that a book review should be part of a conversation with the author and other readers. Here are a few snippets of conversation.*

Penetrating Pearson's Secret Self

(*Toronto Star*, November 25, 1989)

Shadow of Heaven: The Life of Lester Pearson, Volume One: 1897–1948
John English (Lester & Orpen Dennys)

When Mike Pearson made the transition in 1948 from senior civil servant to politician, as Louis St. Laurent's secretary of state for external affairs, he was already a distinguished public figure, the embodiment of Canada's postwar prominence in international diplomacy. Before long he was "the best-known Canadian in Canada and beyond," then a Nobel Peace Prize winner, opposition leader and prime minister from 1963 to 1968. Outwardly his rise seemed charmed and untroubled—until he met the rough and tumble of domestic politics as leader of the opposition in 1958. His last decade in public life was strained and turbulent, his achievements as prime minister decidedly mixed.

The surprises and disappointments of that decade revealed a man more human and fallible than the previously unblemished myth, and much more complex. In this first volume of his biography, John English sets out to trace the development of that complex man, and does so with splendid grace and insight.

The task was formidable. Pearson was literate and articulate, leaving copious diaries, letters, memoranda, articles and speeches to ease the biographer's work. But he was also curiously reserved, and skilful in disguising his less attractive traits behind a facade of engaging wit and affability. He was substantially the author of his own myth. The challenge for a biographer was to penetrate that carefully composed facade. John English has done so with skill, just occasionally showing discretion when he might have pushed understanding slightly further.

There is brilliant irony in the book's title, drawn from John Milton's lines:

> *What if earth*
> *Be but the shadow of Heav'n, and things therein*
> *Each to other like, more than on Earth is thought?*

For Lester Pearson, the parson's son whose faith faded in the 1920s, the shadow remained when heaven evaporated. That shadow of Ontario Methodism always marked his worldly pursuits. Pearson's idealism, complacency, geniality and calculating ambition were a typical inheritance in the first generation of Canadian secularism. John English reveals how much Mike Pearson took, in character and instinct, from his parson father Ed, from Victoria College and from his helpful Methodist patrons.

There were other notable strands in his formation: Above all, his experience of England and Oxford during and after World War I. There his horizons expanded beyond the parochialism and intolerance of Ontario; and in the decades that followed he helped to carry Canada itself beyond its old limits. After a mildly frustrating test of university teaching in the University of Toronto (where his sporting prowess outshone his academic), he entered the Department of External Affairs in 1928 and found his vocation.

From the mid-'30s until 1948, Mike Pearson found himself at the centre of international diplomacy, in London, Geneva, Washington and, from time to time, Ottawa. He quickly revealed his capacity for hard work, diplomatic compromise and the inspiration of colleagues, and was noticed and appreciated both by the Canadian prime ministers R.B. Bennett and Mackenzie King and by foreign diplomats and politicians. By 1946 he was the candidate of the United Kingdom and the United States as the first Secretary-General of the United Nations, barred from that eminence only by a potential Soviet veto. When he entered the cabinet in 1948, Mackenzie King already prophesied that he would become prime minister. Perhaps Pearson did too, although John

English does not speculate on that point.

The author weaves his narrative with vivid evocations of time and place, and almost always balances detail with background and reflection in perfect harmony. He is a bit unsure of himself in some of his descriptions of Pearson's life in England. In one passage, he devotes too much space for my taste to a description of Maryon Pearson's wedding dress; in another strangely defensive section, he responds at length to the preposterous claim that Pearson was a long-time Soviet agent of influence. In doing that, English perhaps fails to devote sufficient analysis to Pearson's too-aggressive anti-communism in the late 1940s. Professor English is scrupulous in assessing Pearson's own story of his life in the *Memoirs* against the historical record when the evidence conflicts, and reaches his own conclusions. He draws a discreet veil over family matters and affections, and thus perhaps misses full entry into what Arnold Heeney saw in Pearson as a "compartment of his mind [that] was hermetically sealed," the source of his deepest impulses.

But what great man does not remain a mystery? John English surely comes close to penetrating this one when he notes that Pearson, like Mackenzie King, acted on emotion and intuition rather than reason: "Both men scanned the surface with political antennae of exquisite sensitivity, and their feelings largely shaped their deeds." This book is a fine introduction to Mike Pearson's emblematic Canadian life, and promises much for the second volume.

Dief and JFK: Two Antagonists in Conflict

(*Toronto Star*, November 10, 1990)

Kennedy and Diefenbaker: Fear and Loathing across the Undefended Border
Knowlton Nash (McClelland & Stewart)

Knowlton Nash spent the '50s and '60s in Washington as a well-informed and industrious correspondent for the CBC. He was an early acquaintance and fan of Senator John F. Kennedy, and enjoyed close access to him during his campaign for the presidency and afterwards in the White House. From that base in Washington, Nash frequently came north to report on Canadian politics in the turbulent era of John Diefenbaker. He was thus able to watch both sides of a conflict that revealed "the lasting and deep-rooted personal hatred and contempt between the 35th president and the 13th prime minister."

Nash kept his notes and files from that time, perhaps in the hope that someday he could tell the story again. He has done so in this lively narrative, which is enriched by fresh interviews with the major players.

The focus of conflict between Diefenbaker and Kennedy was Canada's failure to accept nuclear warheads for weapons that the Diefenbaker government had freely chosen in 1958. But Nash reminds us that the dispute was broader, and in a sense simpler, than that. In the background was Canada's long history of insecurity and uncertainty beside the American colossus. By the mid-1950s Canada had entered a new phase of national self-assertion, marked by widespread suspicion of the Liberal party's cooperative approach to the United States. At the same time, the Conservative party gambled with its fate by selecting a Saskatchewan maverick as its leader.

To everyone's astonishment, the gamble paid off twice: in 1957 with the election of a Diefenbaker minority government; and in 1958 with a Conservative landslide. In those campaigns John Diefenbaker proved himself to be a passionate performer on the hustings and made himself, for a time, undisputed master of Canada's destiny.

Diefenbaker incarnated Canadian ambiguity toward the United States. He was an avid and romantic admirer of the American system, American leaders, and American parties. But he was at the same time jealous, suspicious and fearful of American power. If he had possessed greater skill and confidence in administration, those internal conflicts might have been manifested in measured policy. Instead, they resulted in indecision, incoherence and chaos.

For Diefenbaker's first three years in power, Canada's relations with the United States were cushioned by the avuncular goodwill of the American president, Dwight Eisenhower. But as Nash shows, American diplomats were already deeply worried by the Canadian prime minister's indecisiveness and anti-American prejudice. Once Kennedy took office in January 1961, the collapse of the relationship was virtually foreordained.

Diefenbaker seems to have been both overawed and intimidated by the bright, witty, stylish, activist new president. For his part, the president thought the prime minister bombastic and boring, and after their first meeting in Washington, Kennedy avoided Diefenbaker as much as possible.

Mere personal dislike was one thing: political leaders often put up with it in their diplomatic dealings. But by early 1962 Kennedy felt that Diefenbaker had betrayed his commitment to accept nuclear warheads for Canadian weapons in North America and Europe. When Canada (alone among America's allies) hesitated in its public support for President Kennedy during the Cuban missile crisis of October 1962, Washington's sense of betrayal deepened. Now Kennedy was eager to see Diefenbaker defeated, and had few scruples about nudging defeat along. A Liberal government under Mike Pearson was infinitely preferable. Kennedy's aides (and Pearson himself) had to restrain the president's interventions meant to bring that about.

The heart of Nash's story is his account of Diefenbaker's fall in 1963.

According to Nash, the real precipitant was the State Department's press release of January 30, which rebuked the prime minister for lying about the warheads affair. He calls the press release "the instrument of an unintended coup d'état," leading directly to defeat in the House and loss of power in the general election. Without it, Nash thinks, defeat in the House might have been averted. (But he notes also that when Pearson met Kennedy at Hyannisport after becoming prime minister, Pearson told the president that the press release had cost him a Liberal majority in the House.)

Although Nash blames both antagonists evenly for the Kennedy-Diefenbaker conflict—Diefenbaker "with his visceral, ancient fears of the grasping Americans and his obsessive detestation of the Kennedy style," Kennedy "with his arrogance and contempt at what he considered Diefenbaker's old-fashioned humbuggery"—it is clear that Nash's sympathies, both personal and political, lie with Kennedy and Pearson. That seems reasonable. Despite his talents, Diefenbaker gratuitously damaged Canada's interests. Another Canadian leader, more in control of his emotions, more decisive, and better able to understand military policy, might have avoided the whole messy business.

In his accounts of interviews, Nash shows that many of Diefenbaker's close advisers and confidants viewed his acts, at least in retrospect, as rash and extreme. Throughout the book, Nash recalls a series of extraordinary incidents in the prime minister's office that kept the country diverted and distressed for six fast-paced years. For anyone wishing to relive those contentious times, this is a good place to start.

PET: The Canadian Lone Ranger

(*Toronto Star*, October 27, 1990)

The Outsider: The Life of Pierre Elliott Trudeau
Michel Vastel, translated by Hubert Bauch (Macmillan)

Trudeau and Our Times, Vol. 1: The Magnificent Obsession
Stephen Clarkson and Christina McCall (McClelland & Stewart)

He haunts us still, say Stephen Clarkson and Christina McCall: "Pierre Elliott Trudeau and his ideas remain dominant in the northern attic of the continent, a standard against which other political actors, thinkers, theorists, and hopefuls . . . measure themselves and are measured." These two books are compelling evidence of that haunting presence.

Michel Vastel's work, published last year in French as *Trudeau le Québécois*, is a sharply etched account of Pierre Trudeau's bitter relations with his own Quebec nation. The original title is more appropriate than this one, since the book is far from a full biography. But despite its large gaps, this tale of a loner always ready for a brawl gives us revealing glimpses of a troubled man seeking to work out his complexes on an entire country.

Vastel pays Trudeau the compliment of taking his writings of the 1950s seriously as real indications of his convictions and guides to his acts. Those writings reveal Trudeau's contempt for the Quebec society of his youth, his condescending view of its political immaturity, corruption, ignorance, and self-absorption. They contain sweeping condemnations, seldom rooted in specific example, sometimes amounting to little more than smear. Vastel relates these judgments, with reason, to the easy simplifications about Quebec that were later common in English-speaking Canada, at a time when Quebec was already engaged in a broad democratic revolution in which its former habits and beliefs were discarded. By then, as Vastel notes, Trudeau had taken a separate road leading away from Quebec's new movements of reform; he disdained them as much as the society they had replaced.

Vastel's case that Trudeau was not a useful dissident, not simply a progressive reformer, but rather a destructive rebel against his own Quebec community, is strongly made, with frequent touches of sarcasm to match Trudeau's own. But it is part of a domestic Quebec debate, too one-sided to be fair for an audience beyond that distinct society and unaware of the full context of discussion.

The unusual ferocity of Trudeau's combativeness, and its sources, are obviously puzzles. What was it in his character and surroundings that produced so explosive a personality? Vastel responds with an uncertain venture into psychobiography, suggesting that Trudeau's rages and antagonisms were the result of a missed stage in adolescence, a failure to work through the normal phases of hatred and reconciliation toward his father, who died when Pierre was 15. This explanation is incomplete and not entirely convincing, too much centred on the warring side of his character. Still, real gems of insight are there, and Vastel tells the story with verve.

Trudeau and Our Times, by contrast, is an epic work of great power, matching the full range of its subject's life and character and the complexity of his country. This Trudeau is not just Vastel's brawler, but a man of generous vision and spirituality as well.

Clarkson and McCall, like Vastel, use a theory of personal development to explain Trudeau's life; but theirs is more subtly woven.

"Throughout his adolescence and adulthood," they write, "the carefully controlled Pierre would be subject to sudden outbursts of rage or displays of sarcasm that would have a devastating effect on his victims and on himself. It was as though another powerful shadow personality would always be lying in ambush waiting to sabotage with sudden displays of aggression or combativeness what he was trying to accomplish with modesty, reason and calm detachment."

For them, Trudeau's unresolved conflict of adolescence arose not only from the teenager's loss of a father, but from his over-protective relationship with his mother, from the contrasting qualities of the two parents and two languages he had inherited, and from the accident of a privileged life in which he was free to choose eternal youth.

The prime minister's emotional immaturity, they judge, lasted until his political defeat and collapse of his marriage in 1979, at age 60, events which brought on "a professional and personal crisis of truly heroic proportions." Beyond the public events, their evidence for this trauma is indirect and anecdotal. I would say, rather, that he was slightly more "integrated" than they suggest before 1979, and slightly less "integrated" than they claim after 1979. His outbursts on the Meech Lake Accord since 1987, for example, must match any of his earlier ones for their bitter and uncontrolled immoderation. The shadow personality has not yet been discarded; the spoiled child still lives. Clarkson and McCall, though, relate the belated balancing of his personality to Trudeau's constitutional successes after his return to power in 1980, when he was at last able to engage in realistic political compromise. (But didn't he do that as well in the minority parliament of 1972–1974?)

Their careful analysis is never forced or obtrusive. It is expressed sometimes in the revealing literary metaphor used by Trudeau himself, who absurdly emulated Cyrano de Bergerac, "a brilliant wit and poet, a protector of the weak, enemy of the pompous and powerful, a fighter against tyranny, capable of taking on a hundred bullies and winning against all the odds, a man who refused compromise, fripperies, and flattery." That theatrical, romantic visage is certainly one part of the cold, sarcastic, and cruel rationalist we saw staring us down so often.

But *Trudeau and Our Times* is much more than a study of personality. It is also a rich account of the Quebec and Canada in which Trudeau came to leadership: of the easy corruptions of office after 1968; of the marriage to Margaret and its relationship to power; of friends and foes like Gerard Pélletier, René Lévesque, Claude Ryan, Jim Coutts, Joe Clark, Bora Laskin, Richard Hatfield, and William Davis; and of Trudeau's skillful political political triumph in the Quebec referendum of 1980 and its aftermath.

Clarkson and McCall show that every one of Pierre Trudeau's victories had its price, which was sometimes high. But they allow us to see the drama of his career with an enlarged sympathy and intelligence appropriate to its subject. The authors make a superb team, combining long political experience, intuition, scholarly talent, and great literary flair. The second volume, due late in 1991 and titled *The Fateful Delusion*, should offer equal fascination. In it, I hope they will try to explain why the country responded so passionately to Pierre Trudeau's flawed vision. Meanwhile, we will continue to be haunted by the twilight of a life that may well end in a sadness as deep as Cyrano's.

Pierre Elliott Trudeau died in September 2000, two years after his youngest son Michel, aged 23, was killed in an avalanche.

Mike Pearson: Blessed Are the Peacemakers

(*Toronto Star*, December 19, 1992)

The Worldly Years: The Life of Lester Pearson, Vol. 2, 1949–1972
John English (Knopf Canada)

Three years ago John English offered us the splendid first volume of his biography of Mike Pearson, *Shadow of Heaven*; now he completes the story with an equally graceful account of Pearson's mature years as secretary of state for external affairs, leader of the Liberal party and prime minister.

There is less novelty in this volume than in the first, because Pearson had become a leading public figure by 1949, and remained in the public eye until his death in 1972. As a politician, his style, his words, his triumphs, his distresses, and his failures were our daily companions for two decades. Canadians thought they knew him well.

In this volume John English finds no hidden quirks or skeletons. Instead he brilliantly recalls the unpretentious, self-deprecating, thoughtful, and decent man we knew, a lapsed Methodist thriving on his devotion to public service. In his earlier life Pearson disguised ambition behind a facade of casual charm and humor; in the 1950s, he had the good luck to cloak it in his role as external affairs minister and budding world statesman. That meant he could avoid the partisan abrasion and slogging labor of domestic politics normally faced by candidates for the party leadership.

By 1954 (probably earlier) Pearson was certainly thinking of the succession; but beside Paul Martin, he never looked "overly ambitious." Pearson had the advantage because "in that peculiar political atmosphere of the mid-1950s, to be too political was unseemly." He survived the collapse of the Liberal St. Laurent government in 1957 with a reputation transcending the party, and coasted easily to the Liberal leadership in January 1958.

The charmed life of the Nobel laureate ended instantly. On his first day as leader of the opposition, Pearson took bad advice and was humiliated by John

Diefenbaker. Sensing triumph, the Tory prime minister dissolved parliament at once. In the ensuing election, the Liberal party suffered its worst defeat since Confederation. For ten years thereafter Pearson struggled valiantly in the snakepit of domestic politics—most of the time unhappily.

John English suggests that one source of his difficulties was his unusual road to the top: "Mike's position meant that he received a poor education in the details of the Liberal party and the Canadian political system." Another was a matter of temperament as well as training: Pearson could see the complexity of issues, and was a genial conciliator ready to embrace the best features of an opponent's case. That gave him no leverage against so jealous a competitor as Diefenbaker, who sought not compromise but victory. And Pearson was a dreadful administrator. He could not organize the work of his cabinet or deal decisively with faltering ministers, either to support them or to discard them cleanly.

So he stumbled through five-and-a-half years as prime minister from 1963 to 1968, facing the Conservative ogre across the aisle of the House, disappointing one minister after another, never achieving a parliamentary majority. Despite these trials, Pearson's reforming government had major achievements. *The Worldly Years* makes clear that these were the fruit of his own convictions.

English recreates Pearson's crowded life in broad sweeps rather than close detail, with occasional focus on leading events like the Korean War, Suez, the Norman case, rebuilding the Liberal party, the flag, the emerging Quebec crisis, and the American relationship. His prose has a relaxed and reflective tone that echoes the thoughtfulness of Pearson's own writings. He gives full recognition to Pearson's critics and treats them generously, sensing wisely that this was an unusual man whose faults did not diminish his great virtues.

Pearson's greatest legacy was that he spoke to English Canada about its place in the world in the civilized words of a practical visionary, and lived those words as well. Beyond his talents for compromise and accommodation, he defined standards of international conduct and national reconciliation that enlarged Canadian horizons. In his quiet way, he applied the same genius to world problems—and made an impact that can still be seen as UN peacekeeping forces proliferate.

The last chapter of this fine book opens with James Eayrs' engaging word picture, written after Pearson's death: "Lester Bowles Pearson should be borne in spirit to the Pearly Gates by a large black limousine. If St. Peter challenges credentials, all is soon resolved by firm yet quiet negotiation: the gates swing open, the limousine glides through, from its rear seat a cheerful, rumpled figure waves a greeting and then returns to perusing memoranda to aid in facing Final Judgment."

John English has done Mike Pearson proud.

Kissinger: What History Can Teach the New World Order

(*Toronto Star*, August 27, 1994)

Diplomacy
Henry Kissinger (Simon & Schuster)

Next to Richard Nixon, Henry Kissinger has been America's longest-surviving and most morally doubtful celebrity.

As Nixon's national security advisor he was the president's partner in duplicity over Vietnam; and later, as secretary of state, he cultivated his own interests as the president went down. He survived in office into the brief administration of Gerald Ford, and since then has prospered as a foreign affairs consultant, lecturer, writer and intimate of presidents—a courtier who mastered his devious trade. He is perhaps the only winner of a Nobel Peace Prize who can plausibly be described as a war criminal.

Kissinger was an academic before he was a diplomat, and his historical interests have always been obvious in his politics. He is the assiduous student of Metternich and Bismarck, the old-world advocate who preached the national interest, the balance of power and spheres of interest to the new Wilsonian world of self-determination and collective security. This out-of-placeness has always been one source of his interest and his notoriety. How could such a European cynic prosper as a diplomat in idealist America?

Kissinger gives his impressive answer in this massive study. *Diplomacy* is a sweeping history of international relations since the time of Cardinal Richelieu, which nevertheless concentrates its focus on the twentieth century. It reaches a climax in the Cold War and Kissinger's own direct experience (about a tenth of the book is devoted to the diplomacy of the Vietnam War), and ends by applying the lessons of history to the post-1989 "New World Order."

Kissinger writes with clarity, vividness and profound insight about power, war and the moral intricacies of relations among states. Readers are bound to look for self-justification in his chapters on Nixonian diplomacy; and here, especially, they will have to look to other sources for balance. But for a statesman, Kissinger writes with remarkable range, dispassion and objectivity. In this vocation he is a European scholar in the best sense. One critic has compared his dual talents as writer and politician to those of Winston Churchill—and the comparison is apt. This book, like Churchill's *Second World War*, should have a long life as a standard account, to be consulted and quoted routinely by students and historians.

One of Kissinger's shrewdest narratives is his account of Franklin Roosevelt's effort to bring the United States to the aid of Britain after 1939, despite the formal American commitment to neutrality. Roosevelt, it seems clear, was Kissinger's most admired American model, the one leader who could combine European guile with American high-mindedness: "Roosevelt's methods," writes Kissinger, "were complex—elevated in their statement of objectives, devious in tactic, explicit in defining issues, and less than frank in explaining the intricacies of particular events. Many of Roosevelt's actions were on the fringes of constitutionality. No contemporary president could resort to Roosevelt's methods and remain in office." Richard Nixon (one might add) was proof of that; or perhaps it was just that Nixon lacked both Roosevelt's good cause and his charms in selling it. What's more, Nixon's closest aide may be more skilled as historian than diplomat, where his gift for intrigue and his enjoyment of power too often triumphed over his good judgment.

At the end Kissinger can see few signposts in the chaotic post-Cold War world. He hopes America has learned to temper its idealism with his own hard realism. He suggests that the U.S. should not count too much on Russian good intentions; that it should maintain its solidarity with Western Europe; and that it should not rush into conflicts everywhere.

He recognizes that American cannot remake the world in its image, and concludes with the words of a Spanish proverb: "Traveller, there are no roads. Roads are made by walking." As a guide for presidents, Henry Kissinger seems finally to have come to the end of his journey. But if words can save, *Diplomacy* may at last have earned him a controverted ticket to heaven.

Chrétien: The Outsider Who Came into the Fold

(*The Globe and Mail*, November 11, 1995)

Chrétien, Volume One: The Will to Win
Lawrence Martin (Lester Publishing)

As Canadians reflect on Quebec's fatal split down the middle, Jean Chrétien's role in bringing us to this pass becomes a subject for intense and necessary scrutiny. Lawrence Martin's timely biography—which carries the Prime Minister's life, in this first volume, just to the point of achieving the Liberal leadership in 1990—is an indispensable source for that inquiry.

Chrétien: The Will to Win is a scrupulous and thorough journalist's biography of a political life-in-progress, based primarily on widespread interviews, rather than on the documentary record. The author acknowledges the example of John Sawatsky's *Mulroney: The Politics of Ambition* (1991), and Martin's work matches the earlier one in its convincing portrait of an outsider driven by relentless ambition to the centre of Canadian political power. But

Martin has an advantage: He had generous access to the subject himself, while Sawatsky did not. The contrast is stark. If Brian Mulroney's quest revealed a desire to obscure his purposes and baffle his audiences, Chrétien has always been open and naive about his objectives. As Martin writes: "The Chrétiens are direct people. When they talk to you, their eyes don't shift." However the achievements of Mulroney and Chrétien may compare, there isn't much doubt that Chrétien will win the historical popularity contest. That doesn't mean he can save the country he believes in.

Martin makes it clear that Jean Chrétien always had a sense of his ideal country. It was a sense gained through inheritance and feeling rather than reflection and analysis. His family were Quebec *rouges*, believing in Wilfrid Laurier's transcontinental, French and English nation living in creative union. For Chrétien, accession to Pierre Trudeau's bilingual and bicultural federation came naturally. His mother's parents emigrated to Alberta, and in his childhood Jean heard stories of vast western landscapes beyond the borders of his native province. Those family stories eventually blossomed into his Rockies speech, claiming all of Canada as Quebeckers' shared inheritance.

Until he came to Ottawa in 1963, however, Chrétien's experience of Canada outside Quebec was slight. He was the rebellious product of a tough industrial town and a church-imposed classical education, more interested in baseball and the Kennedys than in English-speaking Canada or the English language. His politics was learned in the rough-and-tumble of Duplessiste authoritarianism. While he rejected the Union Nationale's isolation from Canada, he absorbed its political techniques in his bones. His own local machine in La Maurice adopted many of the habits of the old Quebec, and was still practicing them (as Martin reveals) in the 1970s.

Jean was "a leathery and rugged kid," short-tempered and competitive, a street brawler who always wanted to take charge; but he was never noted for his ideas. When he entered Parliament, Martin recalls, he was an instinctive federalist, a fiscal conservative, and a liberal on social policy. But he lacked specific policy goals, or patience for detail. He had already shown his talent for speaking as a populist while at the same time cultivating his ties with the local Shawinigan elite, and in Ottawa he did the same. His ambition made him serious. "He was hungry," Martin writes, "for knowledge, for power, for prestige, and though it was something he might not want to acknowledge, for wealth."

His goal was to spend ten years in politics, to become the first French-speaking minister of finance, and then to retire to a Quebec City judgeship. But his zeal for power and his hyperactivity kept him in Ottawa much longer than that. Chrétien's "devouring ambition" made him a faithful apprentice to his political patrons—first L.B. Pearson, then Mitchell Sharp, then Pierre Trudeau. They soon recognized his rough-hewn popular appeal, especially in English-speaking Canada where he played to affectionate, old-fashioned stereotypes of the Quebec backwoodsman. But as early as 1967, that caricatured role and his dogmatic opposition to the independence movement had begun to alienate him from the Quebec mainstream.

Lawrence Martin gives us colourful background on the Chrétien family, Quebec constituency politics, Chrétien's long but mixed ministerial record under Pierre Trudeau, his deepening antagonism to Quebec nationalism, and his bitter sense of betrayal at losing the 1984 leadership to his rival, John Turner. Chrétien's political talent seemed to centre on his skill in negotiation, his common-sense judgment, and his popular appeal as a sentimental Canadian patriot. By the mid-eighties—when he withdrew from politics to rearm—he had established his reputation as "the faithful soldier" rather than as a leader of proved vision or great accomplishment.

Martin sums up the man as he stood at the brink of power in 1990. He had shown the toughness to endure, and he had broad appeal as the spokesman of the Liberal centre. Yet "he was not an articulate or profound man; he had a terrible impatience for detail; and he showed few signs of being able to understand, as perhaps the greatest of leaders must, the great currents of change, both the dismal and the grand, sweeping the world around him."

After October 30, 1995, those limitations must put Jean Chrétien's capacity to lead the country more bleakly into question. Is he, like Pierre Trudeau and Brian Mulroney before him, English-speaking Canada's latest false prophet from Quebec (but this time, the last one)? Lawrence Martin's graceful book should help us to answer that question—though perhaps not soon enough.

Frum Fights the Foe

(*Toronto Star*, January 26, 2003)

The Right Man: The Surprise Presidency of George W. Bush
David Frum (Random House)

Toronto journalist David Frum has a neat way with words. His polemical talent carried him to Washington a few years ago as a leading advocate for the new right; and on George Bush's accession in 2001, the Canadian catapulted into the White House as "special assistant to the president for economic speechwriting." The job gave him occasional access to the Oval Office when the president's speeches came under discussion—and a lot of free time. "Being a White House speechwriter," he admits, "is a lot like being a fireman, without the heroics: Much of your time is spent waiting around in case you are needed." Even when he was needed, most of his words disappeared on the cutting room floor. But not that infamous phrase, "axis of evil," and a few short paragraphs to back it up in last year's State of the Union address.

The speechwriting job, as the author makes clear, was pretty low on the White House totem pole. Frum seems to have had no access to most of the presidential staff, to members of cabinet or the National Security Council. There is no evidence in this book that Frum ever spoke to Colin Powell, Donald Rumsfeld, Condaleeza Rice, or Dick Cheney (or any of their staffs) unless he brushed past them accidentally in the hallways. As an insider, Frum was pretty much an outsider. He relished the few perks like a White House parking space, some rides on Air Force One and a pass to the White House cafeteria, but had to endure an uncomfortable workspace in the Old Executive Office Building.

Frum lasted in the job for a little over a year, and has now provided us with his reflections on the Bush presidency in a time of world crisis. But don't look for profound argument and analysis here: David Frum knew much less about what was going on around him than any experienced White House correspondent.

The early chapters, written in a "Gee whiz, I'm in the White House" tone, give us shallow second-hand gossip and speculation about a presidency that lacked vision and soon bogged down in confusion and compromise. There is nothing in them about the substance of policy. Frum tells us that all the president's staff are exceptionally nice guys who go to daily bible class and never swear or put down the opposition. And all of them love the president. The author repeats the suggestion of a friend that George Bush's self-discipline is the result of personal victory over his "drinking problem," and guesses that Bush's policy advisor Karen Hughes gained her influence over the president because she gave him "the unqualified admiration his mother never did." For the rest, we can learn more from the newspapers.

The Right Man would be forgettable if September 11 had never happened. Because it did happen, David Frum has some significant—and frightening—things to say about the character and policies of George W. Bush. Those terrible events, he argues, brought clarity and vision to the White House—and the greatest reversal of American foreign policy in thirty-five years. After 9/11 there would be no more appeasement, no more compromise, no more treatment of terror as a crime or an irritant. With those atrocities, President Bush decided belatedly that the United States was at war, "not merely [with] the terrorists who committed them, but also the governments that aided, abetted, financed, and shielded terrorism."

For David Frum, this means that the president now shares his own conviction that extremist Islam has been waging war against the United States for decades. Frum doesn't quite credit himself with George Bush's conversion to reality, but comes close enough by claiming that he gave Bush the essential words he needed, and the courageous president then "followed where his words led."

Frum links every terror attack on Americans since 1968 in a seamless web that leads us straight to today's preparation for preventive war against Saddam Hussein—and beyond. Syria, Iran, the Palestinian Authority, Saudi Arabia, Iraq: all of them together form "the epicenter of world terrorism." Don't bother about fine distinctions or evidence: take his word that they all hate America out of resentment, envy and failure. Now the whole region must suffer upheaval at the command of a new and righteous crusader-in-chief in the White House, a determined and persistent man whose strength will be applied "without remorse."

Frum insists that George Bush has big plans. He is about to lead the world into "an ambitious campaign to undo and re-create the repressive and intolerant Middle East status quo." Afghanistan was Bush's first victory. "The others," Frum assures us, "will follow each in its turn." Then (if America succeeds) there will be freedom and stability in the region—"and new prosperity [for] us all, by securing the world's largest pool of oil." And if America bungles it . . . well, let's not think about that.

David Frum describes himself simply as a conservative. He reveals himself in *The Right Man* as a dogmatic American triumphalist. If Frum's depiction of George Bush is as accurate as events suggest, then the president is leading us on a frightful journey. Pride is bound to have its fall, but who will go down with it, in pain and endless grief?

The Sage

(*Toronto Star*, October 12, 2003)

The Player: The Life and Times of Dalton Camp
Geoffrey Stevens (Key Porter Books)

In August of 1948, a bright young man from Woodstock, New Brunswick attended his first national political convention in Ottawa. Dalton Camp was a tentative Liberal, observing the managed succession in the governing party from Prime Minister Mackenzie King to Louis St. Laurent—just as, today, some sceptical young Liberal outside from outer Canada may be preparing a trip to another coronation in Ottawa.

The young man of 1948 came home feeling disillusioned and suffocated. The Liberal party, he believed, was stagnant, complacent, indifferent to new faces and ideas. A year later, after nourishment at the London School of Economics, Camp found himself briefly employed as secretary of the New Brunswick Progressive Conservative party—until it went broke and closed its offices. From there he went on to a remarkable career in advertising, political management and journalism which broke new ground wherever he turned. When he died last year at the age of eighty-one, he was revered as the virtual creator of modern political campaigns in Canada, a democrat who reformed the party system, a brilliant political journalist, and a decent man of rare and gentle grace.

If that sceptical young Liberal attending this year's leadership convention chooses a path of similar independence, he will have a model of unusual quality to emulate. (He will also face challenges just as daunting as those confronting Camp when he set out to rebuild the Progressive Conservative party in the early 1950s.)

Geoffrey Stevens' new biography of Dalton Camp is a warm and sympathetic account of a fascinating Canadian life. Stevens does not hide admiration for his subject, and the pleasure he takes in the story is infectious. The author's comfortable and elegant prose gives us an authentic portrait of a complex man.

As Stevens shows, Camp always protected his privacy. His career (and his ambition) made him a public man—a celebrity, even—but he had no great interest in that side of politics. He did not need the pretensions of fame. He relished political life as an intellectually challenging game, a conflict for fairness and decency, and a realm of friendship and loyalty. Beyond all that, he needed constant withdrawal to refuel and reflect, to broaden his ideas, to confront his moods, to live his own life away from the limelight. His private life was never as controlled and reasoned as his public life, and often, in his later years, it fell into disorder. But even the worst spells of depression and disarray were relieved by his philosophic spirit, his wry humor, and his enduring friendships.

Stevens identifies Camp as an American Canadian and a Red Tory. His father, Harold Brainard Camp, was a film projectionist in Woodstock who received a call to the ministry, studied divinity at Acadia University, and led Baptist congregations in New Haven, Connecticut and Oakland, California. For seven years Dalton soaked up the mood of 1930s California while his father's fame as a revivalist preacher and pacifist blossomed. In 1937, Harold Camp died suddenly. The destitute family returned to Woodstock. But the son's appreciation for America—for baseball, basketball and football, for American openness and generosity, for American politics—never left him. That grounding gave Camp an uncommon ability to comment on the strengths and absurdities of American life without any hint of envy or malice.

In the late 1940s, Camp took a year of postgraduate journalism at Columbia University, and spent another year in Labour party Britain under the guidance of Harold Laski at the London School of Economics. When Camp returned to Canada in his late twenties, his political views were fully formed. He believed in civil debate, competitive politics, and progressive reform. He said later that he was a Red Tory in the same sense that Winston Churchill was a Red Tory: "I'm in favour of people, and I'm in favour of trying to alleviate the problems people have, and I think that's one of the functions of government, and I just don't want to see us abandon that role."

For fifty years Camp honored those convictions, ending his life in full cry against the neo-conservatives who had kidnapped his party and brought the Common Sense Revolution to Ontario in the 1990s.

In those fifty years Camp had three careers, and missed having one more. As an advertising man in the 1950s, he began to run provincial Conservative party election campaigns, gradually rebuilding the party in the Maritimes and eventually extending his skills westwards to Manitoba. He engineered provincial electoral victories in New Brunswick, Nova Scotia, Manitoba, and Prince Edward Island, and in 1957 he provided the advertising genius behind John Diefenbaker's surprising triumph in federal politics. Although Diefenbaker took personal credit for his own successes in 1957 and 1958, he could not have done it without Dalton Camp at work behind the scenes.

In the 1960s, as the Diefenbaker government imploded and collapsed, Camp stepped forward to hold the party together. In 1964 he accepted a two-year term as party president, hoping to contain the bitter internal divisions created by the leader and to oversee the transition to a new one. But Diefenbaker's intransigence made that impossible, so in the spring of 1966 Camp set out to persuade the party to review and change its leadership. He achieved his goal at a tumultuous party meeting in November, 1966—there would be a fresh leadership convention in the following year.

Stevens makes the events of 1966–1967 the heart of his book, as they were, undoubtedly, the dramatic high point of Dalton Camp's life. As the party prepared for the leadership convention, Camp sought to recruit two provincial premiers, Duff Roblin of Manitoba and Robert Stanfield of Nova Scotia, as candidates for the succession. Both initially refused his entreaties.

As a fallback alternative in the event that Diefenbaker chose to run to succeed himself, Camp and a team of loyal supporters prepared for Camp's own entry into the race. On the very eve of an announcement of Camp's candidacy, Stanfield reversed his decision and put himself into the contest. Camp suppressed his disappointment, declared for Stanfield, organized his campaign and wrote his nomination speech. Stanfield won the leadership, and then felt forced to shun his friend and organizer in order to appease Diefenbaker's vengeful loyalists in the parliamentary caucus. Camp withdrew from federal politics, his ambitions frustrated.

Stevens briefly speculates on the might-have-beens, but does not labour the point. Could Camp have won the leadership? Could he have become prime minister? Or would he have taken Stanfield's place as the best prime minister Canada never had?

Probably none of these things. The divided party would never have accepted Camp as leader, and the country would never have chosen his tattered party to govern. (Diefenbaker was still around to vilify him.) But even if he had won an election, Camp, the loner, would have hated the job of prime minister and fled from it before it consumed him. Stanfield saved him from greater misfortune—and Camp must have known it.

Aside from brief excursions to Ottawa to manage Stanfield's failed election campaigns of 1972 and 1974, to Toronto for Ontario elections and a couple of major provincial commissions, and a wasted interlude as chief political advisor to Prime Minister Brian Mulroney in 1986-1989, Camp lived after the 1960s in rural New Brunswick.

But his life was not over. He became the country's leading political commentator and columnist, writing for the *Toronto Star* and its national syndicate for twenty years.

He was also part of a broadcasting gem—an entertaining weekly political debate, with Eric Kierans and Stephen Lewis as sparring partners, that aired for a decade on CBC Radio's *Morningside*. At age seventy-two he became the oldest Canadian to have a successful heart transplant. He lived a vigorous life for nine years more, until his last few months of failing health in 2001–2002.

Camp was the most influential unelected politician the country ever had. As his son David said at his celebratory funeral: "He challenged the accepted wisdom of the moment, challenged you to think again, to not lose sight of common sense and common decency, while he infuriated and tormented those wrongheaded, hardhearted people so determined to make Canada into something alien to his heart."

Stevens' admirable biography shows that Dalton Camp's hearts were in the right place.

Chrétien: Tough Guy to the End

(*Toronto Star*, November 9, 2003)

Iron Man: The Defiant Reign of Jean Chrétien, Volume Two
Lawrence Martin (Viking Canada)

The first half of Lawrence Martin's engaging two-part biography, which appeared in the dark days just after the near-loss of the Quebec independence referendum of 1995, was a revealing portrait of Jean Chrétien up to his accession to the party leadership in 1990.

Martin's *The Will to Win* brought the Shawinigan tough guy vividly to life as "a leathery, rugged kid," an outsider eager for knowledge, prestige and power, one who had learned his politics in the brawling school of Duplessiste Quebec.

He arrived in Ottawa as a young Liberal MP in 1963, eager to be coached and guided by Mike Pearson, Mitchell Sharp and Pierre Trudeau. They saw in him the valuable instincts of a populist—and soon, a defender of Canada against the growing dangers of the Quebec independence movement. He was in politics for the long haul. By 1990 he was a veteran of ten ministerial offices (though still rough-hewn), now deeply resentful after rejection as leader of the party in 1984 in favour of his rival John Turner.

Martin's new book takes up the tale from there. He uses the same journalist's techniques of close observation and widespread interviews, and from those sources he tells the story of a stubborn and not very complex politician.

Martin's prose has a street-smart edge that often echoes the manner (though not the grammar) of his subject: Chrétien is described variously as "this floor-scrubber," a "broken-down Chevy," "a brawler," "a sore winner," "mule-headed," "shockingly cynical," and "a schoolyard bully." Sometimes, Chrétien deserves the insults. But he was also a prudent, thoughtful and unostentatious man who kept his head while others were losing theirs.

In 1990 the Liberal party gave Chrétien the leadership without great enthusiasm, and in 1993 the country gave him the prime ministership, in the same doubting mood. His garbled language and lack of grand vision brought with them low public expectations. The country hoped for a quiet interlude after the turbulence of the Mulroney years, and Chrétien was happy to offer it.

He had few ideas and no great plans—whether constitutional reform, social programs or foreign initiatives. He would simply enjoy power and ride out the tides. The shattered opposition parties that emerged from the 1993 election allowed him that privilege.

Perhaps because Chrétien was by then fully-formed and unchanging, the early chapters of *Iron Man* have a flavour of routine about them—as though Martin had grown weary of the man, if not the task. How long, after all—unless you're a political junkie or a pure flack—can you maintain intense interest in someone who says only that "politics, for me, it's a sport . . . it's scoring points. It is winning seats and winning votes," and nothing more. (This makes for special dullness if there's no real threat from any political opponents, as was the case in the general elections of 1993, 1997 and 2000.)

When Martin recounts the early years of Chrétien in power, he skims the issues without much context, detail or sense of engagement. His account comes to life, by contrast, whenever he deals with the incendiary political genius of Lucien Bouchard (the subject of an earlier Martin biography).

Bouchard really made his challenge toward the end of the 1995 Quebec referendum campaign, when he displaced Jacques Parizeau as leader of the secessionist forces and almost succeeded in breaking up the country. From this point (about a third of the way into the book), Martin's story takes off.

Chrétien, the counterpuncher, had been hit hard and was deeply wounded. Now he would fight back with all his will in a struggle that really mattered. "You know, at fifty (per cent) plus one," he told Martin, "I was not about to let go the country. . . . You don't break your country because one guy forgets his glasses at home."

Chrétien's recovery from that near-disaster took several years. It was risky but patiently calculated, with aid—from his new intergovernmental affairs minister Stéphane Dion, from the Supreme Court, and from the Reform party, which backed him in passage of legislation giving Parliament a key role in any subsequent decision on provincial secession. Quebec would never again have the choice it exercised in 1995. In the end the hare was overtaken by the tortoise, and in 2001, Bouchard retired as premier of Quebec. The long sovereignty campaign had failed, and Jean Chrétien was the architect of its defeat.

By that time the prime minister was also in full combat with his other political challenger, his own finance minister Paul Martin Jr. Martin was the hero of the government's successful battle to wipe out the huge annual deficit, a man of ideas and the obvious heir apparent. Chrétien intended to deny him his reward, or at least to withhold it as long as possible. This was a grudge battle revealing Chrétien at his worst (and Martin not always at his best). Martin the author recounts the sordid story with a master's skill.

Paul Martin, it appears, won the war last year, when he left the cabinet and effectively forced Chrétien to announce his retirement. The coronation takes place this week.

But the aging lion is not yet dead. Every day the old brawler has been teasing us with mischievous hints about the uncertain date of his departure. When Martin embraces his predecessor on the convention platform this week, he will have to look out for the knife.

How should we judge the long political career of Jean Chrétien? Until the archives reveal the full documentary record, it is well chronicled in Martin's fine biography. There was nothing much that was noble in the prime minister's public behaviour.

Chrétien's record of indifference to scandal, inefficiency and mismanagement in his government was monumental. His neglect of the armed forces was irresponsible. He had a thuggish presence when under attack. He never admitted error. He fought one election too many and was finally described in his own caucus as "a bully, a dictator, a man so power-hungry that he was placing his own welfare ahead of everything else."

Yet he calmed us all down. He had the wisdom to corral separatism and the deficit. He believed resolutely in the humane use of state power when others preferred to trash it. In his final few months of decaying authority he ratified the Kyoto treaty, reformed electoral financing, reinvested in health care, defended the Charter of Rights and calmly defied the criminal adventurism of the Bush administration in Iraq.

Martin deftly summarizes this mixed record: "He'd been covered from head to toe in abuse since his earliest days, but it only served to harden his resolve. He'd weathered it, and if further evidence was needed to show that he was one of the toughest men ever to occupy the Prime Minister's Office, it came when his own Liberal family 'showered him in shit,' as a friend of his indelicately put it, ordering him to leave. Chrétien defiantly stood his ground, doing more in his final year and a half than in the several shameful seasons that preceded it."

The man's stubborn human faults were also his virtues. But it is time, past time, to say goodbye to a tough guy who delivered the goods.

Frum and Perle Save the World

(*Toronto Star*, February 2, 2004)

An End to Evil: How to Win the War on Terror
David Frum and Richard Perle (Random House)

Since 9/11, no one has beaten the drums of war more insistently than our man in Washington, David Frum. In January 2002, as a lowly presidential speechwriter, he took credit for George Bush's warning that the world confronted an "axis of evil." In January 2003, as the President prepared to invade the first country on that list, Frum laid out America's case for war in his book *The Right Man*.

And now—on cue for the 2004 presidential election campaign—Frum joins with his fellow hard-liner Richard Perle to stiffen everyone's backs for more war. A few days after publication, the President thoughtfully added his own claim in the State of the Union address that it would not be a good thing to throw him out of office in the midst of battle.

Observers may be tempted to wonder, innocently, who is calling the shots here. In *The Right Man,* Frum modestly admitted that the President was wise enough to take his advice; others have pointed to the usual suspects in the office of Defense Secretary Donald Rumsfeld, where Richard Perle himself serves as a member and former chairman of the Defense Policy Board.

But to avoid any possible misunderstanding, Frum and Perle insist in their new book that the "war on terror" is not the result of a "neoconservative cabal in the halls of power in Washington." Instead, they put us right about this canard: it is an expression of "liberal opinion's persistent and pervasive disdain for President Bush." Dubya's critics just cannot accept "that it was the president's determination that was pushing the war forward. Somebody else *had* to be responsible. Hence, the myth of the neoconservative cabal." Good to have that cleared up.

But there are two curious blurbs on the cover of *An End to Evil*. One says: "A not completely crazy case can be made that the most influential thinker in the foreign-policy apparatus of . . . George W. Bush during its first two years was . . . a forty-two-year-old Canadian named David Frum." The other says that Richard Perle, "the intellectual guru of the hard-line neoconservative movement in foreign policy . . . has profound influence over Bush policies and officials. . . . " I suppose that—despite their disclaimers—we'll never know for certain whether Frum and Perle believe their own publicity.

Now, back to the main and deadly business. According to the book, the United States is in a war against evil, and must set its own rules to fight it. In a sweeping survey of America's plight after September 11, the authors aim to reinvigorate the President and the American electorate for the continuing struggle. (Unfortunately, in the authors' eyes, both Bush and the voters show signs of flagging zeal.) Everyone should remember that "we are the terrorists' first target, so this war is first and foremost our war. We are fighting on behalf of the civilized world. We will never cease to hope for the civilized world's support. But if it is lacking, as it may be, then we have to say, like the gallant lonely British soldier in David Low's famous cartoon of 1940: 'Very well, alone.'"

The tone is one of injured righteousness. September 11 showed that the world faces an implacable enemy in militant and terrorist Islam, its fanaticism turned outwards in resentment against the free and prosperous nations of the west—chiefly the United States and Israel. Militant Islam is beyond redemption and beyond appeasement; it is "an aggressive ideology of world domination," willing "to commit murder on a horrific scale." It must be driven out of existence. "There is no middle way for Americans," these Jeremiahs tell us: "It is victory or holocaust. This book is a manual for victory."

The first stage of the "war on terror," in Afghanistan, was accomplished quickly. The next, in Iraq, was more difficult, because critics at home and abroad could not see the connection. But (the authors tell us) Saddam Hussein was a lingering nuisance; ignoring him would show that America was a paper tiger. Iraq's links with al-Qaeda and with weapons of mass destruction were really an irrelevance. The war was above all a matter of symbolism.

"By clutching Saddam Hussein's regime by the throat and throwing it against the wall, the United States demonstrated... that it was overwhelmingly strong, that the terrorists' hopes of somehow toppling the American government were delusions, and that attacks upon the United States would bring nothing but destruction on the attackers." (Not many hints here that the war goes badly in Baghdad.)

Once into America's "war on terrorism," Frum and Perle see no way out short of total victory or apocalyptic defeat. They try to be comprehensive in laying out the campaigns to come—and the schedule is long.

Some of the battles will be fought at home. Immigration rules must be tightened and enforced, biometric identity cards must be issued, bogus charities must be closed, American Muslims must accept and promote American ideals. The authors perhaps underemphasize the dangers such bureaucratic sternness poses for a free society. Weighed in the balance (they might say), what are a few lives tossed away to Syrian torturers or a few hundred "enemy combatants" languishing without rights in the sun at Guantanamo Bay?

Abroad, what Frum and Perle propose could be the agenda for a Hundred Years' War. Terrorists everywhere must be denied money and refuge, hunted down and destroyed—sometimes by preventive war against the states that harbor them. Iran and North Korea both present "intolerable threats" to the U.S. and must be confronted at once. The Syrian, Libyan and Saudi Arabian regimes, all sponsors of terror, must be suppressed. Evil forces lurking in dark places like Lebanon, Palestine, Pakistan, Venezuela, Paraguay, Brazil, the Philippines, Indonesia, Sudan, Nigeria, Yemen, Somalia, and Sierra Leone require hard but varying responses, from radical intervention to political management. Whew!

But the revolution can't stop there. The French, the Chinese, the Russians must always be treated with suspicion. The UN must endorse America's inherent right to wage pre-emptive war, or the U.S. must discard it. The FBI, the CIA and State Department must be transformed into fighting institutions. A new American paramilitary force must be created. Above all there must be "a reform of the spirit" in America—which sounds suspiciously like a call to silence dissent, since according to the rules of war all enemies are outlaws, and dissenters can be subversive.

The struggle to "end evil" we are offered here looks so permanent, the diagnosis so obscure, the means so uncertain, that George Bush will be long dead of natural causes before the day of deliverance finally arrives. Perhaps the non-existent neoconservative cabal should lower its sights to match Bush's flagging zeal.

Stand on Guard, but for Whom?

(*Toronto Star*, February 25, 2007)

Whose War Is It? How Canada Can Survive in the Post-9/11 World
J.L. Granatstein (HarperCollins)

In the preface to his new book, the prolific historian Jack Granatstein reflects that he is now old enough "to begin reflecting on the big picture." As his title suggests, "the big picture" is that Canada is engaged in "a war against terror that will affect us even as Canadians hope in vain that it will not." Within that broad (and contentious) frame, Granatstein looks at six issues bedevilling the country's foreign and defence policies—and offers his pungent views on how to confront them all.

The book ranges widely. Granatstein opens and closes with a bit of twice-imagined fantasy—a catastrophic earthquake on the west coast and simultaneous terror attacks in Montreal and Toronto. On first telling, the Canadian military response (using current equipment and personnel) is pathetic. Thousands die, panic sweeps the country and a hostile American administration reacts by closing the border and devastating the Canadian economy. On second telling (assuming that Ottawa quickly adopts the remedies he proposes), Canadian politicians and the military respond magnificently, the crisis is contained and the Americans are impressed. Bold leadership triumphs.

Between these reveries, Granatstein beats the drum for some of his most familiar tunes. Canadians, he insists, are foolishly addicted to the myth of UN peacekeeping while neglecting the harder realities of military preparedness. They reject the thought of asserting national interests abroad, while romanticising the pursuit of "humane values" in foreign policy.

They are victims of a deadly (perhaps congenital) virus of anti-Americanism. They neglect the looming threats to Canadian sovereignty in the Arctic just as the melting icecap opens the Northwest Passage to international trade and tourism. Among the Québécois, a pervading pacifism inhibits any muscular assertion of a Canadian military role in the world.

Across the country, a heavily promoted policy of multiculturalism inhibits commitment among new Canadians to any shared core of beliefs and values. For more than a decade, the softheaded governments of Jean Chrétien and Paul Martin deprived the country of leadership and allowed its military to atrophy. For Granatstein, as for General Rick Hillier, the Chrétien/Martin era was Canada's "decade of darkness."

Meanwhile, the neighborhood has grown more dangerous: Western nations were plunged into a borderless "war on terror" against Islamic extremism, the United States took the lead in responding to terror and the Canadian military—through calculated political negligence—lost its ability to protect Canadian interests.

Granatstein writes as a hard-headed political realist, deriding those who promote "soft power" and "values" at the expense of interests. Lloyd Axworthy, Bill Graham and Jack Layton draw his particular scorn. As foreign minister, Axworthy's successful promotion of the anti-land mine treaty and the International Criminal Court, though faultless in principle, imprudently defied the will of the United States; in fact, "almost everything Axworthy has said and written since he left the government in 2000" has been "sharply anti-American."

For Granatstein, Axworthy's brand of anti-Americanism is the ultimate Canadian failing, since the country's prosperity and defence depend above all on the goodwill of American governments. The anti-American virus has turned us into moralizing fools.

On matters affecting American security (as judged through American eyes), the author's "realism" means that Canada must almost always embrace American foreign policies. The Chrétien government's decision to stand aside from the Iraq War was "deeply flawed," "confused" or "more likely, driven by its ministers' anti-Americanism and domestic political considerations." (No thought here about the inherent madness of the enterprise.)

The Martin government's refusal to join the Ballistic Missile Defence program was equally misguided. (But somewhat surprisingly, Granatstein concedes "we are not obliged to join the coming war with Iran"—although we may suffer for such waywardness. The Americans "might shout at us," but "they won't bomb Ottawa.")

By insisting, as a general rule, that America's wars must be our wars too, Granatstein leaves some yawning gaps in his "big picture." He never defines the "war on terror"—a war programmed instead for us by the Bush administration—nor raises questions about the best means of fighting it. The terrorist enemy remains for him an ominous and ghostly phantom, sometimes blending with the forces being confronted in Iraq and Afghanistan, sometimes lurking in the shadows closer to home.

Granatstein fails to imagine the possibility that Washington, in its pre-emptive spasms abroad, is engaged in a fatally misconceived and self-destructive adventure. Could it be that Canada's commitment to this particular cause contributes to our insecurity rather than to freedom, democracy and order in the world?

Granatstein doesn't ask whether there are better means of confronting global terror than Washington's Manichean rhetoric and brutal militarism. By now, even a majority of Americans and members of congress seem to think so. Canada's reasoned resistance could offer more benefits and fewer risks to our national interest than the author is willing to concede.

On the other hand, he makes an utterly convincing case for the comprehensive rebuilding of Canada's armed forces for both domestic and overseas use, and an equally effective case for the (primarily military) assertion of Canadian sovereignty in the Arctic. As the book reports approvingly, the new government of Stephen Harper has endorsed and begun to implement both these projects. Granatstein suggests that no other Canadian party can offer similar pledges—indeed, at times his sweeping survey can be read as a Conservative political manifesto on foreign and defence policy.

Granatstein's package of complaints and remedies doesn't always hold together. His extended reflections on the occasional stridency of anti-American expression in Canada, the persistence of a pacifist streak in Quebec rhetoric and the dangers of a multicultural dilution of Canadian identity seem more like echoes of bygone attitudes than useful guidelines for the coming decades. These domestic sermons recall a country we will never see again. His explicit endorsement of the "war on terror" seems more like a convenient means of justifying an enhanced Canadian military than a fully examined vindication of George Bush's War.

And when Granatstein endorses Harper's strong-armed leadership, we should be cautious about the ideological blinkers that may come with it.

Canada's Man

(*Toronto Star*, September 30, 2007)

John A.: The Man Who Made Us
Richard Gwyn (Random House Canada)

This is the season for prime ministers. Only days ago Brian Mulroney launched the massive story of his political life, and in a few weeks Jean Chrétien will have his turn, each of them burnishing his record and flaying his enemies. In a sense they are still in the political battle—if not for the future of their country, then, at least, for their places in the Canadian pantheon. The scars and resentments of the struggle still show.

As we catch our breath between rounds of this heavyweight slugfest, Richard Gwyn offers pleasurable relief with the first volume of his new biography of Canada's first prime minister, John A. Macdonald. No need for disputation and putdown here: Macdonald's reputation is established and cannot be shaken—and Gwyn does not try to diminish it.

More than fifty years have passed since publication of Donald Creighton's eloquent two-volume life of Macdonald, *The Young Chieftain* and *The Old Politician*. In the Canadian tradition of neglecting the country's past, Creighton's great effort—which Richard Gwyn describes as "magisterial and encyclopedic"—might seem to be enough. But as he reminds us, there can never be a definitive biography: "times move on, new evidence emerges, attitudes and assumptions change and open doors . . . to new interpretations of old givens."

When Donald Creighton wrote in the early fifties, the country was just beginning to play an independent role in the wider world, and needed to establish its firm footing and confident perspective for that task. This required a detailed and mature sense of the past, as Creighton and the historians of his generation understood. With his vivid depiction of Macdonald's wily and pragmatic boldness, Creighton helped to establish the nation's self-assurance at mid-century, and to make Macdonald the icon of that confidence in ourselves.

In his new biography, Richard Gwyn seems to have a dual—or perhaps a triple—purpose in mind. One is to remind more recent generations, unschooled in national history, of the country's origins and founding attitudes: "Our history, as we know perfectly well, lacks the drama of revolutions and civil wars, of kings and queens losing their heads. But it is our history. It is us.

It's where we came from and, in far larger part than often is recognized, it is why we are the way we are now. . . . Moreover, as was always Macdonald's core conviction, human nature itself changes little." As much as the country has grown and changed, Gwyn tells us that we remain the same. The past offers grounding and compass bearings for the future.

Gwyn's second purpose is to sketch an admiring portrait of a politician in his times, to celebrate Macdonald's political skills and human warmth and expansive generosity of vision. These are rare qualities worth recalling and emulating. And finally (whether entirely consciously or not), Gwyn's further purpose shines through these pages too. The book is his hymn of praise to what he sees as a miraculous country: miraculous in its peacefulness, its diversity, its tolerance, and its determined un-Americanness. Despite all the missteps and diversions in the nation's history since 1867, Richard Gwyn suggests that those positive national qualities can be traced back unmistakeably to its first leader. That is the personal and contemporary insight that distinguishes this biography from the mid-twentieth century scholarship of Donald Creighton.

John A.: The Man Who Made Us traces the life of John A. Macdonald from his birth in Scotland in 1815 to his assumption of office as prime minister of the new Dominion of Canada on July 1, 1867. The book is not, like Creighton's *Young Politician*, a detailed, sometimes moment-to-moment account of personal and political life in the colonies of the two Canadas that eventually became Ontario and Quebec. Instead it is a genial broad-brush portrait. Gwyn offers faithful summaries of Macdonald's early life and the racial, sectarian and personal conflicts he confronted after entering politics in 1844, but does not dwell intensely upon them. This may have the effect of underrating the difficulty and sordidness of political life in the Canadian colonies at mid-century. But it allows Gwyn to give his attention to the ideas and instincts that moved John A.'s life in politics, and to emphasize the wider forces that turned Macdonald, finally, towards the great project of unifying all the British North American colonies.

John A. Macdonald was no ideologue. He was a practical politician who rarely framed his policies in grand, visionary language. Nevertheless he had a profound—though only slowly emerging—sense of his country's spirit and destiny, coupled with an unmatched instinct about political timing.

As Macdonald committed himself to a political life in Canada, he found three enduring themes: that his country and its institutions were (and should remain) British, but in a North American setting free of the class and national biases of the homeland; that as a union of English- and French-speaking citizens, the emerging nation must respect the interests of both communities; and that, in origin and essence, the country was un-American. These convictions gave Macdonald his direction in politics; and by 1867 they gave Canada its new life. Gwyn quietly but firmly reminds us that Canada is anti-American by definition. There is nothing extreme or unbalanced about that: it is our *raison d'etre*.

As Naomi Klein tells us, crises are the midwives of political change, whether for good or for evil. In the 1860s the Canadian colonies were in crisis. Politics in the Province of Canada were paralyzed by the double majority rule; Britain seemed ready to retreat from further duty as imperial protector in the colonies; and to the south, the United States flaunted its Manifest Destiny and looked northwards. John A. Macdonald, with the assistance of a few political colleagues, seized the moment by undertaking what Gwyn calls "an absurdly romantic project." They chose, as *The Times* of London said then, "to raise a barrier of law and moral force extending near three thousand miles between [themselves] and the most powerful and aggressive state in the New World."

Once the path was chosen in 1864 the way forward to Confederation seemed remarkably easy. "Macdonald," writes Gwyn, "hadn't so much created a nation as manipulated and seduced and connived and bullied it into existence against the wishes of most of its own citizens. . . . By whatever combination of deviousness and magic it took, he had done it. He had made Confederation out of scraps and patches and oddments of thread and string, many frayed and few fitting naturally, but at last it actually existed."

The harder work of weaving those scraps and patches together was about to begin. Richard Gwyn promises to tell us how Macdonald did it in his second volume, due in 2009.

A Patient Prophet Speaks

(*Literary Review of Canada,* January–February 2011)

Becoming Canada: Our Story, Our Politics, Our Future
Ken Dryden (McClelland & Stewart)

In the early years of Stephen Harper's rule, Ken Dryden's face—as he sat through daily question period in the House of Commons—revealed more than most of those around him. His expression ranged from distaste to disgust. As the days passed, he seemed less and less attracted to the mob scene that engulfed him. I wondered what was going on behind that living mask, and how long he could put up with Ottawa's demeaning game.

As a prominent MP and former candidate for his party leadership, Dryden has not been a frequent participant in parliamentary debate. In a recent exchange with Susan Delacourt of the *Toronto Star*, he said that "he decided about eight months ago to pull himself out of the political fray because he hated how he sounded to himself." Now, in *Becoming Canada*, he tells us about his recent political experience, and how he coped with it. While he writhed uncomfortably through question period, he was also thinking—and dreaming too, trying to understand the maelstrom in which he found himself. His new book is a kind of poetic diary of the Harper years, a reflection on the evolution of the world beyond Parliament Hill, and an urgent appeal to our better natures.

Ken Dryden is not a typical party politician, and *Becoming Canada* is not a partisan polemic. It is, he hopes, a contribution to a national conversation in which the country will recognize its mature character and live up to its possibilities. Politics, as he has experienced the game in Ottawa, has failed us, diminished us, reduced our horizons as a national community. He asks for more than that. Rather than a cautionary tale of the worst fates that may await the country (although he knows that the warnings are clear), in *Becoming Canada* Dryden offers us, more positively, what he calls an aspirational tale. The tale is quietly compelling—but in this book he can also be glib and sometimes confusing.

Before he arrives in Ottawa at chapter four, the author takes us on a meandering journey through "America" (not a real place, but the vision that has inspired Americans over generations), the disenchantments of Washington during President Obama's first year in office, and the failure of the Copenhagen summit on global warming in 2009. The purpose of the trip is not entirely clear, though it has something to do with hopes and disappointments, the new scale of our problems, and our inadequate responses to them. We have been prepared for a hard landing, and in Ottawa we get it.

Ottawa, in Ken Dryden's view, is a place where great things once happened. But today, one of the two governing parties "has been for many years out of synch with the times", while the other does not believe in doing anything unless there is "an overwhelming public clamour for action": and even then, it can "do small and spin big", so that "no one will know enough with sufficient certainty to have the confidence forcefully to oppose" it.

The four-chapter core of the book is as much about Liberal failure as it is about Stephen Harper's small-minded Conservative success. Beneath the country's occasional changes of government in the postwar period, Dryden sees a conventional pattern: periodic rounds of political refreshment followed by "cyclical fatigue". But by the time Jean Chrétien became prime minister in 1993, the Liberal party had already exhausted its creative inventory of ideas. That victory was, in a sense, undeserved. The Liberals won because the

Progressive Conservatives had splintered into three regional fragments, and then remained in power out of inertia and fiscal discipline through a further thirteen years. A party whose generous policies once expressed the spirit of the nation lost touch with its electorate, and came to enjoy its entitlements too much.

In 2006, if the Liberals had genuinely believed that Canada would be better off with a Liberal government, and if they had genuinely believed that child care, Kelowna, and Kyoto mattered, they wouldn't have fought among themselves and brought themselves down. If they had genuinely believed, they forgot.

When Stephen Harper reunited some of the Conservative fragments, Ken Dryden argues that Harper was acting on a profound grudge, bringing together voters who felt ignored, neglected and insulted by the Liberal party's use of power. That was Harper's Big Idea. Dryden appreciates the strength of this negative. There was no grand scheme beyond it. Stephen Harper had no larger vision of the country, and still lacks one; he despises visions. He wanted to throw out the Liberal party, and to reduce the national establishment of policy and institutions that it had created. Once in office, he understood that the key to retaining power was, simply, to hold on and gradually convince the public that Conservatives, by being there, deserve office while Liberals do not. He too could govern by guile and inertia. His object was to destroy the Liberal party and keep his non-Liberals in power. (And if that happens, paradoxically, because Liberal MPs have chosen to vote with the minority government in the last two parliaments, all the better for him.)

Ken Dryden is patient about Canada's political cycles. He accepts that popular opinion moves slowly and usually cannot be rushed. The Liberal party should not expect an easy or quick return to power: it has no entitlement. Instead, it must slowly rebuild its reputation and its program. But under the leadership of both Stéphane Dion and Michael Ignatieff, "that never happened."

Dryden sees Dion as "a person of purpose and substance" who could never adjust to the role of a critic in opposition. "Having to win over an audience he couldn't be sure of, he would speak faster, his voice pitching higher, making him look and sound like a little boy who couldn't get his way. With Dion sounding like someone who anyone would want to tune out, people tuned him out."(p. 95) When Ignatieff replaced Dion in the confusion after the fiscal update of November 2008, he too failed to adjust quickly to the party's new role; and in two years since then, Dryden remains unconvinced that the new leader has given the party any reason to believe in itself. Ignatieff has shown no consistency, and has allowed Stephen Harper to define the message for him: the Liberals are the tax and spend party.

The vapid game of politics, now exhausted of all content, continues in a House of Commons that has lost touch with the country. But beyond his party's routine ambition to ride the electoral cycle back into power, Ken Dryden is moved by deeper currents. While the parties play their tired games, he sees that the contest must change. The whole world is shaking.

> Islands disappearing under rising waters, the shorelines of great coastal cities pushed inland permanently, people pushed out—Hurricane Katrina was our cautionary tale. Imagine a hundred Katrinas. Imagine thousands and thousands of people unable to stay where they are and with nowhere to go. Imagine millions of people affecting hundreds of millions more, affecting billions more. It is not possible that we are powerless, that we cannot make a deal on climate change. It is not possible that we cannot overcome our politics, both international and national, and that we are unable to stop ourselves from heading down a path that can end only in one place. We are human beings. We evolved a capacity to think—to analyze, to understand, to act. By working together, we can survive. We can stop. And we refuse to let anyone make us believe it is impossible.

For half a century, Canada has lived "a safe, secure, prosperous life with our eyes closed, no matter what the state of our politics" (p. 181) because the country has been rich in resources and close to the United States. If our eyes remain closed, Canadians can go on enjoying our comforts for a while because "any foreseeable world of the future will need our resources, our peace, our stability, and our security."

But our expectations for ourselves have been too modest. Dryden sees more and more Canadians beyond the tight circle of the political class who now demand more from our politics. They no longer see Canada as the complacent suburb of the postwar years, pursuing its modest aims in the comforting shadow of America. Young and old, immigrant and home-grown, they see America in decline, mankind in distress, and this large nation without a compelling common story to inspire its action in the world.

The story, he is convinced, is already here to be proclaimed. It is not the old story of French-English and East-West that no longer reflects or excites us. It is no longer a story about emulating the American dream. We come from every country, we speak all languages, we have learned to live together in peace. We believe in both individual *and* collective rights. We have passed through an era of multiculturalism "to something else, to something new in the world."

> Newcomers to Canada are not only changed by Canada, they are changing Canada. They are making Canada into something it has

> never been. The dynamic of Canada is not one of groups existing and functioning separate and distinct from one another. It is not one group disappearing into another with little effect. The Canadian dynamic is far more interesting, far more challenging, and far more important. It is a blend, a mix, neither English, nor French, nor Italian, Chinese, or Indian, but something new. In an increasingly global world, Canada has become the world's first global culture. Canada has become a "multiculture."

Ken Dryden's last chapter is titled "Canada" just as his first was titled "America". Like the first, the last speaks of a land of the imagination, a country that exists only in the mind, where it can shape the future. He has chosen to make the audacious claim (or perhaps, more modestly, just to hint at it) that "Canada" offers a myth to itself and the world—and even to America—as powerful as "America" was in its time. He does not suggest that this "Canada" already exists in the country's neighbourhoods and classrooms (and certainly not in our politics), although the mixed population out of which it is being created clearly does. There are tensions and conflicts among us; but he insists that "although this multiculture existence can seem always to be on the edge of breaking down, it doesn't break down. We are not France; we are not Britain. . . . The difference can seem subtle; it is profound."

Dryden argues that the country should discard its modesty and accept that it can do great things. He knows that the problems of the world are complex, but insists that this complexity can be confronted with the simplicity of a powerful myth. It is time for his "Canada" of the imagination to become the Canada in which we live and act. He challenges us "to believe this, to see this, to be what we are."

His uplifting prose can leave us with good feelings. But where does it get us in our politics? Has he offered us a program? He would argue, of course, that the purpose of *Becoming Canada* is not to provide a program: first of all, there must be some unifying belief in ourselves out of which a program may grow. The need is to begin the conversation—and he has done that.

Once we have learned "to be what we are," what follows? There are enough hints in the book that Ken Dryden's program would be confident, generous, progressive, reformist, activist, both at home and abroad. But would his program somehow—as he seems to imply—be everyone's program? Would there be no rude and divisive debate about it in the House of Commons? Would it require no transformation of our parliamentary parties, no reform of our institutions, no revolution in our assumptions about oil sands policy, immigration and refugee policy, environmental policy, Afghanistan policy, the dilemmas of foreign investment, the deficit and the debt? There is nothing of any of these specifics in *Becoming Canada*.

It is one thing to share Ken Dryden's anxiety about the failure of Canada's political institutions, and to see encouraging signs in the kind of mixed community that the country has become. But it is not so clear that a freshly shared dream about the country can both invigorate and unite its citizens. Conrad Black, writing recently in his *National Post* column, also sees what he calls "Canada's immense potential as one of the world's very important countries." Black, though, would certainly produce a political program at fundamental odds with one produced by Dryden. Our shared beliefs about the nature of the country, in 2011, are unlikely to solve our complex problems. We will still have to go on, day by day, confronting (or postponing) one hard issue after another, provoking opponents, making compromises, doing the best we can in an unforgiving world.

In his book *A Fair Country*, John Ralston Saul recently invited Canadians to see the nation's past in a new and creative way. Now *Becoming Canada* offers a companion guide for living together in future. These works both disturb our complacency and anticipate a radical reshaping of the Canadian imagination. In the meantime, who will rid us of this dysfunctional parliament?

III / Polemics

Occasionally I have been moved to offer quick and emphatic judgments against the tide of impending events. "Reason and Democracy" and "Between Two Solitudes" appeared as editorials in The Canadian Forum. The comments on the Pepin-Robarts commission, the American way of war, the Governor General's powers, and advice for the new Harper government of 2006, appeared in the Globe and Mail, the Toronto Star, and the Ottawa Citizen. The lament on the eve of the invasion of Iraq was submitted to the Globe but not published. I confess that Jean Chrétien's apparent confusion and indecision before the war outsmarted me: I can see in retrospect that he was shrewdly, if awkwardly, telegraphing his opposition to Canadian participation in the war. When it began, Chrétien made his clear choice to reject a Canadian role and regained my respect. As the war began, "Music and war in Barcelona" was also declined by the Globe. Stephen Harper, after a brief bow towards openness and accountability as prime minister in 2006, ignored my early advice in the Globe—as he did again in 2008 when I counselled against a premature dissolution of parliament. My jeremiad against Michael Ignatieff is the text of talks in Toronto, Peterborough, Ottawa, and Montreal at book launches for my polemic Ignatieff's World.

Reason and Democracy

(*The Canadian Forum,* June–July 1977)

After six months, there can be no doubt, even among the most incredulous, that the victory of the Parti Québécois has broken the mold of the Canadian political system. Those Liberals who sought comfort in the piety that this was a government of reform and nothing more are now inclined to rage that it proved them wrong. They should show more restraint. (The wisest among them, like Claude Castonguay, have understood and patiently explained the meaning of the victory from the beginning or, like Robert Bourassa, have kept a seemly silence.) While Ottawa frets and fulminates, the Quebec government drops irritants on its flanks, consolidates its power with a conservative social and fiscal program, rallies its forces with the language bill, and rolls on toward the referendum with all the conviction of a liberating army. If it makes generous concessions to the English language minority in the course of debate on Bill One (as it should), it will strengthen rather than weaken its case for independence, by demonstrating its capacity for justice and magnanimity. If it does *not* do so, it may still strengthen the commitment to independence among the French-speaking community while risking the dangerous alienation of non-French-speaking Quebecers. The reality for other Canadians is that the debate over Quebec's future is engaged *within* Quebec, and that all contributions to that debate from the rest of the country (except perhaps the most extreme or the most subtle) are of no significance.

The sense of impotence which this realization creates for politicians has a double risk. For one thing, it drives them to desperate imprudence in the hope of proving their influence on events. Prime Minister Trudeau tells his audience in Saskatoon that the PQ needs their help to win its referendum (what it does need, as we all do, is their goodwill *afterwards*), and that they should therefore send the missionaries of separation rudely home when they come west to preach. How that will contribute to "national unity" remains obscure, since it seems to be a call for distrust and rejection. The federalist rationale for this kind of advice is a condescending theology familiar to Africans at the end of the European colonial period: the nationalist leaders of Quebec, according to this vision, are bad and unrepresentative, somehow placed in power by accident or deceit; they are to be reviled and isolated. The good citizens of Quebec, on the other hand, are to be flattered and pitied as helpless victims, and appealed to directly for their loyalty. The theology is as inappropriate in Quebec as it was in Ghana. National leaders are not undermined by denying their popular roots.

The second danger of impotence is that it tempts politicians to use the issue loosely for political gain in their own constituencies outside Quebec, in full knowledge that they are powerless to influence events within. Both William Davis and Stuart Smith have played the demagogue on this issue in the hope of arousing passionate support for their parties in Ontario; and there is strong pressure on Pierre Trudeau and the federal Liberals to do the same in a federal general election campaign. The public should reject such irresponsibility with contempt. If such demagoguery persists and finds a popular response, it will narrow the range of manoeuvre open to Canadian politicians when they finally come to the bargaining table with Quebec over constitutional change. They will find themselves prisoners of their own outdated rhetoric.

Such an impasse must be avoided. The task of responsible politicians, in the face of a fundamental democratic challenge to the stability of the country's constitution from Quebec, is to widen, not narrow, the opportunities for accommodation. They must do so not on the specious ground that they seek to protect Quebec from itself, but rather that they wish to serve the interests of the remainder of the country. While English-speaking Canada has not yet made the kind of explicit judgment that Quebec has in favour of major constitutional readjustment, there is growing evidence that the public does not reject that readjustment but welcomes the prospect. The polls indicate an overwhelming popular rejection of force as a means of confronting Quebec, and a strong willingness to discuss the proposal for continuing economic association after independence. In addition, the PQ victory seems to have stimulated a deep-set, latent political frustration in the regions of English-speaking Canada by its example, and opened minds to the possibility of a general rearrangement of the constitutional balance without limiting preconditions.

The country's politicians should recognize these new circumstances. To pretend that, somehow, the *status quo ante* can be restored is to engage in fantasy, and that kind of fantasy can lead to political disaster. The course of reason is not to deny reality, or to utter inflammatory and nihilist words about Canada's imminent breakup, destruction, disappearance, and the latest sin against humanity, but to enter calmly and confidently into the discussion of constitutional change in a genuine effort to satisfy the aspirations both of Quebec and the regions. By such acts Canada may finally, in the 1970s, take its destiny into its own hands.

Some persons in Ottawa and the provincial capitals recognize the need but balk at the means, hoping that the adventure can be safely managed by keeping the new institutions of change out of public hands. To attempt to do so would be self-defeating. Canada is a North American democracy, and it cannot produce a new constitution in the late twentieth century through discreet management by the mandarinate, political or bureaucratic. We have had enough evidence of failure in fifteen years of efforts to avoid the main issue and divert the independence movement through existing institutions—parliament, the federal parties, federal-provincial conferences, and a massive royal commission. The quest was misdirected but it was perhaps one that had to be followed to demonstrate its inadequacy. Now, with all its risks, the democratic path of constitution-making must be chosen, and chosen soon. Quebec has established the timetable. The rest of us must rise to the occasion.

The same issue of The Canadian Forum *contained a joint declaration, "Canada and Quebec: A Proposal for a New Constitution," signed by forty-seven Canadian writers and academics. Prime Minister Pierre Elliott Trudeau's response to the PQ election victory, later in 1977, was (among other actions) to create the Task Force on Canadian Unity under the dual chairmanship of Jean-Luc Pepin and John Robarts, which issued its report,* A Future Together, *in early 1979. That report is the subject of the following piece.*

An Ingenious Constitutional Package: Why the Proposals of the Pepin-Robarts Task Force on Canadian Unity Could Work

(*The Globe and Mail*, February 5, 1979)

The Report of the Pepin-Robarts Task Force is the most constructive and realistic initiative on the constitution to emerge from Ottawa in a decade. In spirit and substance, it offers the governments a unique chance (perhaps the last chance) to escape from an aimless and paralytic cycle and to begin constitutional bargaining on comprehensive terms that could, conceivably, produce agreement on a new constitution.

Like the Preliminary Report of the Bilingualism and Bicultural Commission, *A Future Together* is designed first to shock Canadians out of any complacency about the state of the federation. Fifteen years beyond that initial warning, Pepin-Robarts sees the country close to the point of disintegration.

Faced with this prospect the Task Force offers a mood, a set of principles, and a carefully related group of constitutional reforms as the means of averting the worst. In one sense, the Report is yet another defensive effort directed against the challenge of the Parti Québécois, telling Canada once again the sorts of things it must do to keep Quebec in. (That certainly was the initiating purpose that created the commission.) But to see the result only in this way would be grossly inadequate. For the Report has a larger vision; it perceives that constitutional change is being forced on the country from many sources; and above all, it is open enough to contemplate the possibility of Quebec's peaceful departure from the union on the Parti Québécois' terms if the Quebec public decides, "definitively and democratically," that the province should secede.

This democratic generosity, in turn, permeates the Task Force's approach to its own preferred proposals for accommodation. It does not want to see Quebec leave; but the recognition of Quebec's practical right to self-determination means both "the renunciation of the use of force to maintain the integrity of the Canadian state and a commitment to seek constructive political institutions which will reflect the will and aspirations of the citizens concerned." The vision of Pepin-Robarts does not permit the suppression of "the will and aspirations" of the Québécois (or any other Canadians); one way or another, the Report takes for granted that they will be satisfied.

The Trudeau government, of course, has always claimed that it, too, knows and respects Quebec's will and aspirations; but it does so as the defiant antagonist of the Parti Québécois' mandate, and it elevates those aspirations to a pan-Canadian forum. The Task Force instead discards federalist defiance of Quebec in a convincing effort to enter into the spirit of Quebec's blossoming; and it concludes that the Quebec people must gain their main satisfaction as citizens within the boundaries of the community in which they form a majority. This is something startlingly new from Ottawa in this decade.

The genius of the document is that the commissioners have absorbed discord and complaint, and discovered in them the germs of reconciliation. There was no consensus in the country on which they could build, and the Report has certainly not created it. The task of reconciliation is more basic than that. The Task Force's job has been to clear away the underbrush; to emphasize the extent of our misunderstandings, to reduce the confusion and emotional charge of current catch-words and stereotypes, to describe the realities of our various isolations, and to show how we might begin to reconstruct a political union without fear across the real boundaries of geography and spirit.

The Report offers an ingenious constitutional package in which the major elements of novelty are carefully related to one another in a persuasive pattern of argument. It is possible even for a sceptic to see the logic of the case and to conceive that these principles and institutions might give us a constitution that works as the present one does not. But, of course, the package will not be adopted unchanged; in the process of bargaining some of the proposals are bound to be transformed, others to be jettisoned.

The federal-provincial conference, meanwhile, begins discussion today of a small package of constitutional reforms in response to the desperate chivvying of the Trudeau government. How should the conference react to the Pepin-Robarts Report? The Task Force itself is unequivocal: ". . . change that is not predicated on a careful reading of the current crisis could easily undermine rather than enhance Canadian unity. Consensus on constitutional patriation and amendment plus a limited number of matters unrelated to Canadian duality and regionalism would not, in our judgment, be a sufficient response to the constitutional implications of the present crisis." (This stricture undoubtedly applies equally to the government's Referendum Bill now before the House of Commons.)

Instead of piecemeal reform, the Report urges Ottawa and the provinces to undertake, through federal-provincial discussion, the systematic drafting of a new constitution, which should then be ratified by popular referendum. If that process fails, the Task Force contemplates the advantages—of necessity—of a more radical undertaking, a constituent assembly.

The federal-provincial conference should suspend its previous agenda and endorse the Report as the starting-point of negotiation and agreement upon the creation of a continuing body to prepare a draft constitution for its consideration in a year or eighteen months.

Between Two Solitudes

(*The Canadian Forum*, April 1979)

Between the solitudes, once again, there is silence. In Quebec the Report of the Pepin-Robarts Task Force was greeted with close and extended analysis and general enthusiasm. In the other provinces, with rare exceptions, it was reported superficially and discarded. At the February constitutional conference the Quebec delegation made repeated, positive references to the Report while all the other participants ignored it. The federal cabinet gives the impression that the most it foresees for Pepin-Robarts is a quiet burial. The fate of the Report itself is thus a vivid illustration of the malaise that saps the country. In Quebec there is a lively and sophisticated debate on the constitutional future of the community as the forces that shape it shift and strain for predominance. There is life and movement and thought. Any literate contribution to the debate is grist for the mill. In the provinces of English-speaking Canada there is perceived the contrast. While Quebec moves on towards its fateful rendezvous, the partner it assumes will keep it company does not know of, and makes no preparations for, such an historic encounter. For Quebec the constitutional crisis will come to full term within the next two or three years; for the rest of the country there is scarcely awareness that a crisis is near.

This contrast deserves reflection. There is, possibly, more than one explanation for the flatness of the English-Canadian response. The country has, for one thing, been inadequately prepared by its politicians. The Trudeau government entered only grudgingly into constitutional discussion in 1968, until very recently insisting that, aside from the extension of official languages, there was nothing seriously wrong with the constitutional balance. It denied and ignored the growth of Quebec nationalism, and the country was prepared to accept Ottawa's reassurances on that subject—especially since neither opposition party had any distinct vision of its own to offer instead. On the two occasions of high drama when the country's attention was attracted to Quebec (October 1970 and November 15, 1976) the federal government's response was excessive—even paranoid—and after absorbing the initial shock English-speaking Canadians sensed that exaggeration and ceased to share in it. Beyond business-as-usual, the Trudeau government's constitutional devices have consisted only of crisis management and propaganda, neither of which carries much conviction. The country is wisely dubious; but because its leaders make no further and more convincing response, a large part of the public seems to assume that the crisis is wholly fictitious.

The Task Force was one of the Trudeau government's propagandistic responses to November 15; no other major royal commission has had to overcome as much scepticism about its serious intentions and its independence as this one. Careless and shallow reporting (which may be partly the fruit of that scepticism) has made it difficult for the Task Force to demonstrate that the doubt is, finally, undeserved. But close readers of the Report will know that that is true.

Beyond these initial barriers of an ill-prepared and sceptical public, there is a more profound difficulty. In substance, the Report is almost certainly too much for the present federal government to accept. In mood and approach, the document is far more sympathetic, not only to Quebec nationalism, but to the aspirations of the other provinces and the native peoples, than the Trudeau government has ever allowed itself to be. The special genius of the Report is that it foresees the possibility of a new federation, reconstructed on the basis of recognizing the sovereign equality of the provinces with Ottawa. In spirit, the Report almost suggests that Ottawa should stand aside and let the provinces recreate the federation, in the faith that men of good sense will endow the central authority with adequate powers to regain a role of national leadership which it has lost. The endeavour would be risky, and it would involve Ottawa's abandonment of deeply ingrained attitudes of paternal and imperial superiority. No government is likely to make such psychological concessions voluntarily, before it is forced to the wall. The Trudeau government perhaps knows that it has a subversive document in its hands: which is reason to keep it quiet. (This does not explain, however, the silence of the provinces. They may just have been struck dumb in disbelief.)

The single striking weakness of the Report is that it fails to deal realistically with the *process* of constitutional change. This may have been a tactical choice, to avoid raising a complication that was regarded as premature; or it may have been a decision taken in the last-minute rush to produce a document before the February conference on the constitution. In either case the Task Force made an error and lost an opportunity. The failure already seems serious, because the conventional means of discussion in federal-provincial conferences had become a confusing charade even before February, and that conference, by its failure, has now killed the discussion until the next and more serious round of crisis. There is good reason for the general lack of enthusiasm for federal-provincial conferences as constitution-makers; since 1971 it has been evident that they can only produce paralysis. The Canadian public, in its intuitive wisdom, may have sensed that any Report which does not confront the matter of how to go about adopting a new constitution will not get us far in resolving the crisis. That would be an unusually optimistic reading of English-Canada's indifference, because it suggests that there could be a creative response to proposals which involve sensible devices for bringing constitutional discussion to a successful conclusion. In any case, such proposals are not contained in the Task Force's Report and will have to emerge elsewhere.

For all these reasons and more, a good Report has fallen on barren ground. As Canada approaches the federal election and the Quebec referendum, the fragile climate of reason and decency seems destined to degenerate. At the point when events force the country to stand back, to reflect and finally to bargain seriously about a new constitutional settlement, the Pepin-Robarts Report will still have valuable things to say to us. It would be better if we could attend to it now.

Making War the American Way

(*Toronto Star,* November 5, 1990)

When Brian Mulroney made his quick visit to George Bush in early August, and committed Canadian forces to the Gulf alongside the Americans, he acted instinctively as a loyal American. He allowed no time for reflection from a distance, but rallied to the President's cause more rapidly than Mackenzie King did to the United Kingdom in 1939.

Once our ships, then our aircraft, were committed and placed on forward duty in the Gulf, we were irrevocably committed to war if that breaks out. The crowds on the Halifax dockside as our ships set sail knew what had been done in our name.

The choice of war, if it is made, will be made by the United States. For the Prime Minister, apparently, that poses no problem. For Joe Clark it may, but he is a loyal minister who seems to accept that second guessing serves no purpose now.

The early act of solidarity earned us credit in Washington—something the Mulroney government values very highly. If we are to exercise any moderating influence on George Bush's actions in the Gulf, we will be seeking it from a position of demonstrated intimacy and solidarity, not of independent distance. In a war, that probably gives this government no leverage whatsoever.

Canadian closeness to America is a traditional stance, evident in our military role in the Korean War and in NATO. In both those cases, it did not prevent Canada from pursuing a second, diplomatic line as an intermediary and potential peacemaker. It probably served as a spur to action in that second role, out of a lingering sense that total engagement in the American cause was not our proper vocation.

In the Gulf Crisis, too, Canada has set out initially to play this dual role of ally and independent mediator, but only within bounds acceptable to Washington. At the United Nations, the U.S. has made strenuous and praiseworthy efforts to assure that the response to Saddam Hussein has developed under the authority of the Security Council; and the Canadian delegation, at every stage, has worked to keep the UN ahead of the buildup of international forces in the Gulf. The Security Council's decisions through the last three months have given the world fresh hope that the international security system designed in 1945 to prevent war and redress injustice may at last be working as originally conceived.

But there is a shadow background to the UN effort which is much more worrying and potentially tragic. The whole framework of common response to Iraq's invasion of Kuwait seems likely to collapse in catastrophe, the result of a fatal division in the reasoning of western leaders. On one side, the UN resolutions denouncing Iraq's aggression, declaring an international embargo, and authorizing military enforcement of the embargo, are peaceful measures that would only be broken by an Iraqi attack. Formally, the buildup of forces in the Gulf has occurred under that mandate alone.

There is no safe means of responding to Saddam's aggression; but there are more or less acceptable risks. The UN's hesitation has been a reflection of that judgment. For the time being, an effective embargo offers the only means of keeping risks and objectives in reasonable balance.

Historically, embargoes have an ambiguous record of success. But when an embargo is almost universally accepted and tightly enforced as this one is, the prospects of real impact are high.

Whether that impact (even if it is severe) will persuade Saddam Hussein to withdraw unconditionally from Kuwait is another question, with a more doubtful response. The result is only likely to become clear after many months of suffering within Iraq and great patience abroad. But patient enforcement of the blockade is all that the Security Council has authorized, or should authorize for several months more.

There is a double game going on in this affair, and it is not a hidden game. Under UN cover, the U.S. and its allies have also, from the beginning, been preparing a vast offensive force for a potential attack on Iraq. In a sense, the U.S. has used the UN's authority as a means of drawing other nations into the buildup, knowing that once in, they will inevitably be blooded in a war and thus forced to participate. Joe Clark has now warned us to prepare for it; but his warning only makes explicit what was implicit in our acts from early August.

At the point of war, however, the UN's absolution becomes irrelevant. The object then will be to reoccupy Kuwait, defeat Iraq, drive Saddam from office, and impose stringent terms on a defeated power so that it will be unable to threaten stability in the Middle East again. Those are large ambitions, and desirable ones at a certain price.

But they are probably unobtainable without a series of further consequences: thousands of casualties among the forces involved, the destruction of Jordan, the involvement of Israel, disarray in the original alliance against Iraq, disruption of the world economy, mounting protest within the U.S., renewed deadlock in the UN, and no short way out. Will all that be justified if shattered Kuwait is restored to its rulers?

The commitment to use force against Saddam Hussein was made, in effect, when George Bush opted in August for a massive American buildup rather than a naval embargo and a small, tripwire force in the desert. It was aided by a bellicose Margaret Thatcher, who was there in Aspen, Colorado in the days after the Iraqi invasion to bolster George Bush's resolve at a crucial moment.

Once the decision had been made, Brian Mulroney and then others threw in their lot as well, with varying enthusiasm and clear-headedness about the implications.

The hurried decision to deploy overwhelming force was typically American, and narrowed rather than widened Bush's options because it catapulted him beyond peaceful persuasion. More than a quarter-million American fighting men do not sit in the Arabian desert to enforce a naval blockade. George Bush is just one more American president since 1960 who is recklessly inclined to use force abroad without counting the cost. To do so now will be an act of destructive primitivism rather than of principle. The cost will be vast and disproportionate.

If John Updike is right to think that the U.S. must have its little war in every generation, must Canada have it as well? These two countries remain very distinct places, and one reason why is that our experience of violence has been so different.

In Vietnam, in Nicaragua, in Grenada, in Panama—all those recent American wars of principle—we stood aside according to our lights. But now the Canadian government seems to be wishing us into the American experience.

As Brian Mulroney and Joe Clark lead us into battle, let us hope that afterwards the terrible lessons will have taught us other ways. If the Americans cannot learn them, is it now too late to hope that we can still do so by ourselves? Perhaps.

This piece, which appeared three months before the Gulf War, is a companion to the address in the first section, "The Gulf Crisis: Chaos or New World Order?" which was delivered just after the war ended.

How Adrienne Clarkson Could Oust Jean Chrétien

(*Ottawa Citizen,* June 5, 2002)

When Jean Chrétien spoke to the media after his latest cabinet shuffle on Sunday, he told them he had been elected prime minister only eighteen months ago by the people of Canada, and has the right to serve another full term. But he hadn't and he doesn't.

Mr. Chrétien was elected as the member of Parliament for Saint-Maurice, and remains as prime minister because his party commands a majority of seats in the House of Commons. If the government loses a major vote in the House in the next few weeks, he could be out of a job.

The prime minister and members of the Liberal caucus should now be consulting their constitutional advisers. Until last Friday, the Chrétien cabinet possessed a rock-solid parliamentary majority, but that rock may now have turned to flowing lava. If twenty or so Liberal backbenchers decide to absent themselves from the House for one of its supply votes in the coming weeks (the first ones come tomorrow), there is more than one possible outcome.

Faced with the possibility of parliamentary defeat, Jean Chrétien's claim will certainly be that he is entitled to ask the Governor General for a dissolution of Parliament, that the dissolution will be granted, and that he will fight the ensuing election as an incumbent prime minister. If that claim is correct, his challengers in the Liberal caucus will avoid putting the government at risk. After all, the prime minister's power over his own MPs derives from this crude ability to dissolve the House and deprive them of their seats and their livelihoods.

Since the King-Byng crisis of 1926, the prevailing assumption has been that the Governor General must grant a prime minister's request for a dissolution of Parliament whenever it is made. In that crisis, then-prime minister William Lyon Mackenzie King's request for a dissolution was denied by the Governor General at the time, Lord Byng. Instead, Byng invited Arthur Meighen to form a government. When Meighen's government was defeated in the House, Byng granted him the dissolution denied to King, and King won the ensuing election by arguing that Byng had acted unconstitutionally in denying the first request.

For 75 years since then, the conventional argument has been that a government defeat in the House justifies a dissolution of Parliament. Through the prime minister's eyes, that means he takes for granted that he is the one who decides when to call an election. When the House shows lack of confidence in him—or at any other time he chooses—he can go to the voters to renew his power.

In most parliaments, those assumptions are correct. In 1963, when John Diefenbaker's government lost its majority, only an election could sort out the confusion. In 1974, when Pierre Trudeau's minority government faced defeat in the House, the condition was the same. In each case, the Governor General had no choice but to grant the prime minister's request for dissolution.

This time, however, the situation in the House is not the same. There is a clear party majority, and it is not necessarily a majority committed to Prime Minister Chrétien.

If Jean Chrétien is defeated in the House and asks Adrienne Clarkson for a dissolution of Parliament in the next few weeks, decisive power will shift briefly to Rideau Hall. The Governor General will have to examine her responsibilities with care; and before she grants the request with an automatic nod, she will have to canvass all the options in a search for political stability. The political crisis will become a constitutional crisis.

Since the Liberal majority in the House would remain after the government's defeat (except in the unlikely event of a large defection of Liberals to the ranks of the opposition), the Governor General would find on further consultation that there is a majority in the Liberal caucus favouring the choice of Paul Martin as prime minister. On the constitutional grounds that the parliamentary term is still young and that a stable majority exists, the Governor General could well conclude (and arguably should conclude) that the proper course is to invite Mr. Martin to form a government.

If the Liberal caucus senses this prospect, the party's hallowed tradition of loyalty to its leader might take an unusual twist. The party, so finely tuned to its purpose of survival in power, might suddenly discover that loyalty to the next leader is the key to survival.

Just as the British Conservative party quickly and neatly disposed of Margaret Thatcher in 1991 in favour of John Major, so the Liberal party in Ottawa might do the same for Jean Chrétien and Paul Martin in 2002.

Of course, Mr. Martin would have to seek confirmation as party leader in a leadership convention after becoming prime minister. He would win it by acclamation, and the party would be primed for the election of 2004.

What we don't know now is how Liberal backbenchers will act in the coming weeks, and what the Governor General may be thinking about her constitutional role—not to speak of the prime minister's troubled musings in his time of trial. But if nothing changes on the Liberal backbenches, the country is in for eight months of dirty turmoil.

Under pressure from his caucus, Jean Chrétien avoided defeat in the House by agreeing to surrender power to his adversary Paul Martin in the following year. The settlement saved the Governor General from any precarious descent into an active political role, and spurred Chrétien into a surprising final year of political activism.

Will We Join the Musketeers? Ask Jean Chrétien

(March 18, 2003)

The three musketeers have had their afternoon in the Azores. Their ultimatums have been delivered. The UN and millions of their own citizens have been insulted. The troops and aircraft are poised to strike.

So what have six months of diplomacy been about? Two of the musketeers claim that what they sought all along was peace and disarmament. All that Saddam Hussein had to do—even in the last twenty-four hours—was to declare and give up his "weapons of mass destruction." That is what they repeatedly told their doubting audiences at home in Britain and Spain. Their official line was that one person alone could bring peace—and if there is war, it will be Saddam Hussein's fault, not theirs. But the other musketeer—the organizer and advocate of the whole expedition, George W. Bush—has told us since last summer that his aim is not disarmament at all, but "regime change." That is a goal entirely beyond the range of the Security Council's resolutions. The public, demonstrating in its millions around the world, knew all along that he was playing a duplicitous game.

The night before the latest report of the arms inspectors to the Security Council, George Bush told the world (during a fully scripted, phony "news conference") that Saddam Hussein's time had run out. There would be war whatever the inspectors reported, whatever the Council decided. For the imperial president, such decisions are in his hands, not in those of the UN. It can approve imperial decisions—or, in his words, it can demonstrate its irrelevance and go the way of the old League of Nations. (But we should remember that it was the aggressions of Italy, Japan and Germany that sent the League into irrelevance.)

For George Bush, the entire UN exercise has been a charade and a time-filler, accepted reluctantly under pressure from Tony Blair and Colin Powell: a diplomatic pause that conveniently allowed American armies to mass on Iraq's borders, far from their home bases in Florida and Iowa and California.

At best (as Tony Blair hoped) the detour through the UN would give war the sanction of international legality which President Bush never thought he needed; at worst, it would demonstrate that the Security Council is too feckless to police the world. But one way or the other—a few weeks this way or that—the Bush government would do what it has meant to do from the beginning. It would invade Iraq and overthrow the regime.

The rationale for George Bush's new policy was set out last September in his National Security Strategy. In that document, the Bush administration declared itself the guarantor of world order, ready to engage in "preventive war" when any nation or sect or group threatened American dominance and security (as judged solely by the United States). After al-Qaeda, Iraq became the test case in applying the doctrine. For President Bush, there could be no retreat, no *modus vivendi* short of war with Saddam Hussein.

Once the Bush administration decided where to apply the test, no evidence was really needed in Washington to make its case against Iraq. Saddam Hussein's regime, by universal accord, was cruel, detestable, and tyrannous. It had done terrible things. It had once "tried to kill my daddy." It has lots of oil. It might still have dangerous weapons. It might have ties with terrorists. But it is weakened by twelve years of harsh UN sanctions, contained by close international observation, and offers no obvious threat to its neighbours. After three months of renewed UN arms inspections it is weaker still. No matter: the Bush doctrine requires its sacrifices. American power must be displayed. George Bush's armies will face down the tyrant.

As the buildup to war went on last fall, Jean Chrétien and his ministers showed admirable caution. They refused to join Tony Blair and José María Aznar at George Bush's side. For once, their doubletalk and ambiguity was refreshing.

But as we reach the final hours of countdown, Canadians should expect more than jumbled incoherence from the Prime Minister. Does Canada favor this march to war? Will it join the assault at the last moment? Or will it denounce the attack for what it is, an historic act of unjustified aggression?

A week ago, George Stephanopoulos of ABC's *This Week* tried to get Jean Chrétien's answers to these questions. He failed. Whether by calculation or simple bumbling, the Prime Minister filled the air with confusion, unfinished phrases, self-praise, and halfwit insights that defeat any effort of understanding.

Could the divide in the Security Council be bridged? Jean Chrétien told us that "the question is a question of interpretation of what's going on there. And for me . . . I'm not . . . I don't know all the facts, but I know that we made some progress. . . . . It is because the Americans and the British have moved a lot of troops there. You know it is for me what is moving Saddam to comply otherwise he wouldn't have complied. Will he comply completely? It's a question of interpretation."

What would members of the Security Council need to support a resolution authorizing war? In his wandering reply, the Prime Minister inched towards a last minute plea to George Bush not to go to war: "You know the President has won. I have no doubt about it. He won. . . . . I mean that you know, he has created a situation where Saddam cannot do anything anymore. . . . You're winning it big. . . . I'm talking in terms of disarmament. The question of a regime . . . change of regime is something else. . . . It's something that I'm not very comfortable with . . . because where do you stop? You know, if it's okay that we do that there, why not elsewhere?"

What fresh advice would Jean Chrétien offer to George Bush? "The problem is for him he thinks, probably he's afraid that he has been dragging to ... delays and delays and delays to just postpone a decision. And if he had a date in mind and he has decided, like he seemed to say to the nation when he appeared on TV Thursday night, last week, there's not much I can tell him."

Would Canada assist the U.S. only with the support of a UN resolution? "It has been the position of Canada since the first day and it was the position of Canada in 1990, so ... but I'm not confronted with that.... We have three ships in the Gulf at this moment there and in the summer we have to go and replace some troops in Kabul..... So this is where we stand on the question of Iraq."

Is war inevitable? Despite his sense that America and Britain were about to act, Chrétien offered a lame answer: War is avoidable. Here he fell back to the Blair/Aznar line: Saddam is to blame, and Saddam has lost. He should surrender his weapons without a battle. "I'm telling you that if I were in his ... you know, in his boots I would be shaking."

Now, after the Azores excursion, Canada offers its congratulations to the musketeers for giving the UN and Saddam Hussein a twenty-four hour ultimatum!

So where does this leave Canada as the world plunges into war? Without a position, accepting war, waiting for surrender, rejecting a change of leadership in Iraq, wanting a few more weeks of inspections, wringing its hands, morally helpless. This is not the kind of leadership expresssed through the common sense of mankind over the last few weeks. It is not the kind of leadership that Lester Pearson or Pierre Elliott Trudeau would have given us in this crisis. It is a disgrace and an embarrassment. There are times when Canada, despite the costs, must reject blind and destructive American leadership. We must not endorse this war; we must not aid in this demented crusade.

Music and War in Barcelona

(April 5, 2003)

There was a downpour in Barcelona last Friday morning. By afternoon, as we bussed in from the airport, the bedsheets hanging from thousands of balconies, with their painted messages "Aturem la Guerra" ("Stop the War") and "No a la Guerra!" were half-washed-out. The whitened and stained sheets whipped in the wind, as eloquent as the freshly painted replacements that continue to appear. (These home-made banners have blossomed everywhere in Spain since mid-February, spreading daily by sympathetic contagion. The newspapers call them "balconies that speak".)

At nine o'clock on Friday evening we were in the great gothic Basilica of Santa Maria del Mar to hear Handel, Telemann, and, finally, Mozart's Requiem. Two thousand listeners were thinking of war. The great doors closed behind us and the concert began. At ten o'clock, beneath Mozart's resonating lament, we heard soft and distant murmurings, as though the rain had begun once more. With every moment, the susurrations grew louder, harsher, more insistent, nearer. Suddenly we knew what was happening: the residents of the Barrio Gotico were at their windows, beating their pots and pans against the war. These 'caceroladas' are taking place, now, every evening throughout the city. For fifteen minutes, until the end of the Requiem, the cacophony continued, accompanying Mozart in dissonant counterpoint. The orchestra played on, the audience sensed the symbolism of the moment, no one showed impatience. As we left the church, volunteers beyond the doors handed out stickers that read: "Guerra No! Mozart Si!"

On Saturday evening, the spellbinding Mallorcan folksinger Maria del Mar Bonet performed at the Theatre Nacional de Catalunya. Well into her program, she paused and made a simple statement against the war which brought the audience to its feet for two, three, four minutes of solidarity, the applause rolling on, and on, and on.

The next day, Sunday, thirty thousand people gathered at Plaza Espanya for three hours of protest songs, readings and chants against the war. It was raining again, but that did not matter. Maria del Mar Bonet was there, and Paco Ibánez, and Els Comediants, and the mayor of Barcelona, Joan Clos. Meanwhile hundreds of young people filled twenty thousand black balloons in the Plaza Catalunya, tied them in bunches on the pavements, and at two o'clock, cranked sirens and stamped on the balloons across the square, detonating them to simulate the sounds of bombing on all sides.

We came to Barcelona for a weekend of music. We did not seek out the protests, but could not avoid them in the city that has become the centre and model for European challenges against the war. The anger and the ingenuity of this intelligent metropolis gather force. “Bush, Blair, Aznar,” cry the posters on the hoardings and in the Metro, “Resign!” The universities are in continuous turmoil. Every newspaper opposes the war. The national opinion polls show 91 percent in opposition. The announcements of fresh demonstrations proliferate. This week the city council of Barcelona declared itself an official partner in the protests, and decreed that its buses would fly white flags every Thursday until the war ends.

This revulsion, this wave of outrage, will not be suppressed, not in Barcelona, not anywhere in Spain, until the war ends or the government of José Maria Aznar, with its absolute parliamentary majority, hears the deafening protests of its citizens.

In the Spanish general election of 2004, the Aznar government was defeated and replaced in power by the Socialist PSOE, which reversed the country's role in the war and occupation of Iraq, and withdrew its ground and air forces from combat.

What Can Stephen Harper Learn from Conservatives Past?

(*The Globe and Mail*, January 24, 2006)

After a near-perfect electoral campaign, Stephen Harper will be turning his mind this morning to cabinet-making, the legislative agenda, and a timetable for the new parliamentary term. What signposts from the past should we be watching for as his government comes to power in Ottawa? Are there any lessons to be learned from the records of previous Conservative governments?

As a start, it would be wasted effort to plunge into political theology by questioning whether this new government belongs in the Conservative line of succession. Since the terms of John Diefenbaker, Joe Clark, and Brian Mulroney, the Tory party has splintered in all directions—to the Bloc in Quebec, to Reform and Alliance in the west and Ontario—followed by awkward grafting operations that ended two years ago in the creation of Stephen Harper's Conservative party.

These contortions are nothing new: there have been many changes of name, divisive feuds and reunions in the party's long history, from Liberal-Conservative, to Conservative, to National Government, to Conservative again, to Progressive Conservative, to the two-headed monster of the 1990s, to Conservative yet again. Party policy, as well, has featured its full share of somersaults and headstands over the years, from protectionist to free trading, from anglophone and Toronto-centred to bilingual and multicultural, from centralist to regionalist, from nationalist to continentalist.

As a national party within reach of power, the Conservative party has always been a coalition held together tenuously under a dominant leader and subject to internal compromise as the times seem to demand. Since 1921, it has been the party of the "outs," struggling with only intermittent success to remove the Liberal "ins." Now the party's victory should re-establish its legitimacy, whatever winding path it took to get there.

Once in power, the previous Conservative prime ministers John Diefenbaker and Brian Mulroney sought to transform the party into the natural governing party (while Joe Clark had no time to make the attempt). Both failed. Now Stephen Harper—with the normal ambitions of a political leader—will try to do the same. What guidance can the past offer him?

Diefenbaker and Mulroney created broad coalitions uniting strong elements across all regions of the country. Once in office, their task was to consolidate and maintain those coalitions. Both came to office by challenging the complacency and "culture of entitlement" of the Liberal party. To maintain power, they had to rise above the resentments that brought them to victory. Initially, each leader sensed the impatience of the nation. Each promised national reconciliation, inclusion and fairness. Each, for his time, gained the largest electoral majority in Canada's history. Then both saw their coalitions fall apart because they could not escape the limitations of their personal and political origins.

Diefenbaker lost power in a mood of defiant confusion as the complexity of governing overwhelmed him. He could not understand the blossoming of Quebec and urban Canada, and could not manage the country's relations with Washington. Mulroney lost power out of his ambitious Irish exuberance, going too far, too fast in pursuit of continental integration, constitutional revision and tax reform. In their distinct ways, each lost touch with the changing national temper. Diefenbaker fell behind the country's evolution; Mulroney moved too far ahead of it and offended all his constituencies.

The first thing that the record of previous Conservative administrations should remind Stephen Harper is that his party is *not* the natural governing party. There may not—and should not—ever be one again. Mr. Harper was elected yesterday by a sceptical electorate. He received power by default because the Liberal party was too complacent, too comfortable, too arrogant in office. Diefenbaker, Clark and Mulroney all won power on the same kind of rebound, as replacements for discredited Liberal regimes.

Mr. Harper will be reassured by his victory, but history tells us that he cannot take his achievement for granted. He must prove himself in office - not as a partisan who can do what he wants, but as a trustee for all Canadians. He cannot retain power by satisfying his core constituency alone, either through his policies or his distribution of patronage. Jack Layton is not the first Canadian politician to know about borrowed votes: every Conservative prime minister since R.B. Bennett has depended on them for victory and lost them in defeat. Stephen Harper has won on a lot of borrowed votes, and those votes are subject to return.

This means (if he wants to stay around for a while) that he must govern tolerantly from the broad centre of the political spectrum, listening to, respecting and serving his critics and opponents as well as his friends (a lesson that Liberal experience should teach him as well). Above all, the radical social conservatism that was the trademark of Reform will have to remain as distant and peripheral under a Harper government as it has been during his highly disciplined campaign.

Joe Clark was quickly punished for trying to govern as though he had a parliamentary majority when he didn't have one. John Diefenbaker and Brian Mulroney received their overwhelming majorities in 1958 and 1984, and were subsequently punished because they regarded those majorities as the infallible and definitive judgments of God. To avoid nemesis, Stephen Harper and his party will have to struggle continuously to hold onto their humility and demonstrate their responsibility to the whole electorate.

Mr. Harper's recent Conservative predecessors have one great positive lesson for him as well: build upon, and do not thoughtlessly demolish, what previous Canadian governments have created. Mike Harris, that provincial Conservative renegade, offers no lessons in social cohesion for Stephen Harper to emulate. By contrast, John Diefenbaker, Joe Clark and Brian Mulroney did not come to office to tear down Canada's welfare system, or its balance of central and regional power, or its creative pattern of human diversity, or its (relatively recent) national spirit of tolerance and generosity. Instead they accepted the heritage left by their predecessors, both Liberal and Conservative. They sought to correct failings, to fill in gaps, to broaden the sense of inclusion for citizens previously neglected or ignored. They had generous visions.

For the good of the country and his own party, Stephen Harper should follow their example. In this campaign, he showed signs of the self-confidence, pragmatic sense, and thoughtfulness necessary for that constructive effort. Now those signals of his character will be put to the test.

Ignatieff's World: Why Michael Ignatieff Should Not Be Leader of the Liberal Party of Canada

(November 2006)

I wrote this little book between April and July of this year, once Michael Ignatieff announced his candidacy for the leadership of the Liberal party, because I thought Canadians should know his views on international policy. *Ignatieff's World* is intended, you might say, as a pre-emptive strike against an advocate of pre-emptive war. Unlike the other leadership candidates, Ignatieff has no domestic political record of accomplishment to consider when we try to judge whether he would make an acceptable leader of a national party. But he has a large record in his writings, published while he lived in the United Kingdom and the United States—over a dozen books and scores of articles in leading British and American magazines and newspapers. These writings, I knew, were unknown to more than a few dozen—or at most, a few hundred—Canadian readers. Canadians knew of him only as a celebrity in the UK and the US. He gained his reputation abroad as a television commentator and newspaper pundit, aided by his mellifluous prose, his profile of chiselled granite, and his talent for arriving at scenes of battle and chaos in the midst of destructive turmoil.

Michael Ignatieff himself, I'm sure, does not want to become leader of the Liberal party because he is an international celebrity. He must want the job because he believes the country needs him and can benefit by his leadership. But Canadian voters must ask of him: What character, what ideas, would he bring to the leadership? What I could not predict when the book went to press was that Michael Ignatieff himself would offer such powerful evidence demonstrating that he is unfit for the job. Six months into the Liberal party's endless leadership campaign, we have now heard a great deal from him about where he stands on domestic policy, and what he promises to do for the country. Not incidentally, we are beginning to get a clear sense of his political judgment, his ability to sense the country's mood, his knowledge—or lack of knowledge—of what Canadian politicians can hope to accomplish.

What stands out from his months of campaigning is the ease with which he launches himself into confusion and imprudent controversy. Is this a sign of his prophetic boldness or of his innocence, naiveté and ignorance of Canadian politics? To this point, just one week before the leadership convention, he has committed what seem to be three colossal blunders: first, by voting with the Conservative government in May on its rushed motion to extend the term of our military forces in Afghanistan until February, 2009 without bothering to explain why he was doing that; second, by siding with the government in its unbalanced, pro-Israel approach to the July war in Lebanon, and then, in October, reversing himself before a Quebec audience to declare that Israel had committed a war crime in its bombing of the village of Qana; and third, by committing himself to reopen the constitutional debate in the hope of entrenching the definition of Quebec and the aboriginal peoples as "nations" in the constitution. The newspapers and the web blogs have enjoyed a daily harvest of headlines, outrage and belly laughs from these stories and their accumulating debris. (A few weeks ago, for example, *Maclean's* columnist Paul Wells wrote on his blog: "A stout refusal to believe what Michael Ignatieff says has become the central condition for supporting his candidacy for the leadership of the Liberal Party of Canada. The opposition to Ignatieff now comes exclusively from people who fear his words have meaning.")

The candidate's recent blunders must have thrown his closest advisors into fits of surprise and annoyance—for at the least they reveal the loner's difficulty in taking advice and controlling his whims. His public response to such cries of alarm is that he is an honest man who speaks his convictions, and that he will go on doing so whatever his advisors may say. I say, instead, that he is a fool.

Each of Ignatieff's gaffes has its background in his previous writing. I don't mean that they were predictable in detail, but that they are quite consistent with his record, and not surprising when they are seen within that framework. The keys to understanding his beliefs and his judgment as a politician, I think, lie in his prolific writings.

These writings are not bland; they are controversial even when they seem straightforward and direct. His descriptions of scenes and events are often compelling and persuasive. His way with words is powerful. But his arguments and his moral judgments are complex to the point of obscurity and self-contradiction—and when he is forced to clarify them, he plunges into still thicker, swirling mist. He rarely apologizes or admits he was wrong; he just slogs on into greater complication. To speak as a typical reader, I'm often left thinking "Now what is it that he really means here?" (To give him the benefit of the doubt, I begin by thinking that he must mean *something*.) But too many times I end up thinking that he means nothing of practical consequence at all, or that he means something he doesn't want us to understand clearly, or that he means both one thing and its opposite at the same time.

For many of his readers and listeners, I suspect he weaves a web of persuasion by convincing them that he knows more than they know, can see more nuances than they do in the big problems he faces, has been to places they have not been to, has consulted (or been consulted by) the great and the powerful, and brings an overwhelming intellect to the issues he confronts. My warning to Liberal delegates (and to all those who may influence them in the next ten days) is not to let his claims, his credentials or his celebrity mislead them: instead, listen to his words, read his writings, treat him as an intellectual equal and not as some superior oracle, and judge, directly for yourselves, the value of his words. On analysis, I think, Ignatieff's words do not have the weight or the depth that he claims for them.

I'll try to illustrate my concerns by grouping them under three main themes.

1. *Ignatieff is (or, he might say, was) an American imperialist.*

To put this more politely, perhaps I should say that Michael Ignatieff is an apologist for, and promoter of, an aggressive American military policy abroad, designed to protect American interests and save the western world from the barbarians who threaten it along its fringes. Ignatieff's views on the American empire developed after the year 2000. They seem to reflect his own disappointment with the UN's efforts at peacekeeping and peacemaking in the mid-1990s, his personal move to America and the orbit of Washington policy-making, and especially his disorientation after the terrorist attacks of September 11, 2001. In a stream of articles and addresses, he moved away from his earlier writing on ethnic wars and collapsing states to consider "the imperial struggle to impose order once intervention has occurred." His empire of choice was the United States, and he called its new mission a "nation-building enterprise," to be conducted boldly by the use of overwhelming military power. His fresh commitment to the American imperial project was not hesitant or reluctant: it was repeated and emphatic—and it did not change (but only intensified) when George W. Bush and his neo-conservative hawks replaced a more vacillating Bill Clinton in the White House. His advocacy of the new empire reached its peak in 2003 and 2004, as the Bush administration launched (and soon lost) its war of aggression in Iraq.

As he told readers of the *New York Times Magazine* in January, 2003, being an imperial power meant setting the world's rules. (If there is any irony in this assertion, it is deeply hidden.)

> It means [Ignatieff wrote] enforcing such order as there is in the world and doing so in the American interest. It means laying down the rules America wants (on everything from markets to weapons of mass destruction) while exempting itself from other rules (the Kyoto Protocol on climate change and the International Criminal Court) that go against its interest. It also means carrying out imperial functions in places America has inherited from the failed empires of the 20th century—Ottoman, British and Soviet. In the 21st century, America rules alone, struggling to manage the insurgent

> zones . . . that have proved to be the nemesis of empires past.

Now the imperial course was set: it was too late for America to turn back even if it wished to do so. Since September 11, 2001, the United States could only be safe by policing abroad. "Iraq represents the first in a series of struggles to contain the proliferation of weapons of mass destruction, the first attempt to shut off the potential supply of lethal technologies to a global terrorist network." The White House's conclusion that containment would no longer work "is not unreasonable." Waiting would only increase the danger that Saddam Hussein would become master of the entire region and manipulator of the world's energy supplies. Years of sanctions had punished the Iraqi people, rather than the regime, and UN weapons inspections could easily be evaded. "That leaves us, but only as a reluctant last resort, with regime change."

For George Bush, Dick Cheney and Donald Rumsfeld "regime change" in Iraq was anything but "a reluctant last resort": that was a transparent deceit, and Michael Ignatieff (as a close observer of events in the lead-up to war) must have known it. Yet he deceived himself. He allowed himself to be duped. Three and a half years after the attack on Iraq, Ignatieff has never conceded that the invasion was a mistake, a political and moral disaster in its very conception, a gross violation of international law. He has only said, during the present leadership campaign, that he underestimated American incompetence *after* the invasion—as though that admission is enough to excuse his prominent role as an advocate of war. What measure of responsibility does he bear for the Iraq catastrophe—not just as a passive supporter who went along with George Bush and Tony Blair, but as one of the leading public voices of war in the United States?

2. Ignatieff is an advocate of odious violations of human rights.

I'll do little more than mention Michael Ignatieff's contorted justifications for the use of extraordinary powers by the American government in its misconceived "war on terrorism." (I discuss them in twenty pages of *Ignatieff's World*.) He argues his position at great length and in great obscurity in his 2004 book *The Lesser Evil*. What seems to move him is a deep sense of alarm about the terrorist attacks of 2001, a sense that Islamic fundamentalist terror has no political goals, allows no room for negotiation, has as its purpose a complete and violent transformation of an entire, corrupted world, and can only be countered by war and the emergency measures that accompany total war. That is simply to accept at face value the most extreme claims and objectives of Osama bin Laden as though they were real and immediate possibilities. (This is just what extreme anti-communists in the 1950s and 1960s used to say about the Soviet Union: that its immediate goal was world conquest. The result, sixty years ago, was to promote fear against entire communities and to inflate Western defence budgets. The result today has been the same.)

Michael Ignatieff has played an unusual role in promoting the new climate of fear, never more starkly than in the last chapter of *The Lesser Evil*, which bears the title "Liberty and Armageddon". In it, he worries that the modern state system may disintegrate as nuclear and biological weapons pass into the hands of terrorists. They do not seek recognition or conventional power, but aim only to punish the United States and its allies: negotiation, concession, and appeasement will not pacify them. These are his "undeterrable terrorists. "Evil," he warns, "has escaped the prison house of deterrence."

Ignatieff insists that this claim is no lurid piece of sensationalism and then proceeds to make it more lurid. Sooner or later, an attacker will slip through the security barriers with a terrifying chemical, radiological, bacteriological, or nuclear weapon and set it off. In this way, democracies could lose the war on terror. They need not be invaded or conquered. Rather, "a succession of mass casualty attacks, using weapons of mass destruction, would leave behind zones of devastation sealed off for years and a pall of mourning, anger and fear hanging over our public and private lives." Emergency laws would be made permanent, borders would be closed, detention camps would hold suspicious citizens and aliens. Official torture and assassination could become matters of policy, nuclear weapons could be used in retaliatory attacks abroad, and vigilante gangs could patrol the streets. This would be "the face of defeat.... We would survive, but we would no longer recognize ourselves or our institutions." His brief offering of hope pales before his predictions of fresh terror and its disheartening results.

That is the background—an utterly imaginary world of horror—that Ignatieff sets out as his justification for the use of unusual emergency powers for the long-term. "Since the politics of reason," he says (that is, normal democratic politics, with normal protections for rights and liberties), "cannot defeat apocalyptic nihilism, we must fight," and we (whoever "we" are) must fight dirty.

To counter what he sees as this pervasive threat of terrorism, he argues in favor of American pre-emptive and preventive wars, preventive detention of suspects, selective assassination, and what he calls "coercive interrogation." (In more direct language, that is, he justifies American/British military aggression, imprisonment without charge, official murder, and certain techniques of torture.) In defending each of these exceptional measures, he lays out rules that should be followed by American presidents for their use. Significantly, Ignatieff makes these arguments for the suspension of human rights and liberties in writings published in 2003 and 2004, *when every one of these unusual measures was already being used by President Bush.* Ignatieff was not writing as an independent critic of an administration that needed challenging for its abuse of power: the main effect of his writings, on the contrary, was to provide cover and apology for the White House's indifference to human rights, not to impose public restraint upon it. Ignatieff was acting as a propagandist for George Bush's misguided "war on terror" and its repugnant techniques.

3. ***Ignatieff has an inability to judge Canadian interests from a Canadian perspective.***

Given that background of commitment, influence and intense experience in the politics of American imperial adventure, I think there must be serious doubts about Michael Ignatieff's ability to see the world wisely and knowledgeably through Canadian eyes. Intellectually, he has admitted in the past that he is a Canadian of convenience, a cosmopolitan or a post-nationalist who does not put much store in the role of nations (including his own) beyond the need to impose minimal order. His previous writings on civic and ethnic nationalism, as much as his recent comments on the need for renewed constitutional discussion in this country, reveal profound confusion about nations and nationalism. His absence from Canada for most of the last thirty-five years means that he is unfamiliar with the constitutional trials that this country has gone through—and left behind. He seems unable to read the signs of public concern, or discontent, or anxiety that politicians who have lived here have absorbed in their bones. Since 2004, in addition, his emphasis on a forceful Canadian role in the world has closely echoed General Rick Hillier's campaign to integrate the country's military forces more intimately into American operations abroad. I worry that Ignatieff's long record of support for power in the United Kingdom and the United States reveals something profound in his character: he wants too much to please those with power in the world. That means, in 2006, pleasing the American administration above all, at a time when the Bush administration has lost both its authority and its sense of direction. Ignatieff, the public intellectual, has never spoken truth to power. This is not a constructive stance for a Canadian party leader elected to serve Canadian interests.

The American expatriate writer William Pfaff wrote wisely in last Sunday's London *Observer* about the abstract world in which the Bush administration and all those who share its illusions have been living for the last five years:

> In America, it's as though Bush, his inner cabinet, and the neocons have been playing a video game, with fictional characters and victims, virtual death and torture. Now the disc has suddenly finished, and it's time to shut down the player.
>
> This is not just a figure of speech. American policy has been running on images rather than evidence of real nations and people doing

> things for real human motives. It has been populated by abstractions: Global Terrorist Conspiracies, Rogue Nations, Fanatics Who Hate Our Freedoms, Generations of Terrorism and The Global Menace of Al-Qaeda.
>
> The U.S., where actual people live, has been turned into an abstraction: the Sole Superpower, which everyone in the world knows is a Righteous Nation.... We are the tranquil Elephant... which by its very presence guards the smaller beasts of the savanna from carnivorous predators.
>
> This is what we exist to do. We are the leading nation, the most moral, born with the redemptive mission to create... "the 'City on the Hill', the democracy... that originated the modern world..., establishing the greatest of republics, saving the Four Freedoms for the world by winning (alone!) both First and Second World Wars, then the Cold War, and now confronting the ultimate test of the 'long war' against Evil itself, incarnate as Terror.

This fantasy world sounds remarkably like the one described and promoted by Michael Ignatieff in his *New York Times* essays of 2003 and 2004. William Pfaff calls it a "post-Orwellian" world, because now "Big Brother has become a part of his own creation. He is imposing it on others by acting as though it were real, at whatever cost to others. This is our problem today. In some measure we have all been drawn into this virtual world. How do we leave?"

At the very moment when the United States—after its mid-term elections—seeks desperately for some path of escape from the "virtual world" in which we have all become trapped, this is no time for the Liberal party of Canada to choose a leader who helped to create and sustain George Bush's nightmare world. When Michael Ignatieff speaks to us these days, he talks about his good intentions with an air of frightening plausibility. But it would be a mistake to forget his record—a record that is out of tune with our needs and interests. Instead, I believe it would be safer, more prudent for us, if that spinner of dreams were to remain on the Liberal backbenches through this and the next parliament, where he will have enough time to come down to earth, to get to know the real life and real possibilities of this country more thoroughly.

Ignatieff's bid for the Liberal party leadership failed in this first round of 2006 but succeeded three years later, leading to the fumbled national electoral campaign of 2011 and his immediate resignation as leader.

Can Stephen Harper Dissolve Parliament When He Chooses?

(*The Globe and Mail,* August 21, 2008)

When Parliament amended the Canada Elections Act to establish fixed election dates every four years, government house leader Rob Nicholson insisted that this was "an idea whose time has come." The idea, he said, was to limit the prime minister's ability to dissolve parliament at a time of his own choice. The change "would help to level the playing field for general elections." The public would no longer face surprise elections; all political parties would benefit from a regular electoral timetable; parliament would be free to plan its business over stable four-year terms; and voter turnout would increase. In future, the prime minister would only retain the power to seek dissolution if his government suffered defeat on a confidence vote in the House of Commons.

MPs from all parties supported the bill, though a few opposition members doubted that it would achieve its purpose. The catch was in the first clause: "Nothing in this section affects the powers of the Governor General, including the power to dissolve Parliament at the Governor General's discretion." Since the Governor General acts only on the advice of the prime minister, if the power of dissolution is unchanged the prime minister's power to choose an election date short of the new four-year limit also remains unchanged. Liberal MP Marlene Jennings put the criticism most bluntly: the bill was "clearly duplicitous"; the government was simply "trying to blow sand in our eyes."

The government responded with vehement denial. The theoretical power of dissolution might remain, but the bill was a solemn declaration of Stephen Harper's intent. "This prime minister," Rob Nicholson insisted, "will live by the law and the spirit of this particular piece of legislation." Another Conservative member declared that Harper was giving up a power "that past prime ministers . . . have used like a club." Months earlier, the prime minister himself told the House that "the government is clear that it will not be seeking an early election. At any time Parliament can defeat the government and provoke an early election, if that is what the opposition irresponsibly chooses to do."

The government's refrain echoed repeatedly until earlier this year. There is a fixed election date in October 2009; the prime minister is bound to respect that date (in honor if not in law, since the terms of the Act seem self-contradictory); in the meantime Parliament must get on with its work.

Now something seems to have changed. Is there a decent way for the prime minister to slide away from that commitment? In April the government whip, Jay Hill, gave warning that if Stephen Harper decides to call an election because Parliament has become "dysfunctional", he will give ample notice. "If Parliament was not functioning well, that would show a lack of confidence in the government. It's a no-brainer that we'd have to go to the people to try and settle it."

Last week the prime minister confirmed that the key to the use of his power would be parliamentary "dysfunction." And who would make that ruling? "I think quite frankly," Mr. Harper tells us, "I'm going to have to make a judgment in the next little while as to whether or not this Parliament can function productively."

What frustrates the prime minister is that he now wants an end to the life of a tiresome Parliament, but he can't be sure that the Liberal party will join the other opposition parties to ensure it. In Mr. Harper's words, "Mr. Dion says he doesn't support the government but won't say, you know, whether he will defeat us or not. I don't think that's a tenable situation." As they tease one another in their August war of words, both leaders may now see advantage in forcing the other into an election—without quite wanting to say that openly.

So the fixed election law—which the government probably introduced with half-innocent good intent in its early months of power—has become an awkward burden for the prime minister. Stephane Dion's erratic conduct on votes of confidence in the House—whether it is cute, or confused, or just weak—has riled the prime minister. Does that justify him in violating the spirit of the election law?

The Governor General is no doubt taking fresh advice on that question from her constitutional advisors in these waning days of summer. Could she reject the advice of the prime minister to dissolve Parliament without a government defeat? Does the new law make any difference? There is only one answer: despite the law, she would be obliged to do what Stephen Harper asks. She has no power, in this situation, to challenge the political judgment or the moral subtlety of her prime minister. Stephen Harper, like other prime ministers before him, can still wield the big club. The new law is a nullity without prime ministerial self-restraint.

A few weeks later Prime Minister Harper asked for and received a dissolution of parliament from the Governor General. He failed to win a majority in the October election, faced early defeat in the new House and prorogued before a confidence vote could be held, precipitating the collapse of a tenuous opposition alliance. He governed with a minority until the general election of 2011, when he won an absolute majority of seats.

IV / Diversions

Sometimes the absurdities of life and politics have moved me to fantasy—more often in this century than in the last, which may indicate my own aging or the world's decline (or both). In 2002, observing a vicious internal battle for leadership of the Liberal party and the Canadian prime ministership, I imagined an exchange of letters between a beleaguered Jean Chrétien and the wily Robert Mugabe, lifetime president of Zimbabwe. A few months later, in Spain, I struggled to understand the English text of instructions for a new mobile telephone, and took a few liberties in writing my own fractured but similar version. Back home in 2012, I imagined what Canada might face in the event of a second Harper majority victory in 2015. Among other things I foresaw the creation, in Three Hills, Alberta, of a new national capital and an awe-inspiring memorial to the country's permanent leader. By 2014–2015, I knew that only satire could divine the governing spirit of the Harper cabinet in what turned out, by miraculous good fortune, to be its receding months of power. Aside from the Three Hills piece (which appeared in The Globe and Mail*) these essays are published here for the first time in print.*

The Mugabe-Chrétien letters

(August 2002)

Copies of the following letters were recently discovered blowing in the wind below Parliament Hill or thereabouts. I cannot vouch for their authenticity.

Dear Robert,

I hope you won't mind this letter. Though we've met just a few times, I've been feeling close to you in spirit over the past few months, and need your advice. (I'm encouraged that people jokingly call me "Prime Minister Mugabe," which I'm determined to take as a compliment.) But first, I must apologise to you for supporting your country's suspension from the Commonwealth after your recent elections. You will appreciate that this was a bit of harmless public relations, meant to appease a few nuisance-makers here at home. It means nothing, and will soon be reversed. Meanwhile, my admiration for your political skills only grows.

You may have heard that I have some difficulties in Canada. You know, I won three glorious election victories like yours; and then I won a grand triumph in my battle with Conrad Black. He left the country, renounced his citizenship, and sold his newspapers to my good friends when I refused his elevation to the House of Lords. But since then I have problems. Those friendly papers have been good to me, but I need more forceful defenders in the coming months. Some people object to my party's right to rule, and a few fanatics even object to me. A few weeks ago I had to say farewell to my finance minister because he would like to be leader too. (And as you well know, a country can have only one leader at a time.)

Even though I have an ironclad five-year contract, I face what is foolishly called a "leadership review" in my party, and after that I must hold another general election. I always love a good fight, but this is getting tiresome. Of course I will win both, but I could use the advice of another old pro to guarantee my place in history. I know you have more than twenty years in power, and me, I aim at that too. Right now, I have about ten.

Tell me, my friend, how should I deal with my critics in the party, my opponents in Parliament, and my enemies in the press?

Your great admirer,

Jean

* * * * *

Dear Jean,

I knew you would finally understand. Power is comfortable, isn't it? And the longer the better. Twenty years is good. Don't ever believe that old canard that power corrupts.

Here are a few thoughts about the vicious enemies you mention. On the party: You probably know this as well as I do. The keys to success are simple. Reward your close friends lavishly (minor office, big pensions, and diplomatic postings are always helpful; but have you also tried foreign bank deposits and gifts of public lands?) Build superhighways in friendly districts. Demand loyalty and freeze out your critics. Most of them will go silent in the hope of favours, or in fear of losing those they already have. If you haven't tried all this, do it at once.

On the parliamentary opposition: Treat them roughly. Remind them constantly of their own corrupt records and their squabbles. Ridicule them.

Tease them. Taunt them. Insult them. Limit debate. Deny all their motions and amendments, even the reasonable ones that you supported at election time. And since they can challenge you in elections still to come, do what you can to restrict election advertising and disruptive public meetings. Hire your own vigilantes to assure that public meetings *are* disruptive.

On the press: This can be most inconvenient. Get your friends to buy newspapers and television stations. Then watch them carefully (they tend to get an exaggerated sense of their own power). If you can, ban critical comments on politicians and the State, and especially any slights against you personally, the living embodiment of the State. (If that's too difficult under your bill of rights, then depend on quiet threats against the owners. They usually work.)

Well, that's a start. I can give you more details if you need them.

With warm fellow-feeling,

Robert

* * * * *

My Dear Robert,

Your advice is priceless, and I'm using it when I can. But still, I'm beginning to have nightmares of defeat. Please send more details.

Yours affectionately,

Jean

* * * * *

Most Respected Jean,

You must be in trouble if things are failing so fast. But as our old friend Richard Nixon used to say, "When the going gets tough, the tough get going." Here's how I'd advise you to get going.

On the party: Demand pledges of loyalty. Fire a few more ministers, and consider putting some of them in jail. Snarl at them, but only in private. Flaunt your own impregnable virtue, strength and good health. Make big promises to regional loyalists, and deliver on a few of them for good effect.

On the opposition: In future, meet Parliament as briefly as possible - say, for a couple of months a year. Hire some agents to work within the opposition parties to throw them into endless infighting. (Though I hear that they do it in Canada without provocation. Count your blessings.) Accuse the opposition leader of treason. (I can suggest a good public relations firm to set this up for you.)

On the press: This is a specialty of mine. Prosecute critics for disloyalty to the State. Limit newsprint or ink supplies. Have a few publishers, editors, and reporters fired for insubordination or anything else. Hijack a few newspaper delivery vans. Appoint friendly owners to the Senate. Ban foreign journalists from entering the country. Close down the internet.

Would all this be going too far in Canada?

With concern,
Robert

* * * * *

Dearest Robert,

Many thanks. I've put my staff to work on all this. But there are signs of rot all around me. The caucus is two-faced. What more can I do?

Worried,
Jean

* * * * *

Highly Revered Jean,

As a last step, while you still have a majority in caucus, declare a national emergency and introduce a bill to postpone the next general election for several years. (You once told me you are all-powerful and could do that. Can you?) And when the party meeting votes non-confidence in your leadership next winter, just ignore it. If my party is any example, they won't do anything about it if you do. After all, you have a mandate from the people, and in your system no one can take that away from you.

If necessary, go to war.

Isn't democracy wonderful?

Ever your faithful friend,
Robert

P.S.: Leak these letters. That'll throw the fear of Mugabe into them.

Jean Chrétien was forced by his party to retire in the following year. Robert Mugabe remains in power in Zimbabwe, fourteen years on and counting.

Guide for the Cell Phone Use (Europe)

(November 2002)

Please first to read the instructions. The factory is not responsible for any improper activities with the telephone.

Your telephone is really a radio and meets all rules for the safety and security of everyone young and old. The emissions are always lower than necessary, even when higher. (Limit 2 watts per kilogram of human weight.)

1. PUTTING IT TO WORK

Insert and remove the credit card by the picture.
Insert and remove the battery by the picture.
Charge the battery by looking at the picture.
Turn on the telephone by pushing for a long time the button. In the meantime do not go away.

2. MAKING A CALL

Ask the number to the telephone you want. When replied, press the button short. Bla, bla, bla. Close the button when you want them to stop.

3. MAKING AN INTERNATIONAL CALL

See the prefix and ask the number. Select the country when visible and begin talk. When complete, then stop soon.

4. RECEIVING A CALL

See the picture of the caller and hear the noise, or feel the telephone shake. If you press the button long, the caller is rejected. If not, they are okay. To end, say “goodbye” and give up the phone.

5. IN THE MIDDLE OF A CALL

Here you may do many things, for instance: Bringing the voices louder by pressing the “OK”; make the loudspeaker but keep away so not to damage the ears; call another while keeping the first waiting; memorise a number by keeping it repeating in your mind; look at the directory; talk to the operator; playing music soft or loud in background for pleasure; and so on.

6. CONSULTING THE MEMORY

In this is all that you have ever done. Press the button long and look at the menu. Move to which memory you want (ex.: Personal, local, world, political, environmental, garbage days, etc.). See and consider the memory for what you want to do with it. To leave, press "OK" or speak "Forget it."

7. EVENTS
Everything that happens is in the telephone already. To see them, press the button very long. Choose one and press it. (Ex.: Bush speech to Iowa farmers.) Listen close (or not). (There is in this also all your friends' birthdays to remember, or if so you can even create new ones.)

8. TO PHONE FROM OTHER COUNTRIES
Beware. Doing this must have permission of the phone.

9. MISCELLANEOUS
Other things:

1) To engage the vibrator in a public place, press # almost long. To disengage, drop phone and ignore.
2) To hear messages, always go them in the screen.
3) For more problems, ask the operator if on 24 hour duty. (Operator has same guide book as you.)

THIS IS THE LATEST TECHNOLOGY AND ALWAYS UP TO DATE. CONGRATULATIONS AND GOOD TO HAVE YOU AS OUR FRIEND!

(WARNING: IN CASE OF VAST NATURAL CATASTROPHE, DO NOT USE TELEPHONE AS IT WILL TEND TO CLOG.)

Stephen Harper's Generous Legacy: A Glimpse into the Future

(*The Globe and Mail,* May 11, 2012)

Shortly before writing this piece, I had visited Ankara, Turkey and toured the mausoleum of Mustafa Kemal Ataturk, Founder of the Turkish Nation. My reading of the future had not anticipated the 2014 collapse in the world price of oil.

In the aftermath of Stephen Harper's 2015 election victory, Canada faced troubled times. The Northern Gateway pipeline, approved by the federal cabinet despite an adverse environmental review, faced construction delays resulting from public protests along the route. The government of China, as a major participant, expressed its impatience. In the United States, President Obama lashed out at Prime Minister Harper for his refusal to sanction more oil exports across the 49th parallel. ("We don't want the Americans draining all our sacred reserves at less than world prices," he was heard muttering to an aide.)

When the drone attack and parachute drop on Parliament Hill by U.S. special forces occurred, no one expected Canada's vigorous raid on Washington that ended in the burning of the White House. The President's surprise offer of an armistice was graciously accepted by the Prime Minister, who insisted that he never really opposed new oil exports to the United States, and offered unlimited contracts at a fixed price of $200 a barrel for ten years. Peace returned to North America.

That was the point—as an Access to Information request now reveals—when Ottawa began its covert planning for a new capital city. "Prudence demands that we move the capital further away from the American border," wrote one adviser in the PMO. "We have the perfect alternative: a pleasant town in the province that holds our wealth, which will signify our status as a world energy superpower. It's a small and historic place called Three Hills, Alberta."

Planning and building the new city proceeded in deep secrecy under direction from the Prime Minister's chief of staff. The Defence Department assisted by designating most of central Alberta as a restricted military zone, accessible only by special permit from the PMO.

For four years total secrecy was maintained. The completed capital city was to be unveiled on the eve of the 2019 federal election, as a special gift to the nation; but we can now reveal this astonishing project as it nears completion in 2018. "We never mentioned it before, because no one ever asked," the Prime Minister's spokesman explained.

On one of the three hills that give the town its name, the new Royal Canadian Government Centre will contain all the (substantially reduced) facilities of parliament and the federal public service. On the second hill, the giant Canada Ethical Oil Corporation will refine dirty oil to a high standard for export to China and the USA. On the third hill a National Historic Memorial will be dedicated to the capital city's inspiration and creator, Stephen Harper Canada, Founder of the Nation. It was planned entirely without the Founder's knowledge by staff in the PMO/PCO and his Calgary constituency.

The Memorial will occupy a hilltop area of twenty acres. Four towers will dominate the corners of the square, each containing an artifact from the life of the Founder: in the first, a full-size replica of his birthplace home in Toronto; in the second, the Steinway piano used in his historic performance of Beatles songs at the National Arts Centre; in the third, an illuminated copy of his manuscript on the creation of professional hockey in Ontario; and in the fourth, the original court documents marking the bankruptcy and termination of the Liberal party of Canada. At the top of the square, and dominating it, the Harper Mausoleum will arise, sheathed in marble quarried in Alberta's Rocky Mountains (Inc.). A spokesman in the PMO tells us that flattening the hilltop and constructing the Mausoleum have been financed entirely through private gifts.

The capital's transfer from Ottawa to Three Hills will take place following the Natural Governing Party's electoral victory in October 2019.

Our Leader and His War Cabinet: 10 Despatches

(August 2014 to October 2015)

The secrecy of Stephen Harper's cabinet discussions was impenetrable. By 2014 the damage his regime had done to Canada's democratic institutions and humane policies was self-evident, and the prospect of more was discouraging. Like others—such as The Globe and Mail*'s television critic John Doyle, who had dubbed Harper "Our Glorious Leader"—I turned to satire, knowing that the government and its supporters were deaf to reasoned commentary. I wrote a series of spurious reports on my blog, WordSmith, divining the inner workings of the prime minister's cabinet, as it conducted war against the Canadian electorate and prepared for the 2015 election. Here are ten of those despatches.*

August 16, 2014
Our Leader Consults His War Cabinet

Stephen Harper was on his cell phone with John Baird. "I want you to get home pronto, minister, for an emergency meeting of the War Cabinet. We'll be at the usual secret location at ten o'clock tonight. No excuses."

Baird hailed a cab from NATO headquarters and rushed to Brussels airport where his Challenger jet was fueled up and waiting. "Message received jetting home super supper airborne," he tweeted. "Good chance to think through world crisis in tweets over next seven hours. Will report."

Other members of the War Cabinet (Clement, Kenney, Mackay, Moore, and Poilievre), summoned by flashing red lights and buzzes on their iPhones, hopped the nearest flights to Ottawa. By ten o'clock they were all there, except for Poilievre, who had mistakenly taxied out to the Diefenbunker at Carp. Seeing the parking lot empty, he realized his mistake and hustled back to town, arriving a little late.

"Well, gentlemen, what do we do now?" the Leader asked as they settled into their hard chairs.

"Just what's the problem, then?" said the minister of justice, respectful but confused and a little tentative.

"I don't need to tell you that we're in the midst of a world crisis, Mackay. Sinjar Mountain! Baghdad! Syria! Donetsk! Keystone XL! Ebola! Today, I've despatched two giant transport planes full of weapons to our brave allies in Kurdistan, where they're fighting the Islamic Caliphate. Caliphate my foot! They're nothing but a bunch of desert thugs and fascists. We've got to wipe them out with the help of our British and American partners. Now that Nouri al-Maliki is gone, we can do that and reunite Iraq."

Jason Kenney looked quizzical. "But, prime minister, don't the Kurds want independence? How will their victory reunite Iraq?"

"Minister! Minister! One thing at a time," the Leader responded. "First, total war, then reunification. It's simple strategy. Isn't that clear enough? We've got two planeloads of weapons and we need to unload them. Poroshenko says he doesn't need them after we sent him that load of body armour, helmets, sleeping bags, uniforms, and pup tents. Anyway, it would be a bit foolish to take on the Russians. We may be at war with them, but we can't risk a fight. And remember, this fulfills a heartfelt wish of mine. At last we're joining the Iraq War, as I said we should have done long ago."

"Hurrah! Hurrah!" exclaimed the minister for intelligence and propaganda.

"Thank you, Pierre. Much appreciated," the prime minister replied. "Now, what about a brief summary of the general situation? How is everything related to everything else?"

"Right," said Poilievre, bowing gracefully from his kneeling position in the Leader's direction. "I was hoping you'd ask. As you often say, Canada can't stand idly by while the world falls to pieces. We're a world petroleum power and a warrior nation, and we have to act like one. So, let's see. There's Baghdad under threat of attack; there's Donetsk, occupied by Russian agents; there's Irbil; there's Scotland, with a referendum coming on."

"What are you saying, minister?" the prime minister interrupted. "Would you send the Van Doos to Edinburgh?"

"No, no, Leader. But we can't afford to lose Scotland. Think of all the Scots Canadians! You should follow Tony Abbott's lead in Australia and denounce a 'Yes' vote for Scottish independence. Obama's done it too. That's a first step. We have to use our influence or lose it. That about sums it up for this week."

"Ahem. . . ." Kenney hesitated. "I think you've forgotten one thing, Poilievre. If we're defending the Kurds and the Yazidis from bombardment in northern Iraq, and the Ukrainians from the Russians, shouldn't we be aiding the Gazans as well?"

A chill enveloped the room. There was a chorus of protests from other members of the War Cabinet. "They're a bunch of terrorists, launching rockets every day. Who could put up with that? The Israelis have a right to defend themselves! Don't they have the right to defend themselves? We can't take on every issue in this world!"

The minister's cheeks turned distinctly pink. "I . . . I'm only looking for consistency," he whispered.

The Leader eyed him coldly. "I don't think we'll need your services in the War Cabinet any longer, Kenney. This room is feeling a bit crowded. Please leave, and don't bother to return. I suggest you get back to your temporary foreign workers. That file still needs attention."

There was awkward silence as the minister shuffled quietly from the room.

"Well, I think that's enough talk for today," the prime minister ruled. "We should get a few tweets out of this enlightening discussion. Baird, would you see to that? And then, how about taking the next flight to Irbil with those war supplies? That should be good for a few photo ops. War Cabinet, attention! Dismissed."

September 24, 2014
Harper Consults His Inner War Cabinet

"Get me Poilievre on the phone," Our Glorious Leader told his chief of staff. "I need an emergency meeting right away. We're in crisis mode around here."

"Yes, sir, I have him permanently on an open line to his cell phone," replied the chief. "Here he is."

"Leader! Leader, yes, good morning. How are you?" cried Pierre. "I've been waiting for your calls. How can I help today?"

"Here's the thing," Harper replied. "We're at war in Iraq, now that we're finally a member of the 'coalition of the willing'. And that means we're at war in Syria. Obama is bombing all over the place. Where will he go next?"

"I'm keeping an eye on the world map," said the minister for intelligence and misinformation. "It's quite a big place, the world."

"Well, yes, I'm learning that. So, what we need is an urgent meeting of the Inner War Cabinet—the secret group, not the usual one—to thrash out our new position. Get Baird and Calandra to the underground War Room ASAP."

"Yes, sir! They'll be there as soon as they can get downstairs. And I've got coffee on the boil."

Within twenty minutes, Baird, Calandra and Poilievre were with Our Leader at the war-plans table.

"Now, men, I'm depending on you. It looks as though we're heading into a war effort on many fronts. It should take us right past the election of 2015, whenever that happens. I'm keeping the date open, just in case. Now, Paul, I know you're a new member of the Inner War Cabinet, so you won't know much about our plans so far. I think Pierre should give us a quick roundup of our current position. Go ahead, Poilievre."

"Yes, master. First, we've got our special forces unit—about sixty men—in Lithuania, scouting the Russian border. Then, we've got those three F-18s. I think they're in Poland this week. And our special forces in Iraq, consulting about the threat from the Islamic State for another week or so."

"Wait a minute, Poilievre! Did I hear you calling ISIS the Islamic State? It's not a state, it's a bunch of criminals. Don't ever call that a state. They're just thugs, and we must wipe them out."

"Sorry, sir. I won't do it again. And there's Scotland: we solved that one nicely last week. Chalk up a victory there. Your statement before the referendum did the trick, prime minister."

"You're on the button there, minister. I had a phone call from David Cameron to congratulate me. I think that was before he'd talked to the Queen. Anyway, what were you saying, Poilievre?"

"Well, there's the Ebola crisis, and there's climate change. Everybody's talking about Ebola and climate change."

"Nothing to gain on either front," responded the Leader. "Don't any of you mention those words."

"That's about it, then," the minister concluded, bowing deeply.

"What we need to do is decide about Iraq and Syria. Obama says no boots on the ground, but the defence minister tells me that our 69 men in theatre all have regulation-issue boots on their feet. Will that put us in Washington's bad books, Baird?"

"Gosh. I never thought of that," said the minister for foreign travel. "But we have a C-130 waiting in Trenton, and it could rush a shipment of running shoes to Baghdad before Obama learns anything about it. I'll get those boots back here right away."

"You're a good man, Baird, always thinking on your feet. Once you've done that, we have some time to consider the next phase of the war. I'm mighty relieved. And Palandro, not a word about any of this in the House. Do you understand?"

Calandra, following Poilievre's lead, bowed deeply to the Leader.

"Keep your cell phones charged, men! You can never tell when I'll have to summon you to deal with the next world crisis. Attention! Inner War Cabinet, dismissed!"

September 29, 2014
Boots in the Air = Boots on the Ground?

"Hey, Baird, did I tell you what Obama told me yesterday?"

"You mean about the war?" Baird replied as they lunched on poutine in the prime minister's office.

"Hey, don't call it that," Harper corrected the foreign minister. "He says we can't call it a war. It's a counter-terrorism campaign. That way, he doesn't have to go to Congress to authorize what he's doing in Iraq and Syria."

"That's smart," said Baird. "Why can't we do that too?"

"Well, that's the other thing. Now Barack tells me he wants us to join his air strikes in Iraq and Syria; but I promised parliament I would ask for a vote before we go into combat again. He wants to use some of our F-18s over there."

"Well," Baird replied thoughtfully, "I suppose we could send the six planes we have in Poland down to Baghdad, if Obama promises to use them sparingly. In Ukraine, it only looks like war (as I've said before) but it really isn't. It's just the Cold War. So those guys are mostly enjoying themselves in Warsaw."

"That's a thought," said the prime minister. "But if we send them to Iraq, we'll have to send ground staff as well, say two hundred servicemen or so. And that means 'boots on the ground,' as Obama puts it. Boots on the ground means combat, and that means a vote in the House. I guess I shouldn't have talked about 'combat' in 2007. If I'd only spoken about 'anti-terrorism' we wouldn't need a vote in parliament at all. Everyone knows we can do what we like if we're fighting against terrorism."

"Yeah," reflected the foreign minister. "You're caught in a corner. I think we need to consult the War Cabinet."

"Go ahead then," Harper responded wearily. "Call them to the underground War Room."

Ten minutes later, they were all there—Kenney, Moore, Poilievre, Baird, and Harper.

"Welcome, men. Poilievre, can you sum up the situation for us?"

"It's not looking good," said the minister for intelligence and disinformation. "Boots on the ground means . . . boots on the ground. And we have no boots in Iraq, only running shoes."

"What?" exclaimed the Leader. "Baird, what about that?"

"Well, chief," Baird replied, "It's true. I did as I promised the Inner War Cabinet. I got all those boots—69 pairs—out of Iraq and replaced them with Adidases."

"Baird, Baird, you acted too fast. Now we need those boots, and more. Get them back there."

There was a long pause as the foreign minister consulted his iPad.

"Uhm . . . uhm. I seem to have lost those boots. No one can tell me where they are."

"Listen here, Baird. We're going to need lots of boots on the ground in Iraq. Our brave men can't go shoeless into battle. CSIS tells me there are a lot of U.S. army boots for sale on the streets in Baghdad, sold off by all those deserting soldiers last month. Baird, get on the first plane to Baghdad and buy them up, and keep them there for our forces. Keep a record of where you put them."

"Yes, sir. I love Baghdad. I can report on the situation first hand from there. I'll tweet as often as I can."

"Well, that's a relief," said the Leader. "That should hold the line until we meet again. I can probably delay a vote in the House until we know we have boots on the ground waiting for our men. War Cabinet, attention! Dismissed!"

October 2, 2014
Stephen Harper's Anti-Terrorism Campaign

"Poilievre, quick, call in the War Cabinet. I've consulted caucus and informed the House. Now I need final approval for my campaign plan."

"At the ready, sir. I've rung their buzzers and they're on the way," the minister of intelligence and misinformation replied.

"And by the way," Our Leader added, "make sure Clement and Mackay are on your list. I forgot them for our last meeting. You can forget about Calandra."

In ten minutes the ministers had gathered in the underground War Room: Poilievre, Kenney, Moore, Clement, Mackay, and rushing in breathless, Baird."

"All right, men, take your seats," the prime minister motioned to them. "Baird, I see you're a bit out of breath. What's up?"

"I'm back from that quick trip to Baghdad, prime minister, with great news to report."

"Give us your words, then, foreign minister."

"I've solved the problem of the missing boots on the ground, Leader. It turns out there were never sixty-nine pairs on the feet of our special forces in theatre. Only twenty-six pairs. I went looking for replacements on the streets of Baghdad, and I got a real bargain."

"Well, tell us about it, minister," said the prime minister, urging Baird on.

"The great news is, when I found someone selling standard army boots and told him I wanted twenty-six pairs, he said 'Twenty-six, no good. For same price, $100 (U.S.), I give you twenty-six thousand. All polished, slightly used, various sizes.' So I snapped them up. They're all in storage at Baghdad airport."

"Baird, what would I do without you?" responded the prime minister, patting the minister on the shoulder. "Now, Poilievre, can you summarize the situation up-to-the-moment?"

"Yes, master," he brightened. "You've told us we're under threat in a noble cause, and our allies want us to join them in the war."

"Hold it right there, Poilievre," the Leader interrupted. "Did I hear you calling it a war again? If I hear that word from you once more, you're out like Calandra. Understand?"

"Of course, prime minister. A thousand apologies. A noble, endless, anti-terrorism campaign."

"That's better. But cut the 'endless' stuff. It's only for as long as necessary. Okay, carry on."

"Thank you, prime minister," Poilievre bowed slightly. "So what you recommend is that we send six F-18s, two refuelling tanker aircraft, and groundstaff to the Middle East as soon as we find an airport that will take them. And we'll keep those twenty-six men, in boots, with the Peshmerga."

"You've got it right, Poilievre. Any comments, ministers?"

There was a moment's silence, until Kenney raised his hand.

"Three respectful questions, prime minister. Do we have authority from the UN Security Council? Will we bomb Syria? Will our aircraft be under U.S. command?"

Several ministers shuffled uncomfortably, one said "Tsk, tsk," and one muttered "Shut up, Jason."

The Leader looked stern. "My orders have been given. They're on the way. Now, all of you, get out of here. War Cabinet, dismissed!"

November 23, 2014
Stephen Harper Considers His Future

"Hey, Poilievre, it's time to call in the War Cabinet. I have some thoughts," the prime minister exclaimed.

"At your service, sir," responded the minister of intelligence and misinformation, leaping quickly to his feet and simultaneously dialling up Baird, Moore, Kenney, Clement, and Mackay on his cellphone. (A trick he had learned in his spare moments.) "They'll be at the War Room in ten minutes flat. I'll go by the stairs while you take the private elevator down to the bunker."

In a blink the ministers had gathered at the War Room door, awaiting the Leader's arrival. (Only he knew the access code.) Harper emerged from the elevator, punched in the code, and led them to their places where they stood silently until the prime minister reclined in his alcove and beckoned them to sit.

"First, men, I want to congratulate Baird on his speech to the NATO Council of Canada on 'Ukraine: The Future of International Norms.' That was stupendous. You have a brilliant speechwriter who thinks entirely in one-sentence paragraphs. I haven't seen a better putdown of Poutine and the Russkies since my own face-to-face confrontation last week in Brisbane. I gave him our summary judgment while you spelled out all his self-defeating acts of wanton aggression. He's clearly determined to destroy Russia's greatness with his threats to Ukraine and to all of us."

"Get out of Ukraine! Get out of Ukraine!" shouted the ministers in unison, until the Leader silenced them with a wave of his hand and a modest smile.

"Yes," Baird replied after a short pause. "He's a gem of a speechwriter and I certainly wouldn't want to lose him."

"Don't worry, Johnny, I don't make many speeches and I keep them short. He's safe where he is in your office. Now then, men, I want to discuss two things," said the Leader. "First, should I retire from politics after ten gruelling (though triumphant) years, or—"

"No! No!" came the frantic response.

"Thank you, men. That wasn't necessary. Or—as I was saying—should I call an election for next spring and catch our enemies in the lurch? I know my election law sets the date for October, but nothing in the law prevents me from ignoring it and dissolving parliament anytime. I've done it before."

There was a buzz of animated voices.

"Calmly, calmly, my friends. Think through the prospects, men: we must use a bit of practical science, the kind our antagonists say we always neglect. First, about my retirement. You must admit that I've earned it. I've created our party out of stray bits and pieces, brought us to power, given us our majority, made us a warrior nation, suppressed information in the name of transparency, balanced the budget, and set an example to the world of a nation that acts only on principle. What leader can claim more than that? On the other hand, I'm told that two-thirds of the electorate hate us and some of our own are hesitant about our methods. If I go now I'll pass on the realm to one of you, and give the party a fresh face. If I stay and lose the election, I'll be shamed, my record will be stained, and some of you will be defeated."

"Don't go!" Poilievre pleaded. "You're my idol, my beacon and the very fount of my faith!"

"Don't go!" cried the rest, with varying degrees of intensity.

"Well, then, consider the alternatives," said the prime minister quietly. "If I remain, and we wait for an October election, think of what we face in the meantime: Sona and maybe Del Mastro in prison, a Duffy trial for weeks in the spring, month after month of Mulcair in the House, Trudeau's popularity outlasting all our vitriolic advertising, a storm of fresh insults from the Parliamentary Budget Officer, more extreme weather explained by our foes as the result of our inaction on climate change, continuing struggles against ISIL, more wanton aggression from Russia, our F-18s draining the surplus away as they fly around Iraq and Central Europe, more friction from the First Nations, the prospect of another recession. . . . That's not a pretty picture. It looks to me like total war."

"Oh, horrors," muttered Mackay as the others made glum faces.

"Where's the upside in all that?" said the Leader.

"There isn't any," replied the members of the War Cabinet, in unison again. "Let's dissolve. Let's go to the GG in January. That way, we'll win another victory before the apocalypse."

"Well, you've given me lots to think about in the next few weeks," said the Leader. "So, I advise you to prepare yourselves for whatever the future may bring and I may decide. I'll look at all the alternatives you've offered me in your collective wisdom. Attention, War Cabinet! Session, dismissed!"

December 23, 2014
Stephen Harper Decides to Rebrand

"Quick, Poilievre, I need to consult the War Cabinet! We're heading into election year without a paddle, and I need one badly. Call in the boys!"

"Yes, sir, at your service, sir," responded the minister for misinformation and intelligence. "They'll be in the War Room as soon as I press my instant alarm button. They're all wired up. (I've got the latest technology.)"

"Good fellow, Pierre. What would I do without you?"

"You wouldn't, would you?" cried Poilievre in alarm, his eyes clouding over.

"No, no, look, calm it, young man. I never abandon my friends. Now press your alarm and get on with it."

Poilievre recovered and pressed hard. There were distinct rumbles in the Centre Block, Justice, Foreign Affairs, Industry, and Employment as ministers leapt to their feet and rushed to their secret underground passageways. By that time Poilievre was already waiting at the War Room door. "Mackay, check! Baird, check! Moore, check! Kenney, check! Poilievre, check! All present," he muttered as he marked them in his attendance register.

Inside the Leader looked impatient. "Four minutes and forty-two seconds," he noted. "A new record, but we're still aiming at four minutes. Now let's get to work."

"What's on the agenda, then?" Mackay inquired, hesitantly.

"Two things," answered the Leader. "First, we need a sense of direction. We can't run on keeping the Enemy out of power any more. Now we're the Enemy. Justin stumbles all over the place but keeps popping back up again. We can't run on surpluses and tax cuts, because we've spent the money and are heading into deficits again. We can't run on accountability and transparency because . . . well, just because. We can't claim to be an energy superpower, because we haven't built a single pipeline to anywhere and tanker trains keep falling off the tracks, and no one builds tar sands plants at fifty dollars a barrel. We can't run as a warrior nation because that's too dangerous, what with terrorists and Poutine and Ukraine and the price of the F-35. So what do we do? I think they call that 'rebranding', don't they?"

"Prime minister, with respect," Baird interrupted, tugging at his forelock. "You're right about everything except the warrior nation bit. That's our lifeblood, like hockey. We can't abandon it now. Why, I've visited Kiev and Moldova and the Baltics and Poland and Byelorussia. I've talked to General Trueblood at NATO. I've said again and again that we can't accommodate evil! We have to confront it. Poutine wants to confront *us.* He takes issue with our values. He's an uncontrolled aggressor. We have to chain the bear! After all, we're not a nation where what goes around, comes around. I'll say it again, we can't accommodate evil! Think of the Blitz! Think of Pearl Harbour! Think of Hiroshima! Think of the Light Brigade! Think of the Halifax Explosion! Think of John Diefenbaker!"

"John, John, control yourself," said the prime minister. "You're not addressing a public meeting. You can't order the Russkies around the way you command the National Capital Commission. You could get us into trouble if anyone took your words at face value. Are you really talking about regime change in Moscow? I can see by your red face that you know you've gone too far."

Baird blushed more deeply and hung his head in silent apology.

"That's better," the Leader reassured him. "Now, since no one has any objections, let's talk about rebranding. What I mean is, I'm on the point of an epiphany. Somehow we have to accommodate the Russkies, but we can't accommodate climate change. I've been watching the weather and reading Naomi Klein, and I think she's onto something. I don't want to admit any mistakes, so what we must do is work out how to reverse course without anyone realizing what we've done until they begin to congratulate us. Look, it's just a matter of language. We're not talking about a 'carbon tax' here: that's clear. But how about, say, a . . . levy, or a resource replacement fund, or a rainy day account, or a bow to reality, just in case. Let's see what the Albertans, for example, have been doing about that. Can you put your minds to it? And at the same time, think about some freshening up in cabinet ranks. I'd like your thoughts about whether I should give holidays to, say, for example, people like Fantino, or Agluqqak, or Alexander? Or anyone else?

Gloom enveloped the War Room.

"Take heart, boys," the Leader urged with a beaming smile, "I'm grateful to you all to hear your profound words of wisdom today. 2015 is election year, and we'll meet again in January. War Cabinet, attention! Dismissed!"

January 30, 2015
Stephen Harper Prepares for Combat

"Come on, Poilievre," exclaimed the prime minister. "It's time to hail the glories of war! We've got an election to win. Call in the War Cabinet!"

"At your service, sir! I've rung the alarm and they'll be in the War Room in a moment or two."

"And by the way," the Leader added, "call in Nicholson, Fantino and Calandra as well. They've got lines to deliver and they'll need some coaching. I haven't seen them since Christmas."

At Poilievre's electronic command, Kenney, Mackay, Moore, Baird, Clement, Nicholson, Fantino, and Calandra rushed down to the Bunker. The faithful servant was at the door to check them in, while the Leader waited patiently in his alcove. "All present, sir," reported the minister of intelligence and misinformation.

"Thank you, Pierre. Four minutes and twenty-nine seconds. Improving, but still not fast enough. Suppose we had a real emergency? Now, let's get on with it. Baird, tell us how preparations are going for the campaign."

"Well, Leader," the minister of foreign travel replied, "our special forces are at the front line doing laser targeting, protected by our fine and loyal snipers. As you've said, when the enemy shoots at us we kill them."

"Wait a minute!" the prime minister interrupted. "I'm talking about the *election* campaign, not the *Iraq* campaign. *That one*'s right on track."

"A thousand apologies, Leader. I was just thinking about my next trip abroad. Anyway, it's war on both fronts. Here at home, right on schedule, our rhetoric is heating up day by day. We're frightening the opposition into supporting us when the time comes to extend the Iraq mission at the end of April. As the war intensifies (though not too much, I hope), we'll focus more and more on it rather than the deficit, the dollar, and the price of oil. And there's also Ukraine, of course, where Poroshenko and Poutine are conveniently keeping the pot boiling. With good luck, in a crisis we may be able to avoid a budget altogether. Once you dissolve parliament to fight a wartime campaign, you can finance everything with Governor General's Warrants."

"Good point, minister. Now then, Nicholson, tell us how we're doing in the ministry of war."

"Well, Leader, progress is being made. We're standing up to terrorists at home and abroad. We're engaging with them now and then. I'm keeping the accounts, and no one else knows how much we're spending. Best to keep it that way."

"Great work, minister. Keep the noses of your accountants to the grindstone, as they say. And Calandra, what have you got to report?"

"Well, Leader, I'm back on duty in the House, reminding everyone that the opposition always puts criminals ahead of taxpayers and votes against every benefit your government proposes. I've recovered my self-confidence, and don't need prepared talking points any more. That should save time for your clerks in the PMO."

"Congratulations, Conundrum. Keep it up. Now, Moore, how's business, as they say?"

"A bit dicey, Leader. We let Burger King take over Tim Horton's, and now they're firing people all over the place. That won't look good for you when you visit Tim's looking for votes during the last days of the campaign. I suggest you keep your distance."

"You're damned right I will," Harper replied. "Thanks for the warning. I've never entered a Burger King in my life. And Kenney, how are things with the ethnics? Is that vote all locked up and ready to deliver?"

"Yes, it should be secure. But if I may say so, respectfully, sir, there's still a problem with the budget. Keeping it balanced isn't a sure thing, and I can't trust Oliver's assurances. Maybe we need to fire a few thousand more public servants."

"Clement, how about that?" demanded the prime minister.

"You could be right, Leader," replied the minister for budget cutbacks, deferentially. "But I don't want to say so. Perhaps we should simply put them on warning for after the election."

"Yes, go ahead," the Chief replied, "and don't forget to swear them to secrecy. Well, that about sums up the agenda for today. Remember, men, we're in a war for survival – civilization against the barbarians at home and abroad. Remember, loose talk costs political lives! Up the Empire! Salute the flag! And, by the way, as you go out the door pick up your flak jackets. War Cabinet, attention! Dismissed!"

February 11, 2015
Stephen Harper Circles the Wagons

"Poilievre! Poilievre! I need your help. Call in the Inner War Cabinet right away!" shouted the prime minister in a tone of alarm.

The minister for intelligence and misinformation rose from his customary kneeling position and saluted smartly. "Yes, Leader. I've alerted them all. They'll be with you in the War Room instantly."

The Leader entered his elevator and descended to the bowels of Parliament, where Poilievre, slightly out of breath, already waited to unlock the protective War Room door. Within seconds, Kenney, Baird and Calandra appeared at his heels. Poilievre checked them off as they took their seats at the table, facing Harper in his alcove.

"Baird! Baird!" the Leader exploded. "What are you doing here? You're the reason for this meeting! Get out of here! You're no longer a member of the cabinet, Inner, War, Regular, or Outer. You're lucky to have a parliamentary pension, but you won't collect on any of your air miles. I don't want to see or hear from you ever again! You're an ingrate and a bombastic buffoon! How dare you leave cabinet the way you've done it? Since when is it proper to resign by giving Terry Milewski a scoop on *The National*?"

The ex-minister for foreign travel rose from his chair clutching some notes, took a deep breath and prepared to speak.

"I said I didn't want to hear from you!" exclaimed the prime minister. "Do you know what those words mean? Now get out of here. I told Poutine to get out of Ukraine: do you think I'm afraid to say the same thing to you? You? I'm not afraid of Poutine, and I'm not afraid of you. You don't even have nuclear weapons: only bluster. Now go!"

The ex-minister hesitated briefly, crumpled the text of his prepared remarks in his hands and headed for the exit. As he departed, he half-turned and muttered to himself: "I'll . . . I'll give my speech tomorrow in the House. They'll appreciate me there. Good night and goodbye."

The door slammed and there was an awkward pause.

"I don't know how he got in here," the Leader snarled. "Poilievre, didn't you cross him off the list after you saw the news?"

"Apologies, Leader, apologies. I was awaiting your instructions and you didn't say anything except to call in the Inner War Cabinet. So that's what I did. Oh my God! Am I out? Do I have to go too?"

The Leader offered him a benign smile. "Calm down, Poilievre. It's all right. I need you more than ever now. I only want to be sure of your complete and utter loyalty, come what may. And yours, Kenney, and yours, Calabria. What do you say?"

"Of course, Leader," Kenney insisted, piously. "I am your servant in sickness and in health, until you depart this realm and are raptured up to a better place."

"Never doubt me," Calandra chimed in. "I'm with you to the bitter end."

Poilievre shook his head frantically in agreement.

"Well, look, that's a relief, then," said the prime minister, recovering his *sang-froid*. "Now, let's get on with the job. We have fresh things to consider, like whether I should spend more time with my family, when to call an election, whether we should arm the Ukrainians and send more boots into Iraq. We all know this is a dog-eat-dog world. As Winston Churchill used to say, 'war is the natural condition of mankind.' Remember that."

"Don't go!" cried Poilievre in panic. "What would the country do without you? Have you ever thought of that?"

"Oh, come on, Pierre, relax. We're only talking things through in a reasonable way," replied the Leader. "When I decide to go, you'll be the first to know, and certainly before Terry Milewski. Now, Kenney, what do you think?"

Kenney masticated thoughtfully and furrowed his brow. "I know what a heavy weight you carry as Leader," he said, "and how much you constantly think of the common interest and the common good. I'm sure that the heavens watch out for you, and I know that whatever you do, you'll act only with inspiration. Divine inspiration, I can confidently say. It's a blessing, too, to realize that we have such a strong team standing close behind you. As for an election, I'm always ready for it. In Ukraine, I'm with you all the way; and in Iraq, why, there's a God-given war if ever there was one. When our boys meet the enemy on the front lines (as you've truly said) we kill them."

The prime minister showed pleasure. "Now look, men. It's a relief to hear such encouraging words from all of you. So let's forget about Baird. He's gone the way of Eve Adams. I'll think about your helpful advice, and when I finally decide about my future, and the election date, and Ukraine and Iraq, you'll hear from me. In the meantime, I've decided to make you, Kenney, minister of war, and you, Poilievre, minister of mobilization and foreign workers. Conundrum, stick to your job as chief parliamentary mouthpiece, and never falter. We have to be ready for anything. So, back to the trenches! Salute the flag! Inner War Cabinet, attention! Dismissed!"

May 16, 2015
Stephen Harper Girds for Battle

"Hey, there, Poilievre, it's time to summon the Inner War Cabinet. We need new battle plans. Call in the boys in short pants."

"Yes, sir, prime minister. They're already on their way to the bunker," replied the minister for disinformation, mobilization, foreign workers, and repeated talking points, bowing deeply as he pressed the ALERT! button on his smart phone.

By the time Kenney, Calandra and Bezan had reached the tunnel leading to the Bunker, Poilievre was crouched in the doorway ready to grant them entry as, one by one, they whispered the password in his left ear.

The Leader was already relaxing in his comfortable alcove chair, with a new display of Canadian flags flanking him on both sides. The ministers' hard chairs had been freshly painted in Conservative blue, and a defiant portrait of Dief the Chief had appeared on the wall to the Leader's right.

"I think you'll approve of these new touches to our meeting place, as the day of judgment approaches," the prime minister began, with his familiar sly smile.

"Yes, yes, yes, yes!" cried the ministers in chorus.

"Now to get down to business, as we leave the pre-pre-election period and enter the pre-election period. Remember, we're at war at home and abroad. We need to ramp up our efforts a few notches. We've had a few setbacks—or, to put it another way, our enemies are getting more dangerous. Khadr is free, the Supreme Court says he's only a child, someone on my own staff has published full-face videos of me with our special forces in Iraq, the chief of defence staff is supposed to treat all women soldiers with respect, the information commissioner says it's wrong to pass retroactive legislation making unlawful acts legal, the socialists have sent Jim Prentice to the sin bin in our beloved homeland Alberta. I sense that there may be a slight whiff of public anger in the air. So I need your advice: what do we do?"

The ministers struck poses of deep concern. After a pregnant and respectful silence, Calandra was the first to speak.

"What's necessary, Leader, is to recall the horrors of the sponsorship scandal, spread fear about the epidemic dangers of marijuana on the opposition front benches, and call on Mulcair repeatedly to pay all his party's debts for employing public servants on party jobs."

"And remind everyone," interrupted Poilievre, "that we have a special tax advantage just for you! Just for you, and you, and you, and you!"

"Excellent, Palumbro, and very good, young Pierre," responded the prime minister. "I like all that repetition . . . but perhaps try a bit less desperation in the voice. Now, what about you, Jason? What do you think?"

Kenney ruminated with his usual profundity. "All that might not be enough. We're digging ourselves into a hole these days, and you're right about the hint of public anger. We have to do something to displace it. I think we'd better think about purging the military leadership, and begin to spread more fear. Talk about war and terrorism every day, wherever you can. Think of it: there are unfriendly people all around us, threatening good Canadians. That's why we need more security, more surveillance, more anxiety. The world's a dangerous place, and we're the ones who know how to keep the country safe—and how to lower taxes at the same time."

"Wise words, Kenney. Can you be more precise?"

"Well, now that we've been to Iraq and Kurdistan with our 24/7 television team, what about a lightning visit to our forces training soldiers in Ukraine? Maybe we should risk a visit to the front lines outside Donetsk to deliver flak jackets and sleeping bags, and to greet a few cringing refugees. We could even bring a handful of them back with us on the government jet and grant them citizenship in a special ceremony. On election eve, that might do the trick for us. But keep it secret until the very last moment."

"Sometimes you're a genius, Jason," responded the Leader. "You've given me renewed hope. I'll tell my staff to start planning right away. Obviously, no one say a word about it. Top secret! And now, look, obviously, back to your talking points, all of you, for the next phase of the campaign. But be sure, always, to keep on script. Inner War Cabinet, attention! Salute the flags! Dismissed!"

October 21, 2015
Stephen Harper Meets His Last Inner War Cabinet

"Poilievre! We need a post-election think session. Call in the Inner War Cabinet!"

"At your orders, master," responded the minister for disinformation, etc., dropping smartly to his knees among the movers' boxes at 24 Sussex Drive. The prime minister kicked a hole in the wall as he left the room.

Within seven minutes, Poilievre was crouched at the doorway of the subterranean war room under the Centre Block, receiving whispered passwords as Kenney, Calandra and Novak rushed in. Harper was already slouched casually in his alcove chair, dressed in his CANADA windbreaker and blue running shoes.

"Well, men," the Leader muttered with a slight snarl on his lips. "I need your advice about the transition. What do we do now?"

"Do we really have to go?" Poilievre pleaded.

"I'm afraid you still don't understand the system, Pierre. When we lose our majority of seats, we have to leave office. I know that much about the constitution. But beyond that, we have lots of choices. I want you to think about them."

A long silence echoed through the room.

At last, Jason Kenney raised his hand and spoke thoughtfully. "Did you say we will be resigning on November 4?"

"That's what Ray has arranged with the usurpers," Harper replied.

"Then," Kenney responded, "we have an historic opportunity. You'll remember what almost happened—but didn't—on November 5."

"Jason, you're brilliant. Could you really arrange it?"

"Well, we're lucky to be where we are in this secret cavern. If I'm right, we're sitting directly under the Speaker's chair in the House of Commons. With some careful placement, we could cause a big bang just after we surrender power. The House will be empty, but the noise should resonate with our base. They don't care much for Parliament anyway."

"Kenney, you're a genius," exclaimed Calandra, slapping the minister of defence on his sloping shoulders. "That will put the fear of God into our cowardly enemies. They'll have to blame it on the terrorists. And maybe they'll give us back our power so that we can pursue those responsible for the crime—or, I mean, those we blame for it."

The prime minister brightened. "Well, Ray, what are your thoughts?"

"It's possible," he replied. "But I don't think the new government would resign so easily. It would be their first big challenge, and they'd want to look confident and responsible. Besides, we'd have to engage in a vast cover-up to hide our involvement in the plot. We'd have to arrange with an intermediary to employ a third party to do the job, and then hide our tracks. We haven't got that much time. What's more, we'd be in violation of Bill C-51."

"I suppose that's good advice," Harper replied. "So, what else could we do instead?"

Calandra looked glum. "Well, at least, we can limit the damage to the Harper party. If you have to give up the prime ministership, I think you should keep the leadership and prepare for a victorious return to power four years from now, or sooner. The country will be fed up with tax and spend . . ."

"But," Harper interrupted, "I've already announced my resignation. How do I get around that?"

"Well," Novak said, "you can always drag your feet. Say the party needs a time out. Purge any rebels in the new caucus. Give the faithful ones jobs in the shadow cabinet, and prime office spaces. Delay any meetings of the national party council. Show what a sensible and compassionate man you are when the new House meets. The country will begin to see its mistake, and regret its loss, and soon they'll want you back again. I can foresee it all."

Kenney looked pained, leant low in his chair and clutched his forehead. "I . . . I . . . I want to be sunny and optimistic, but I'm feeling a bit ill. I should lie down for a bit. I think I need to leave now. Excuse me." He rose, backed slowly towards the door, and disappeared.

"I may have a slight problem there," the prime minister mused. "Otherwise, I think I can handle your plan, Ray—unless Loreen can persuade me to build a new house in the foothills. Anyway, let's finish packing up and carry on. We're in the last days, so we might as well enjoy ourselves. Inner War Cabinet: salute the flag, give us a hearty round of 'O Canada' and 'God Save the Queen', and then, for the last time: Attention! Dismissed!"

Acknowledgements

For a lifetime of opportunities to write and to publish, I am grateful to four universities—Toronto, York, Trent, and Western—where I taught politics; to the newspapers and magazines who invited and accepted my submissions; to my book publishers (in the beginning, Mel Hurtig; and then the University of Toronto Press, Macfarlane Walter & Ross, Lorimer, Bev Editions, and Rock's Mills Press); to the family who endured my inevitable distraction to the latest political crisis; and above all, to Dawn, wife, companion, first reader.

DENIS SMITH

Index

www.ingramcontent.com/pod-product-compliance
Lightning Source LLC
Chambersburg PA
CBHW070302290326
41930CB00040B/1807
9781772440423